Due on the 19 OCT

A Parents' Guide

to the Emotional Needs

of Children

A PARENTS' GUIDE

TO THE

Emotional Needs

of Children

BY DR. DAVID GOODMAN, 1894—

With an introduction by

MARYNIA FARNHAM, M.D.

HAWTHORN BOOKS, INC., PUBLISHERS, NEW YORK

First Edition, May, 1959

The Library of Congress has catalogued this publication as follows:

Goodman, David, 1894–
   A parents' guide to the emotional needs of children. With an introd. by Marynia Farnham. ₁1st ed.₁ New York, Hawthorn Books ₁1959₁

   318 p.   24 cm.

   Includes bibliography.

   ✓ 1. Children—Management.   ✓ı. Title.

HQ769.G67   649.1   59–5617 ‡

Library of Congress

ACKNOWLEDGMENTS

THE author wishes to express his appreciation and thanks to the National Association for Mental Health for permission to quote their copyrighted popular folder, *What Every Child Needs*. The eight points in this declaration of the basic emotional needs of children have been used as headings for the sectional divisions of this book. The original was composed by Mr. Edward Linzer, Educational Director of the Association, with the assistance of Miss Isabel Johnson, staff writer.

The author is also indebted to the following authors and their publishing houses for permission to quote from them: Gladys Andrews, *Creative Rhythmic Movement for Children*, copyright 1954, Prentice-Hall, Inc.; Theodor Bovet, *Love, Skill and Mystery*, Longmans, Green & Co., Ltd., 1958, reprinted by Doubleday Co., Inc.; Judson T. and Mary G. Landis, *Building a Successful Marriage*, copyright 1953 by Prentice-Hall, Inc.; David R. Mace, M.D. from *The Encyclopedia of Child Care and Guidance*, edited by Sidonie Matsner Gruenberg, 1958, Doubleday & Co., Inc.; Robert Paul Smith, *Where Did You Go? Out. What Did You Do? Nothing*, W. W. Norton & Co., Inc., 1957; Dr. Edward A. Strecker, *Sex and Your Child's Happiness*, reprinted from *This Week* magazine, copyright 1953 by the United Newspapers Magazine Corporation.

Many of the true story illustrations in this book are taken from the mail coming to my syndicated column "What's Best for Your Child." Others are taken from cases in my own counseling files. Names, addresses, and other identifying facts are, for obvious reasons, changed.

Appreciation is warmly given to the publisher of this book, Mr. Kenneth S. Giniger, and the editorial staff of Hawthorn Books. I am particularly indebted to Mr. Fred Kerner, former editor, whose constant encouragement and many practical suggestions promoted the progress of the work step by step, and to his successor, Mr. Whit Burnett, for carrying on the editorial completion of the book.

The author is grateful to Mrs. Eleanor Shoemaker for help in organizing the material and for many valuable suggestions regarding both content and style. He also wishes to thank his secretary, Mrs. Shirley Engle, for her conscientious preparation of the manuscript.

Finally, the author wishes to thank Marynia F. Farnham, M.D., for the inspirational stimulus derived from the reading of her remarkable book, *Modern Woman: The Lost Sex,* published by Harper and Brothers.

TO MALVINA

wise, good, and beautiful

wife and mother

TABLE OF CONTENTS

Introduction 11
Let's Begin With You 17
BOOK ONE — *Love*
Understand Your Child's Need of Love 25
Parent Love Begins With Married Love 32
Your Parents, Too, Had Parents 38
Appreciate and Prosper — In Marriage and Parenthood 44
Live Your Gender! 51
Your Sexual Happiness Is Your Child's Emotional
  Security 57
Parents Are a Child's Fate: Children Are a Parent's Fate 65
BOOK TWO — *Acceptance*
Rejection: Tragedy of Childhood 73
Rigid Rules: A Baby Experiences Rejection 80
Reject Your Child: Reject Your Self 84
Give Love First, Then Ask Obedience 88
The Accepted Child Acquires a Conscience 91
Teachers, Too, Help Children Acquire a Conscience 96
Orphans of Divorce: America's Legally Rejected
  Children 100
Parents Without Partners 106
True Stories of Rejected Children 117
BOOK THREE — *Security*
Love, Not Things, Make the Secure Home 135
Discipline Gives Your Child Security 143
Courtesy of Parents Promotes Children's Happiness
  And Sense of Security 147
Home Is a Comfortable Place 155
The Good Word Makes the Good Home 162

10   *Table of Contents*

BOOK FOUR — *Protection — Independence*

Protection Precedes Independence 171
First Steps in Attaining Courage and Independence 176
Teach Handicapped Child to be Self-Reliant 185

BOOK FIVE — *Faith*

Your Child's Faith Depends on Yours 197
Moral Trials and Triumphs of Children 211
Only You Can Give Your Child a Sound Sex Ideal 226
Sex Instruction Can Be Easy 234

BOOK SIX — *Guidance*

Your Child's Good Manners Please God and Man 253

BOOK SEVEN — *Control*

Discipline: How Can I Guide My Child 269
Individual Problems of Discipline 275

CONCLUSION

What Your Child Needs 295

Suggested Reading for Parents 303
Index 305
The Author and His Book 319

Introduction

THE reader will, I think, find this a likable book. Perhaps you ask why use so slender or trivial a word. The truth is that many books setting out to help parents find ways of helping their children to grow up happily are far from likable and lose effectiveness from this fact. But beyond being attractive, it has other things to recommend it to the attention of parents. Its approach is positive. It doesn't set out to read angry lectures. It points out the avenues open to parents to influence children in the directions which will help to make them effective, successful and happy. It is particularly useful, I think, in placing substantial emphasis on the great importance which the relationship between the parents has in establishing the kind of emotional climate which fosters and promotes the healthy growth and development in the children dependent on it. It thus succeeds in making the point that the interests of parents and children are really, at many points, identical. Parents' happiness makes happiness and there is no necessity for parents to make a grim business of bringing up their children. They need not sacrifice their all to it but can be happy in it.

11

The author takes the happy position that parents can, by making the effort, change their attitudes, if necessary or useful. He plumps for the use of the will and the intelligence. He believes that parents can learn if they will take the trouble to try to do so. He follows the plan of elaborating on the Rights of Children as set out by the National Mental Health Association, elaborating point by point. This is a convenient and useful scaffold. It promotes the positive approach. The author thus avoids the "problem" presentation. Rearing children is not set out as an immense struggle to avoid catastrophe or rescue the young from calamity after disaster. It is rather seen as a pleasant and not too difficult part of a marriage. Perhaps, at times, one gets a little too much the impression that the whole thing is quite simple and that following the author's helpful guidance will insure success. But this is a fault of its virtue. For Dr. Goodman is concerning himself with the usual child, the child we all expect to meet and have. He is not addressing himself to the parents of a child with problems of any magnitude. His book is not and, I take it, not intended to deal with the pathological or the abnormal. He avoids these areas. It is not that he does not recognize that parenthood is a demanding (and sometimes exasperating) job or that growing up does not have its hurdles. He accepts both these facts. But he insists that neither of them puts the parents in an impossible position. He rather takes the position that parents have the responsibility and the capacity for dealing with what comes if they will see to their own relationship and pay reasonable attention to their children's needs.

Throughout, this book has the two key words: love and common sense. The first is directly mentioned and repeatedly alluded to; the second is there by inference and implication right along. Together they make a mixture which is blessed in the business of bringing up children. If that were all that is needed, it may sound simple beyond the need of any repetition or elaboration. But a present tendency to make it necessary to provide every part of life with a grandiose and complicated set of directions, to believe that there must be a formula for even the simplest operations of ordinary existence, makes it particularly useful to meet an insistence on common sense. It is, as the reader will, I think, discover, very pleasant to find a tendency to simplify rather than complicate the matter in hand. And, finally, the author refrains from any extravagant or excessively delving excursion into the buried reasons for all his suggestions. He does not attempt to lay bare all the complex and devious mechanics of development, all the lines of stress and counterstress. There is a need for such undertakings. They are the foundation for all that the author says and urges. But, too often, they become, in such books as this, the only concern of the writer. Dr. Goodman does not fall into this. He is devoted to his thesis. He stays with it. Parents will be happy with it.

MARYNIA F. FARNHAM, M.D.

A Parents' Guide

to the Emotional Needs

of Children

Let's Begin With You

You ARE a conscientious parent. You love your children and want to do right by them according to your own best instincts and the soundest knowledge available.

But you are not always as successful with them as you would like. You sometimes wonder why you can't be a more effective parent, make your children behave better, feel happier, do more.

You should know that the kind of parent you are depends greatly on the kind of parents you had.

You may have been lucky. You may have had amiable and intelligent parents who easily and naturally raised you correctly, affording you all the love and guidance you needed. That gives you a great advantage. It makes it that much easier for you, in turn, to be a good parent and raise fine children.

But then again, yours may have been nervous and unhappy parents who had so many troubles of their own they couldn't properly love you and look after you. Your parents may have quarreled and left you a legacy of doubt, instead of faith, in people. They may have been too strict. Or they may have been

17

too lax, giving you little or no upbringing because they were too absorbed in their own affairs or pleasures. They may have been divorced, or one of them may have died leaving you to the custody of only one parent—or to strangers—and depriving you of the wholesome balance of both a man and a woman's influence in your life.

Your share of all this you carry around within you, and, of course, it affects your behavior toward your children. But you are a separate and individual person. You have a mind of your own plus the will and the energy to assert that mind. You can start fresh from where you now are, using the good of the past as you recognize it but rising above the bad of it. Thus your life goes forward and not backward.

Also your children's life!

And you are not left alone to carry out your great task. There are "helpers and servers" in the world who will gladly aid you. These are the ideas of many good and wise men who thought hard and long on the problems that beset you and came to useful conclusions about them—all yours to study and apply. Particularly on the subject of raising *good* children is there a lot of knowledge available, some of it old, some of it new.

Don't reject an idea because it is old, but take a new look at it. Many of the best ideas of men of the past have been repeated so often they have become just words—monuments of thought, rather than thought itself. We should remember, however, that these ideas have survived not because they were bad ideas but rather because they were very good ideas. The sophisticated may mock at old ideas—but you will be wise to seek out their meaning afresh and apply them to the education of your children. Solomon said: "Train up a child in the way he should go: and when he is old he will not depart from it." This idea is one of the oldest on child behavior that we have; it is also one of the best.

And don't be afraid of an idea because it is new, either. Parenthood is a living, growing thing. Parenthood can always use good

new ideas. Upon these depends mankind's evolutionary progress.

One of the most useful of the new ideas for healthy, happy
thinking is professionally called Mental Hygiene, but we shall
call it "The Mental Health Way."

Mental Health teachings have many fine ideas for raising
children, as the following pages will indicate. Your job of parenthood—let me assure you—will be much easier and far more successful if you study and consistently apply them.

The beauty of The Mental Health Way is that its aim is
preventive. To avoid ills is always better than to try to correct
them afterward—especially with children. As the old saying
goes, "An ounce of prevention is worth a pound of cure."

The Mental Health Way of raising sound children has been
set forth in various publications issued by the National Association for Mental Health. The most widely distributed of these is
a summary statement entitled, "What Every Child Needs." It
sets forth in the simplest language the essence of Mental Health
teachings on the care and upbringing of children. It has the
special value of comprehensiveness. You are sure to come out
fine with your family if you use its eight principles as your
basic guide.

The origin of the Mental Health Association's statement of
children's needs is interesting and instructive.

A meeting of The Young Parents' Club of Peoria, Ill., had
been called to hear a noted nutritionist discuss "The Needed
Seven," the basic foods every child must eat for good health:
(1) leafy green and yellow vegetables; (2) butter or margarine;
(3) bread, flour, cereals; (4) citrus fruit, cabbage, and tomatoes;
(5) potatoes and other fruits and vegetables; (6) milk, cheese,
and ice cream; (7) meat, fish, poultry, eggs, and legumes.

The speaker emphasized the fact that there is a great difference between a child's getting plenty of food and his being well
nourished. What children need, she explained, is a variety of
foods for body building and repair, for regulating and protecting
their organs, and for energy. All the various nutrients are de-

pendent on each other in a complex and endless interaction. You must supply every one of "The Needed Seven" to make sure that your child's body is truly nourished, that he (or she) will grow into a strong, healthy, vigorous man (or woman).

This was valuable information and greatly appreciated. But the audience did not feel completely satisfied. A child is more than a body. A child is a living spirit. He has emotional as well as physical needs.

"What do you feed a child's mind and soul?" someone in the audience asked, as if speaking for the whole group.

One member of that audience, Edward Linzer, now Education Director of the National Association for Mental Health, was struck by the parent's question.

"What do you feed a child's mind and soul?" How important it is for parents to know that! He determined right then and there to make available a clear and simple answer to that question. With the collaboration of Isabel Johnson, a writer with a genius for condensation and simplification, he composed this guide for parents, "What Every Child Needs for Good Mental Health."

To the needed seven physical nutrients, they added eight needed spiritual nutrients: (1) Love, (2) Acceptance, (3) Security, (4) Protection, (5) Independence, (6) Faith, (7) Guidance, (8) Control. These, too, are dependent on each other in a complex and endless interaction. You must supply all eight of them to make sure that your child grows up spiritually sound and strong.

Most parents understand well enough the physical needs of children, good food, plenty of sleep, exercise and fresh air, and are eager—sometimes too eager—to supply them.

But the emotional needs of children, unfortunately, are not so well understood by the parents. Our own personality distresses prevent our seeing our children with clear eyes and supplying their true needs. As a consequence, they suffer many griefs and acquire spiritual and emotional ills that plague the later years. Nothing is more necessary for parents to comprehend than that their child has an emotional as well as a physical self and that the former must be provided for as well as the latter.

This book will take up these emotional needs of children, one by one. It will endeavor to show you specifically and in detail just what it is your children require of you and how you can best overcome your own emotional disabilities in order to supply it.

Children are like plants. Give them the right nurture and they'll give you the right growth. But the child must be nourished spiritually and emotionally as well as physically.

Children whose basic needs are satisfied grow up well. They are healthy and happy and develop into sound, competent adults who succeed in their marriage and career and add something to the welfare of society.

As a conscientious parent, it is certainly your wish that your child shall so mature. With understanding and effort you won't find it too difficult to help him do this.

This book aims to supply the understanding. It will be your satisfaction to supply the effort. With a good understanding of what your child needs, your efforts should be less arduous and your success more certain.

Summary and Suggestion

Your child is the product of three generations—you, your parents, and himself. For the present, you are the focal and most vital factor—the interpreter—for your child. That is why we said, "Let's begin with you." What gifts or burdens did you receive from your parents? Are you, however unconsciously, passing these on, for better or worse, into your marriage—and from thence to your child?

Think about this as you plan your child's upbringing. If you received fine traditions of family life from your parents, bless and appreciate their memory and make sure that their standards are upheld by you. But, if your parents didn't do too well by you, lift up your heart and—without blaming them—determine that you will do better by your children.

BOOK ONE

Love

EVERY CHILD NEEDS TO FEEL:

that his parents love, want and enjoy him

that he matters very much to someone

that there are people near him who care what happens to him

CHAPTER I

Understand Your Child's

Need of Love

PRIOR TO birth the child lives in a sea of comfort where all his wishes are satisfied as soon as made. Is it any wonder then that his first utterance is a cry of protest at being born? "It is as natural to die as to be born," said the philosopher Bacon, "and to a little infant perhaps the one is as painful as the other." How great is the need of love to still that cry!

Indeed, when you look at your new infant, cast like a lost mariner on an alien shore, his whole being one loud lament, surely you know that only as you create for him another world of peace and comfort can he feel content and secure.

The best of food and shelter, the finest medical care will not suffice him—without love. In a foundling hospital babies have been known to wither away and die, not that the doctors and nurses did not try their scientific utmost to save them, but because there were not enough loving arms to cuddle and comfort them. Better a hovel with love than the most antiseptic sanatorium with impersonal treatment.

In medical books of a generation ago there were frequent

references to a strange infant malady called marasmus, derived from a Greek word meaning wasting away. These books told of newborn children who literally wasted away and died because they couldn't communicate a need for food—the normal exchange of cry and loving response having been denied them by the fact of the absence of the mother.

The infant's cry is a call for love and care and nourishment. If none is afforded, he learns that there is no use to cry. His one way of speech is lost. He lies there in complete apathy, unable to express any need and so is unable to secure any help. He wastes away and dies.

The behavior of two nurses in the babies' ward of a hospital tells a revealing story. Both are well trained, both energetic and competent. But one goes from baby to baby giving not only the needed physical attention but also a warm pat, smile, a hug. The other methodically goes her rounds concerned only to get her work done. The first nurse will quiet and comfort more babies than the second. That's the practical value of love with children.

You can see the same thing in a school for young children. One teacher has the knack of winning the good will of the pupils through her warm-hearted manner, her patience, her constant use of praise. Another, though equally conscientious, is severe of aspect and harsh in speech, frequently expressing blame. The first group of children learns more and behaves better than the second.

To a mother a baby's first smile is like a bit of heaven. She should know that it is also a vitally important first step in his personality development. That smile—and your response to it—may decide much of his later destiny.

All lessons in life are lessons in love. Your baby's exchange of smiles with you is his first lesson in love. Lucky is he who learns that lesson well. For him a happy stay on earth is assured. But woe betide those who don't. All their lives they will wander, like Abraham's son Ismael, seeking their lost inheritance.

Every period in life has its special problem. And each must be learned in its own time, or it will bedevil all the later periods, making the solution of their problems more difficult. Infancy too has its problem. Your child has made his first great step in spiritual growth when he smiled back at your smile. He has learned life's most necessary lesson, how to give as well as to receive love. Only you can teach him that lesson.

As you provide for all his needs, nourishing and comforting him, he learns to look for you, to await your steps. And when you come, he coos and smiles, demonstrating his satisfaction at your presence. That's love going out to meet love.

The child whose emotions have been well-nourished by the love of his parents begins life emotionally stabilized and strong. He steps smilingly out into the world expecting to be befriended and well treated. He is not disappointed. Smile and the world smiles with you, is one of the great truths of life.

It is also true that the child who is well loved, loves back— first his parents and then people in general. He becomes a friendly, outgoing, generous person who enjoys doing his fair part in all human relations. He makes good at marriage and passes his fine feelings and ideals on to his own progeny. All this had its auspicious beginning when your baby smiled at you and you smiled back.

"Won't too much loving spoil my baby?" a young mother asked me one day, explaining the circumstances with serious concern. "Seven months ago my husband and I adopted a precious five-day-old baby boy. So far he is not spoiled and is a wonderfully happy baby. I want to keep him that way, but I know we have a long road ahead of us. It seems so hard not to spoil a child when you love him so much."

One might laugh at this young mother's fear, were it not a sad fact that many parents have the same false notion. "Give a child too much affection," they say, "and you just make a brat out of him. A strict routine is what he really needs."

And so they set up rigid rules for such things as eating, sleeping, toilet training, without consideration of the child's natural rhythms. These are the parents who *do* spoil their children.

They make angry, rebellious spirits out of them who grow up to be the world's worst tyrants.

The truth is you cannot give a child too much love. Love is the very breath of his life. It is on your love that he flourishes and grows—spiritually as well as physically. For in time he learns to return your love and becomes a friendly, outgoing person whom everyone will like because he likes everyone. Thus your love goes its journey through the world, the living memorial of your own fine self.

Furthermore, it is through your love that your child develops a conscience—his sure inner guide as to what is right or wrong. He enjoys your love and will do what you tell him in order to retain it. If your own standards are high, your child's will be also. And how much easier all child rearing becomes if you start with affection and from there work on to training of more formal kinds as he grows up. In time, you see, training becomes a habit and a convenience—and no problem at all!

But to teach your child this first vital lesson of love, you have to be—as all good teachers are—full of the subject matter yourself and eager to impart it. That is why it is so important for parents to be relaxed and happy—in themselves and with each other.

A wife unsure of her husband's love can embitter her baby's milk—and his later life—by her readily communicated nervous tension.

Husbands, too, have their affectional needs, and wise is the wife who steadfastly attends to them. "I had a nice wife until my first son was born. Then Mary became more mother than mate." How many husbands make some such complaint! And with what sad consequences for the children.

But assured that the arrival of a child means no diminution of his wife's ardor for him, the husband is usually more than willing to be a true helpmate in the care of the child—and share the baby's smile. To love both husband and child to their full need may seem like demanding a lot of a woman, but a true daughter of Eve is ready to meet that obligation. She wants to be a complete woman and that includes married love as well as mother love.

Your baby will smile at you and later at the world, if you two will never cease to smile at each other. No fact of child training is truer or more important than this.

The children who are not adequately loved in infancy go through life full of doubts and fears, almost as if they hadn't really been born yet, were not at home on earth. They expect no good of life, never having received any. And they usually get no more than they expect.

That is why it cannot be said too strongly, nor repeated too often, that a parent's first duty is to give love—abundantly and continuously, and without qualifying conditions. So don't hesitate to release to your children all the affection you feel for them. The spiritual and practical benefits can scarcely be measured, as the following case demonstrates.

"Can I sit in your lap?"

Seven-year-old divorce-orphaned Tommy took his thumb out of his mouth and looked at his newly acquired foster mother with hesitant yearning. Would she laugh at him? Would she think him strange, so big a boy to ask for cuddling?

She didn't. She just smiled, stretched out her arms and held and hugged him for a long time.

How good it felt! He was like a parched field drinking in the rain. It wasn't so necessary now to put his thumb back into his mouth. Nor did he wet his bed that night as he had done so frequently before. Love had released the grief-imprisoned self for growth.

The first need of all children is for a warm, physical, cuddling love. If for any reason they have been deprived of it, as Tommy had been, there is a gap in their development that nothing else can fill. Always they will be seeking it, the warm physical assurance of being loved.

Similarly for the other stages of their development. Each has its needs. If they are not met, life forever after is out of joint and forever after they will be struggling to set it right again. That is why it is so important for parents to understand what children need in each stage of their development and endeavor to supply it.

Never say to a child, "I will love you, if . . .!" Nor say, "I will love you, but . . . !" Just say, "I love you!" and mean it, supporting your words with caresses and embraces and care and comfort and merriment and laughter—and all that a child needs to feel absolutely assured of being loved.

Even if your child may seem at times to take advantage of your unquestioning affection, and, feeling absolutely secure in your love, may tease and tempt you into anger or irritability by a bit of wayward behavior—don't get upset. He's just testing the limits of your love. If you keep smiling, he'll know it's for real. And then you can patiently but firmly insist on the duty to be done—and he'll do it!

If only the ego did not get in the way of our love! If only we were not so absorbed in ourselves and our personal problems, how gladly would we give ourselves in love and devotion—in happy talk and play—to our children.

The need of every parent is to learn to let go and love. As you lose yourself in the task of parenthood, you will find your higher and happier personality. You will become more competent in the carrying out of duties, and also more relaxed, more at ease in the universe! You'll be what you want to be—a successful parent.

Summary and Suggestion

At this early point, do you truly understand your child's need of love, not in a sentimental way, but as an absolutely practical proposition? Love gives your child a base for all his future development. The well-loved child is easy to handle, responsive to suggestion, quick to grow. He has what he needs, a comfortable security; he is ready to give you what you want, obedience and cooperation.

If, as you review your past relations with your children,

you conclude that you have been a bit remiss in the actual expression of affection, don't hesitate to begin now—not too suddenly, of course, and certainly not mechanically as a parental chore. Take your children in your arms, pat and caress them, give a good-night or good-bye kiss. Don't be afraid of giving germs! Children can throw off germs, but they can't throw off their grief at their parents' lack of love for them.

CHAPTER II

Parent Love Begins With

Married Love

WE HAVE come to understand that every period in life has its special problem, and that even a newborn baby has a lesson to learn—to receive and give love.

But this problem really began before his birth. It began with you two, his parents. Unless you love each other, you cannot properly love him nor provide a love-warmed home for him. Then how will he ever learn his lesson of returning love, if he hasn't received any to begin with?

True, there is no guarantee that your children will grow up healthy and happy just because you two are in love with each other. You must also have the knowledge and the will to raise them right. One thing is certain, however, the children of parents who do not love each other have a sad time of it.

Their home is a spawning ground for mental and moral ills. Like the sad refrain to a tragic song are the words one hears repeated in children's court, regarding newly arrested juvenile delinquents: "Broken home! Broken home! Broken home!" Less drastic, but no less potentially harmful, are the cases where a man and his wife stay together but indulge in continual quarreling, criticism or nagging.

No study of what every child needs, therefore, can do better than dwell hard and long on the question of how parents can so replenish each other's affections, can so fulfill each other's need of love, that in its mutual overflow there will be more than enough to envelope the children with warmth and comfort without possessing or binding them.

The best way to understand your mate's need of love is to think of your own. Just as you long for some loving heart and mind to be ever present in your life—sharing your joys, sharing your sorrows, sharing the in-betweens—so does your spouse. And in whom but you can he hope to find all this?

If you asked Mrs. Farnham where she found the energy to keep her home so clean, cook three good meals a day, and also romp and play with her three children, she would give you a merry smile and say: "That's my secret."

What was her secret?

Her secret was——well, her secret was greathearted Mr. Farnham, who knew how to make love to a woman.

A man who is a good lover to his wife is his children's best friend. His love upholds her spirit, gives her joy and enthusiasm. Child care is play to a woman who is happy. And only a man can make a woman happy. In deepest truth, a father's first duty to his children is to make their mother feel fulfilled as a woman.

How unfortunate it is that many American men fail to realize this and give up the lover's role too readily for that of the mere provider. Provide a little less and pay court a little more, and you may be agreeably surprised to find that your wife is perfectly content to have fewer things in order to have more of you.

And the children, too, get along fine on limited creature comforts in a love-warmed home. They don't care half so much for the things you buy them, the toys, the fancy garments, the rich foods, as you think they do. But how they enjoy the company of gay, high-spirited parents. Furthermore, what a fine example you set them for their own future marriage.

The wife who is unhappy in her relations with her husband tends to overattach herself to her children and dominate all the aspects of their life. This inhibits their growth in self-reliance. Sons especially are damaged. That mother-bound boy, so uncreative in work and love, is a casualty of his parents' mismating. If his father had not failed his mother in her needs as a woman, how very different might have been his destiny!

If you think of yourself as a husband, you are a husband only because this woman is your wife. And you are a good husband only as you give this particular woman satisfaction of her needs. No other woman—imaginary or real—is your wife. You have to make good with this woman, or admit that you are not, in fact, a good husband. No man is a real man unless he can truly and enduringly love some one woman.

Similarly, if you think of yourself as a wife, you are a wife only because this man is your husband. And you are a good wife only as you give this particular man satisfaction of his needs. No other man—imaginary or real—is your husband. You have to make good with this man, or admit that you are not, in fact, a good wife. No woman is a real woman unless she can truly and enduringly love some one man.

✽   ✽   ✽

"Since the children have been away at camp," said Mary, everyman's dream of a wife, "I've had a lot of time to think. And I've come to the conclusion that, in our devotion to our children, we wives do a lot of neglecting of the man who works to provide for it all.

"So I've sort of extra-special pampered John these days. John likes stews, you know; but Patricia hates 'em and David doesn't care for them either; so we never had stews. But now that the kids are away, we have stews and pudding desserts that John likes and a lot of his other favorite dishes, too.

"And, of course, we have cocktails before dinner, no hurry at all. And after dessert we chat and chat over our coffee and cigarettes, and really get acquainted again. It's nice, real nice." And Mary smiled and blushed a little, almost like a new bride.

"Every summer's a sort of second honeymoon, and when the kids get back they find us fit to live with again."

Hurrah for Mary!

What wives need to know, especially American wives, is that children have to have fathers, not only providers, nice human fathers, cheerful and relaxed. Such fathers are able to cooperate in the care of the children and do the things that only a man can do for their upbringing—like teaching little David how to bat a ball or giving Patricia a cavalier's attention when she's wearing a new frock with which she hopes to wow the boys but isn't quite certain.

A married woman has two jobs: one to care for her children, the other to keep a man happy. Many women object to this, giving up the second job when the first gets too burdensome. But they're foolish. If they balanced their devotion, they'd come out better in the end. Their husbands would reciprocate by being better fathers, and that would make it easier all around—and certainly happier.

Much of the attention that mothers give their children is excessive. These would thrive better, acquire more self-reliance, if left to their own devices. Husbands, however, are often neglected. Some of them feel pretty bad about this, though they don't say much. Some go wandering, and that's never good. Smart wives see to it that it doesn't happen.

Smart wives also know that children grow up and leave the nest. Then it's especially nice to have a really companionable husband around—one you can live alone with, and like it.

No marriage so grounded in faith, love and understanding need ever fear divorce.

Every divorce is a confession, a public confession, of the failure of two people to make a marriage. And neither of them can claim to be entirely blameless in the break-up. Nor can the undivorced but constantly quarreling pair escape sharing the blame of their disharmony.

"If I were only married to so-and-so," you say, "how happy I would be and how happy I would make him (her)." But this

thought is only an illusion. You might, and you might not. Most
likely you wouldn't, because the very tendency to build on fantasy is the mark of a weak character, fleeing from reality because
he cannot handle it. *Those who divorce once readily divorce
again.*

Strong people do well with what they have, where they are.
Strong people say, "Reality, be thou my dream!" And they
mould reality into something that resembles their dream.

So can you with your marriage. And with the children who are
the product of that marriage.

Summary and Suggestion

If you love and understand each other, aiming always to
fulfill each other's man-woman needs, you have a sure base
for building a fine family.

How about your man-woman relations?

Can you, Mr. Husband, honestly say that you always try
to satisfy your wife in her total aspects as a woman? Do you
still speak the complimentary things a woman likes to hear,
do you remember anniversaries, do you bring home flowers
occasionally? Do you make love to the whole woman before
you presume on sexual relations with her and do you stay
with your wife in love and appreciation for a time afterwards? Do you make sure she goes to sleep happy?

And do you, Mrs. Wife, accept your sexual responsibility
as a woman, giving your husband his woman's worth of
coquetry and charm and ardor? Do you help him live up to
his essential greatness by always making him feel proud and
strong through your consistent admiration and praise? Do
you make a pleasant, sweet, orderly home for him? And do
you teach the children to appreciate their absent father's
labors in their behalf and not to take his support for granted?

Good for both of you, if you do! And good for both of you
it will be, I assure you.

But if, perhaps, love and love-making are still problems with you, you should try to understand why. It was your parents who, to a great extent caused that problem. But then, they, too, had parents!

CHAPTER III

Your Parents, Too,

Had Parents

As THE bride and groom step up to the altar, filled with faith in each other and hope of mutual happiness, they do not realize that behind them stand two rows of ghosts. These ghosts speak no words at the moment but will certainly have their say in the actual marriage. They are the complexes, the qualities of mind and character each acquired in childhood in relationship with his or her parents and brothers and sisters. Your parents, too, had parents who made or marred their children's lives, and each other's, depending upon whether they were or were not able to give and receive love.

John Gordon, for instance, complains bitterly that his beautiful wife Nancy is frigid, continually frustrating him by her unresponsiveness to his love-making. What John Gordon did not know was that his wife had been propagandized into a fear and hatred of men by her mother who had been deserted by her husband. It may take many years of patient and gallant devotion on John's part before he can hope to thaw the frozen core of distrust of men in Nancy's soul; a distrust aggravated by several experiences of Nancy's with men who sought to possess her body without loving her. "They only want you for one thing," her embittered mother had told her, "and when they've had their fill of you, they try another."

John Gordon has to make up to Nancy for what her father did to her mother. Will he succeed? He'll try. But John has his own parent-caused inner distresses which make him hunger for an ardor in a wife which he may never get.

As a young boy he had been separated from his adored mother, because the profligate father, after wasting the family fortune in gambling, had died, leaving her the sole support of more children than she could manage. She had sent him to his grandparents on a lonely wheat farm in the West. He was well fed and housed there, and somewhat loved by his odd, old grandparents. But how he longed for his mother! Her vital warmth of love and laughter were essential to her small son's spiritual and emotional well-being. But he was never to see her again. She died the next year. Now all his days and nights are filled with fancies of some woman who would take her place, give him the perfect love denied him in childhood and now insistently demanded by his adulthood.

But Destiny gave him Nancy—beautiful but cold Nancy! With her pretty face and full feminine figure, she seemed the ideal wife-substitute for his mother. And she certainly could have been—if only that same Destiny had not deprived her of the capacity to love.

As he lay in bed beside her, wondering what he could yet recover of young love's dream in his life, visions of other women came into his mind, eligible and available. But divorce would mean the giving up of his two children, and he cared too much for them to inflict a broken home upon them, to have only a visitation relationship with them.

Is John Gordon the only man lying beside a woman who cannot love him and longing for one who can? No, he isn't. And conversely, many a wife lies beside an insensitive, or sodden, husband clutching with hungry arms night's unavailing air.

Not for their own faults do they suffer so, these frustrated lovers, but for their parents' mismating. Indeed, all young lovers have to bear the burden of the cynicism and malice of the defeated lovers who lived before them.

*   *   *

When the handsome, former Air Force Lieutenant married the sweetheart of Sigma Chi, all their college friends commented:

"What a charming couple! Won't they be happy together!"

But it didn't turn out that way at all. On their first anniversary, two sad-faced young people stared across the breakfast table at each other in sullen silence, wondering why—Oh, why!—they had ever married. The night before, as on many other nights, one had slept in the bed and the other on the couch.

What had happened to young love's dream?

It died. The two young lovers discovered that for all their longing to love and to be loved, they just couldn't. The attitudes toward marriage which they had developed in the homes of their parents crept up on their romance and killed it.

The young man came from a mother-dominated family. The father had been degradingly henpecked. "No woman will ever boss me," he avowed to himself in early adolescence. Whenever his devoted young wife showed extra competence, taking over some difficult problem of finances or household management—whenever she expressed a firm, strong opinion at variance with his own—his repressed fears of woman dominance became violently aroused. He denounced her actions while accepting their benefits.

The girl came from a home where the father had deserted. She had observed her mother assume the whole obligation of bringing up the children. How she admired her strong, competent mother! How instinctively she imitated her!

And there you have it! But you, will you too, make love difficult for your children?

Many men and women are caught in this trap of an inherited

inability to love. They must learn a new way, if either they or their children are to be happy.

❋   ❋   ❋

"Never once have I been happy," she lamented. "My childhood was like living in a tunnel. I never could do what I wanted. Always my mother said, 'Do this, do that.' And I did it."

As you looked at her sad, dispirited face, you felt so very sorry for her. This is what a person comes to who has been allowed no sense of her own worth.

But as she spoke further of her own family and its problems, you found that she was doing exactly the same with her children as her own mother had done with her, hedging on their freedom, limiting their lives, never allowing them to be truly themselves.

That's the tragic way one generation influences another. The pattern keeps repeating itself through time. The parent who suffered a beaten-down childhood, in turn beats down her children. This is her first chance to show her power—and show it she will, even though it means the misery of her children and her own failure as a parent.

Somewhere the vicious circle must be broken! Where? Right here and now—and with you!

If your relations with your children are unsatisfactory—if your children don't seem to be happy—pause and reflect whether you are not imposing on them the controls and limitations you suffered as a child.

The need of every child is for freedom to grow as a person of significant worth. It is the duty of every parent to promote his child's growth. The strong, self-confident child makes his own fortune—and above all, his own happiness.

But the ego-distressed parent is always holding his or her child back. He or she wants to control the child, to be the dominating influence in its life. The child becomes the shuttlecock in his parent's emotional game of badminton.

What is the rescue for parent and child in this frustrating situ-

ation? The parent must give up in mind and memory his (or
her) dependence on his own weak yet oppressive parents and
transfer it to a faith in God and an orderly universe governed
by law.

As you thus mature spiritually, you no longer have need to get
ego satisfaction from dominating your children. They will not
be fearsome, dependent nor sullenly resistant. They will step
forth cheerily to take their place in the world.

Better still, when they become parents they will not oppress
their children. The vicious chain of inherited tyranny and ego
distress will be broken if you and your mate establish a new
pattern of parent love based upon married love. All this is assured when parents understand and forgive each other.

*   *   *

When they quarreled about their children, the father would
say: "The trouble with you is that you won't cooperate with me
even in those matters we both agree are right. If I correct one of
the children, I can't make it stick, because I never know whether
you will back me up or not."

But the mother had a different viewpoint: "You are much too
critical. Our children know at least that I believe in them. But
you—you don't let them feel that you believe in them, just as you
didn't let me feel that you believed in me. You let me down, and
that's why I couldn't cooperate with you."

"What do you mean, I let you down?"

"You know very well what I mean. All the times that you made
me think I didn't count as your wife. Your other affairs and
friendships!"

"They were of no significance. You're just arguing."

"They were to me . . ."

This quarrel went on for a long time. It was a repetition of
many previous quarrels along the same line. The sad thing is it
never got anywhere. The children had to go on living their lives
with two strikes against them: a pair of quarreling parents.

Yet these were both good people, who had married for love,

and who really wanted to make a go of their marriage and raise a worthy family.

Why had they fallen out? Why do so many fine couples have a falling out, and thus foredoom their children to the misery of a divided home? Everybody means well, but not everybody does well. Why? *Why?*

The answer is, their hidden complexes won't let them!

Summary and Suggestion

We enter marriage not trailing clouds of glory behind us, as the infatuated believe, but bearing a heavy burden of unconscious conflicts and spiritual dilemmas which we acquired in our own childhood from our parents, brothers and sisters, and other factors in our development. The over-argumentative, for instance, may have had domineering elder brothers and sisters with whom it was a question of argue or submit. The promiscuous may have so lost out in early affectional relationships as to require constant amatory reassurances. All behavior—all misbehavior—has a reason.

And since we're all in the same boat, each having his own inner conflicts, we should learn to be patient and forgiving toward each other. Especially husband and wife! A faithful and ardent love uplifts its recipient and makes him want to do better. If you just go on loving your marriage partner, faults and all, he'll gradually overcome the worst of them. Your marriage will improve.

Who profits the most from this? Your children. By mutual forgiveness, you become more devoted to each other and therefore better able to make a good marriage and a good home for your offspring. In addition, your understanding of life has been deepened, and you know now how to keep your sons and daughters free of some of the pitfalls you encountered.

CHAPTER IV

Appreciate and Prosper—

In Marriage and Parenthood

"You CANNOT love anyone," declares a Spanish folk proverb, "unless you also love his faults."

This is possibly the wisest thing ever said on the subject of marriage. Only as we learn to love our mate "as is," good qualities and bad, can we make a marriage.

If you accept your partner's faults along with his virtues as together composing the person whom you love, you please him (her) with your fair and candid attitude. He feels relaxed with you because he doesn't have to strain to be what he isn't. Naturally he is grateful and shows his gratitude in what ways he can.

But if you are quick to see his faults and to berate him for them, he is tempted to retaliate in kind and tell of the bad traits he sees in you. They won't be hard to find. For aren't we all human and full of faults?

One of the most pleasant feelings in life is indifference to the faults of others. What a luxury! Of course, we are aware that the faults exist, but we don't mind them so long as they are not directed aggressively against us. We live and let live. Such a deal of useless contention and irritability that saves us—the curse of many marriages.

But acceptance is not enough. We must go on to the higher practice of seeking out the good qualities in our spouse and expressing praise and appreciation.

Everyone responds to genuine appreciation. Everyone tries to live up to the estimate which his loved ones have of him. For everyone has a self, and everyone is trying to maintain and, if possible, enhance that self. When you express praise you are encouraging your mate to move higher in his instinctive aspirational endeavors.

In faultfinding, conversely, you dam the stream of growth in the individual. He can't become any better because you don't let him. He cannot behave "big" because you are continually cutting him down to size by your belittling criticism.

The opposite of appreciation is faultfinding, mankind's all too universal failing. It ruins human relationships just as appreciation promotes them.

What we fail to understand in our faultfinding is first that it is futile, and second that it is a defense mechanism against the recognition of our own weaknesses. People's faults are deeply rooted, usually due to remote—even hidden—causes. They are uncorrectable without the cooperation of their possessor, a cooperation we are not likely to get. What folly is it then for us to concern ourselves with people's faults, an evil which we are in no position to change!

More important still is the realization that it is our own faults that makes us so acutely aware of the faults of others. Disturbed as we are by our own unethical behavior, we turn with unconscious relief to a contemplation of the delinquencies of others, particularly of the ones we have wronged. When a husband has been unfaithful to a wife, how easy, and how necessary it is for him to see her as a cold, unresponsive, quarrelsome nag. When a parent has given way to a sadistic impulse to beat a child, how relieving it is to expatiate on the child's general delinquency!

All this constitutes a psychological law: *Appreciate and you prosper; belittle and you lose.* Unless we learn to apply this law, as psychological as it is spiritual, we are doomed to an existence of mediocrity, frustration, and defeat.

A married man told the following intimate story to his psychological adviser:

His wife was young, charming, and beautiful—but alas, also willful. It was a particular source of grief to him that he could not persuade her to retire at the same time that he did, which was usually rather early as he had to get up early to go to business the next morning. His pretty wife, his willful wife, declared that she would not be dictated to as to when she should go to bed. At times she would willingly go when he did; at other times she might want to read, or sew, or dabble in some new cosmetics.

The husband felt hurt, seeing his position as the breadwinner unappreciated. He expressed his hurt. She stayed up later and more frequently. He became quite bitter.

One night as he lay in bed, half-asleep, half-awake—really longing for her, and yet too proud to show that he was waiting —anger overcame him and he gave vent to harsh upbraidings. She answered that no matter what he said or did, even if he beat her, she would go to bed when she pleased.

Suddenly the ludicrousness of his position struck him, and in the midst of the argument, he burst into a gay and merry laugh, calling on his wife to forgive him, and saying that, of course, she had the right to go to bed when she pleased. The resultant effect on the wife overwhelmed her. With a hysterical cry, she threw herself in his arms, kissed and hugged him passionately, affording him a wooing delight that he had never believed was in her.

"Why did she act this way?" he asked the psychologist.

"Why?" The answer was not slow in forthcoming.

"Your allowing her the freedom of choice restored her individuality to her. She felt she was not just a doll-wife but a human being. Now that the choice was not to be forced on her, she could freely follow her own inclination, which was, of course, to be in your arms."

After all, for most of us, life is inherently limited. We have moderate means, we are bound to an ordinary job, we have little opportunity for travel or adventure, our folks are "just folks," our children "just kids," and the one we have married an earthbound mortal. From this curse of the commonplace, the law of appreciation rescues us. We enjoy our work, enjoy our friends, enjoy our families; and we do it all ourselves by the power of appreciation.

Appreciation is no simple theme, no vague or generalized theme. Appreciation is a very real force. It is governed by a principle almost as direct as a law of physics: *We draw to ourselves the good of everything we appreciate.* This law works, and works wonderfully.

What we appreciate is ours, for we have drawn its good to us. What we depreciate is lost, because we have, in effect, thrown it away. Appreciate more than you depreciate, and you will live the abundant life; depreciate more than you appreciate, and you will live a limited life. Such is life's spiritual mathematics and any spiritual second-grader can figure out the correct answers for himself.

Unfortunately, many of us never graduate from life's spiritual first grade. We give way to constant discontent, betraying our lack of self reliance. As appreciation is the beginning of spiritual life, so discontent is the beginning of death. It has killed many a marriage. There's a couple I know, for instance:

They had no talent for love. Yet they were a distinquished pair—well bred, cultured, sophisticated. They knew a great deal about music, literature, and art. They could discuss world affairs and international relations. On the subject of love and marriage, however, they were illiterates. They just didn't know how to be happily married. They led a dull, dry, dreary existence together and provided a dull, dry dreary home for their children, as well as a poor example of marriage. The truly sad fact about this couple is that their number is legion. What, after all, do you do if you are married to someone whom you don't really care for and you have children whom you do really care for?

That's a poignant question. Millions of men and women in America yearn for a sound and honorable answer to that question.

One answer which a great number have taken in the past decade or two is to get a divorce. Some have found something of a solution in that. It is said that many second marriages are better than the first. It is never, however, a completely satisfying answer. No one can desert a child and ever enjoy peace of mind again. Every child is entitled to permanent parents. Ask the four or five million orphans of divorce in this country how they feel about the legal breakup of their homes and you are sure to get some pretty chilling responses. Just look at the grief in their eyes!

Another answer—and the one most frequently accepted—is to grin and bear it. Some don't even grin, they just bear it—grimly bear it. This is obviously a poor answer as the vast sea of marital misery indicates. But your average mortal is inured to accepting poor answers to his problems. He thinks he is not entitled to much joy in life; he goes on living but he doesn't know exactly why. Is there no better answer?

There certainly is, and it's so patent and obvious you would think anyone could see it. And anyone could, except the ones who most need to see it. That answer is to try to improve the marriage.

A generation or so ago there appeared an utterly delightful play on Broadway called "Beggar on Horseback." One of the scenes was entitled "Interlude." Played in pure pantomime, it showed the crown prince and crown princess of the country retiring for the night. They were so completely bored and weary with each other, they didn't even look at each other. But a carnival was going on in the capital that night. Suddenly, as by one impulse, the two young people got out of bed—again without looking at each other—dressed, put on masks, and set out for fun and frolic at the carnival.

Yes, you guessed it. They meet at the fair, are irresistibly attracted to each other, have a deliriously happy time together, break off with passionate protestations of love, and return each to a lonely bed.

The point of the pantomime is pathetically plain. Putting on romantic masks the couple that were so bored with each other find a great joy in each other. Play the game of love with the marriage partner you have and you'll be amazed at the fun there's in it.

"Love," said the great psychologist, Havelock Ellis, "is an art." It's an art that can be cultivated. It involves graces that grow with the willingness to use them.

The married couple that was mentioned first, for instance, how barren and brittle were the extramarital affairs with which each had attempted to console himself! If only they would put on romantic masks and play Cupid's game with each other! What a carnival they could have!

And their children, knowing the joy of a happy, harmonious home, would grow up to be whole and wholesome personalities, free of the twin evils of our time, mental illness and moral delinquency.

Here is your marriage partner—the other parent of your children—who has it within him (her) to give you the greatest joy you will ever know. Or the greatest misery! Or a mediocrity of nothing much of either! Which shall it be?

That will depend on how well you apply the law of appreciation. Remember always: appreciate and you prosper; belittle and you lose.

Summary and Suggestion

What a child most needs is two parents who love and appreciate each other and love and appreciate him. All-round love and appreciation give a family serenity, security, strength. Where love and appreciation rule a home, each individual in it grows. Where love and appreciation rule a home, parents and children enjoy mutually fulfilling days.

You must also learn to appreciate yourself, not in an egotistic, fulsome way, but in a wholesome, constructive way. Recognize your own worth, assume your proper place in the world and in the home, and accept nothing less for yourself. How many people weaken their personality every day of their lives, literally wash it away, by self-depreciation? How quick are our associates—and even the one we have married —to value us at our own estimate. If we belittle ourselves, how can we expect others to respect us? "Right you are, if you think you are," is the wise old maxim. Don't be an egotist, but likewise don't be such a fool as to think less of yourself than you really are, and certainly don't voice such opinion to the world, your mate, or children. If you keep on saying, "Poor me!"—that's what you'll be—"Poor you!"

Here is your day aglow with joy and beauty if you have the mind to see it. Don't let it sink into the night of apathy and gloom. Life calls on you to live this day and live it more abundantly.

The sure means to this abundance is appreciation! The best place to begin this appreciation is right in your own home with your own spouse and children—and with yourself!

———————————

CHAPTER V

Live

Your Gender!

AT THE end of a hard working day, a woman gynecologist sat
in her office smoking a cigarette and reflecting on the many
patients she has seen during office hours. Some had mysterious
functional disorders for which she could find no physical cause.
Others had come just for a pre- or post-childbirth check-up and
had asserted with smiling emphasis that they felt fine.

As the doctor reviewed the two types of patients in her mind,
an idea dawned on her with the shock of a great realization. The
women with the "mysterious" functional disorders had one
thing in common: they regretted being women. They thought
men had the best of it. It was their discontent with their gender
that had caused these functional disorders.

The other women, the happy, healthy ones, were glad to be
women, diaper-dirty babies and tobacco-smelling husbands and
all. Unfortunately, hardly half of modern womankind can be
said to belong to this truly feminine category.

The American woman is suffering from gender pangs—psy-
chophysical unfulfillment as a woman. She rules her husband,

51

she rules her children, and to an ever-increasing degree she is beginning to own, if not rule, American business. But is she happy? That's a question. Does she exert a wholesome influence on her children? That's another question.

A generation or two ago, the lot of woman was more difficult but more satisfying. Her sphere was the home. Husband and children depended on her for meals and clothing as well as spiritual comfort. It was good to be a woman, because it was good to be so needed.

But the role of woman has undergone bewilderingly rapid changes in the past fifty years, and many have come to feel too uncertain about their place in life to be happy. The home no longer requires their full talents and energies. Food and clothing are now factory-processed, and husband and children are to that degree less dependent on them.

Some women may think it very fortunate that food and clothing are now manufactured outside the home. Does it not save them much backbreaking toil?

That it does. But it also deprives them of much ego satisfying importance to their families. "I'm *just* a homemaker," present day housewives say, almost apologetically, for it is no longer the full time job it once was.

Many American women have turned to careers in business and the professions as compensation and gained thereby a kind of satisfaction. But it does not make them feel better as women. Success in a career is not the same as success as a woman. The successful career woman is rarely a success as a woman. And how gladly would most of them give up their careers for a grade-A—or a good grade-B—husband. Discontent is the mood mark of modern woman. Only as she recovers her self-confidence as a woman, will she be happy again. That, of course, includes fulfilling her role as a wife when she becomes one. Take the case of Mrs. B:

"No woman is a true friend to her children who lets her husband 'go wandering.'" the counselor told her.

"What do you mean 'wandering'?"

"Seeking amorous satisfaction outside of his relationship with her. You know the statistical reports on the subject. According to Kinsey and others, fifty per cent of American husbands at some time or other in their marriage 'go wandering.' The ones who lose most by this are the children."

"Why the children?"

"Because they become thereby second-class children. The child brought up in the home of infidelity, even secret infidelity, never enjoys his full rights to his parents' love. These parents are too absorbed in the problems of their own love-life to give him the attention he needs. And sooner or later they may desert him entirely in a divorce or separation."

"But is that the woman's fault?"

"No, not entirely. *But it is the woman's business.* Home and children are primarily a woman's business. If she will attend to her full duty as a woman, keeping herself interesting and pleasing to her husband in addition to taking care of the house and the children, the problem in many instances need not arise."

Of course this is a one-sided argument. The converse of the proposition could just as well be addressed to husbands—and often has been.

But children have always been more closely identified with the mothers than with the fathers. It is presumed that a mother's first concern is her children. She wants them to have the good things of life and to be protected against the evil.

The best thing in life for a child is to have two parents who really love each other and who maintain a secure and happy home for him. And the most evil thing in life that can happen to a child is for his parents to separate and break up his home.

Most mothers recognize this simple and obvious truth, but not all of them realize how much the resolution of the problem depends upon them. It is quite a challenge to a woman to be a full-time sweetheart as well as a full-time mother. A true woman meets the challenge wholeheartedly and with grace and spirit.

And her rewards are very real and enduring. In addition to personal fulfillment as a woman, she wins a willing helpmate in the care and training of the children. Children are most obedient when they see in the actions of their parents the benefits of co-operation.

The role of men in our society has also undergone considerable change in recent years. And not in ways favorable to man-woman happiness!

Because competition is so severe, many men are almost totally absorbed in their business or job. Success is a must, and desperately do they strive for it. It is frequently a nervous, exhausted, irascible man that comes home to dinner in the evening with no heart for gallant play with his wife or companionable fun with his children.

American men provide for their wives, and most liberally, but they do not husband them. Do the American women prefer it that way? Some might say they do, seeing the pride with which they display their material booty: fur coats, motor cars, cultural adornments for their children, and on and on. The discerning eye, however, notes that behind this facade of treasured things there is nevertheless a discontented woman.

"You never bring me flowers anymore," one such woman happened to remark to her husband at the dinner table. Their daughter had just told of a classroom discussion interpreting Wordsworth's poem, "The Yellow Primrose."

"I give you a good allowance," the husband retorted. "If you like flowers, why don't you buy yourself some?"

"I never knew my mother could be so angry," the girl declared, in telling the story next day in the same class!

Because the American husband's one ego-satisfaction is to be a good provider, he frequently overplays the part, becoming in time the good provider, and not much more to his family. He is the missing man in many a home. His wife and children, though humbly dependent on his largess, are strangely unappreciative. They are too weak to refuse his bounty; but love and honor him for it? That they won't! The patronized have been too much hurt in their pride to love the donor.

The American mother married to a business-bound husband,

lives her whole life in her children. Is this good? It certainly
is not. She frequently smothers them with excessive care, affection, and protectiveness, allowing their individuality little
growth. Deriving her whole ego support from their need of her,
she does her utmost by fair means or foul to keep them dependent on her for as long as possible. Is it any wonder that America
is called the land of "Momism?"

But if the American mother enjoyed the companionship of a
romantic-minded husband, she might be more willing to let her
children alone, and they, then, might unfold according to their
own inner necessity and ideals. The psychoanalysts warn: "A
child can never be an adult plaything and turn out well." But
millions of American children are the playthings of their mother's emotions. No wonder we have so many neurotics.

The solution lies in a deeper understanding of our sexual personalities and an endeavor to live up to our gender ideals. We
need more truly masculine fathers, more truly feminine mothers.

The truly feminine mother, fulfilled in her marriage to a truly
masculine father, does not overprotect, dominate, or over-
fondle her children. She lets them judiciously alone. She knows
exactly what they need of food, shelter or clothing, because she
waits until they tell her. The children are secure in her watchful
care and yet free to develop their own destinies. The manly
father is a gallant husband to his wife, a pal to his sons, and a
kind of cavalier to his budding daughter. He devotes himself to
his family as much as to his business. He may get rich slowly,
but success is ultimately his, for his wife and children are a constant inspiration to him to do his best. In the balance of love and
work he finds his health and his happiness.

Summary and Suggestion

"Strength," said Havelock Ellis, the great sage on the subject of sex, "is the charm of a man, as charm is the strength
of a woman."

This is a very wise statement. It can help you establish your proper role in your marriage.

A wife is proud of a husband who shows strength—assuming responsibility, surmounting difficulty, asserting courage and confidence. "I married a real man," she says to herself. And willingly she lets him be the "head" of the home, as she becomes its "heart." And gladly does she give him her best of feminine charm as his due reward. A man enjoys a wife who is all feminine—who wants to love him, not dominate over him.

What kind of parents are best for children? Manly men and womanly women. They provide a harmonious home and a sound heredity.

CHAPTER VI

Your Sexual Happiness is Your

Child's Emotional Security

IF THERE is one pure joy that earth allows to mortal man in compensation for his endless toil and trouble, it is man-woman love in marriage. Yet how many in petty irritability or anger, in ennui or inertia, in stupidity or ignorance, throw away this dearest thing they own as if it were a mere trifle.

The relationship between your sexual happiness and your child's emotional security, is of a great but seldom realized importance. As Dr. David R. Mace, the noted marriage counselor explains, in the *Encyclopedia of Child Care and Guidance:* "The function of sex in marriage is not simply to create the child, but also to generate, and constantly to renew, the love that sustains the child in an atmosphere of warm emotional security. To put it in another way, the creative love that makes husband and wife parents is not adequately expressed in one decisive act of sexual union; it needs repeated expression to go on maintaining the flow of mutual love which should continue to surround the child."

Marriage, one would think, is a game at which one simply

cannot lose. The pleasures and satisfactions are so very rich, and the obligation so light *because shared*. Why the maladjustments then? The answer is simple. It takes two to make a marriage, just as it takes two to dance together. The two cannot dance together if each wishes to make his own steps, and two cannot live in marriage if each—or either—wishes to assert only his own egotistical way.

This is a childish attitude. The child knows only itself. Until we are mature we cannot marry, and this means spiritually mature, rather than merely physically mature. Maturity is not a matter of calendar years. Maturity begins when we rise above self and have the capacity to see and understand another and to live and work in harmony with another. Some attain spiritual maturity with body maturity. Some never attain maturity. At thirty, forty, fifty, they are still children.

Married love is a prize well worth a lifetime's labor. Yet there are some who tire in Cupid's first mile. They do not realize, as the clever French writer André Maurois so succinctly put it, that, "Marriage is an edifice that must be rebuilt every day."

The fact that you were happy in your marriage yesterday is obviously not enough. You have to be happy in your marriage today, and each day. And you can!

But it takes effort. One cannot afford to be slack, inattentive, or careless in marriage. One must give it one's best every day. Inertia, that dread quality that brings out the common in the best of us, so often turns a glowing romance and sexual happiness into a drab, matter-of-fact relationship, or something even worse.

Granted that a marriage was originally consummated in love and not in error, its satisfaction should increase rather than grow less with the years, because each satisfaction is enriched by memory of the previous satisfactions.

So many divorce-bent women complain bitterly that their husbands are conducting extramarital affairs, perhaps even maintaining an extra establishment for the "other woman." Yet, originally the husband thought his wife desirable enough to sacrifice his freedom for her; and in her present relations with him she has none of the handicaps that "the other woman" must bear—secrecy, time limitation, extra expense, social guilt feeling. Why then has the wife, with the odds all in her favor, lost out to the other woman? Because the wife has failed to keep herself sexually interesting to her husband, has thrown away in lassitude, dullness, inertia, the sweet bait with which she originally entrapped him.

The advantages are all with the wife. She has first chance at her husband, endless opportunity, and God and man's law on her side. If every good woman were also a coquette, and if every coquette were also a good woman, how much more marital felicity there would be in the world! Coquetry, however, requires effort, and many married women will not make the effort.

If marriage is an edifice which must be rebuilt every day, then a wife must consider it a daily duty to make and keep herself "interesting" to her husband, to give him such wooing delight as he can obtain from no other woman. How much of a married man's infidelity is the woman's fault, no one has set forth yet; but an interesting article for a woman's magazine might be written under the general heading, "Does your husband supplement?" —meaning does he have to seek outside of his relationship with you for the sex satisfactions which he requires and which you are unable or unwilling to give him? Many a "good woman," fatuously blind to her own sexual inadequacies, thinks that she is living with a faithful husband, but oh, on how many a supposed business trip or club activity does he adroitly disengage himself from his wife and home and slink off to that warmer and more ardent woman who gives him, for his attention and money, his "woman's worth" of passion.

Some time ago there appeared in *Esquire* magazine a wise and witty article entitled: "Why I am Faithful to my Wife." It also was reprinted in *The Bedside Esquire*, which is still available at the local book shops. Would that all husbands in the marital danger-years between forty and fifty could read this article and from it realize the shoddy bargain that constitutes most cases of marital infidelity!

A man has a wife with whom he has lived ten or fifteen years in the cozy humdrum of a good marriage, and then a piquant sexual morsel appears that he can have for the asking. "Well, well," he says, "a good wife, nice children, a comfortable home —and now this sweet thing, too! I must be quite a fellow to have all this coming to me!"

But then he reflects a little and decides that the piquant sexual morsel is not worth the having. When you have a wife *and* a mistress, you soon find that you can enjoy neither. It isn't a question of morality, at all; it's purely and simply a matter of realizing a man's satisfactions in the life he is actually living. Of course, the wife would soon know (trust her intuition to tell her, as well as her women friends!) and then the love life with the wife, the not-too-exciting but nevertheless soundly satisfying love life with the wife, would be over. And the love life with the mistress —well, the piquant sexual morsel might not be so tasty after all. Sex under furtive, hasty, conscience-troubled conditions doesn't have much flavor.

Besides, there's the matter of the children—the fine, intelligent son, the adorable lovely small daughter—what could Aphrodite herself offer to counter-balance their loss?

There is a Spanish folk proverb which says: "He who knows one woman, knows all women; he who knows all women, knows no woman." In love, he who sips many brims never quaffs the cup. If you want the great experience of a true love, you must build it up with one person.

As long as the husband and wife are faithful to each other, as long as the day's harassments are soothed in the night's embrace, the sexual rhythm can be counted on to clear away the petty discords that gather in all marriages. In the light of desire, how readily do the shortcomings of the marriage partner disappear! The sharp voice, the show of temper, the clash of opinion —are all washed away in passion's tide. A new serpent-free Eden arises, vernal, fair, to be the abode of the restored Adam and Eve. The unfaithful have no such insurance.

Just because you want to enjoy your sex life, you should think hard and long on what it means to have an extramarital affair. Disillusionment is almost certain—rarely are the conditions right for sex outside of marriage, with a hundred and one things to fear and worry about—making impossible any true fulfillment. Physical sex can be a most trivial experience, yet for this moment of sensation many risk health and peace of mind, to say nothing of the greatest loss of all, the chance to experience sex with love, the most felicitous of all human experiences.

Time was when the male—"the imperfectly monogamous male," as one sociologist has dubbed him—was most blamed for the breakup of a marriage through sexual infidelity. That attitude is now changing. No husband commits adultery without at least some collusion on the part of his wife, what she didn't do, if not what she did. Modern woman assumes her full responsibility to make the sex part of marriage satisfactory.

It was the pioneering social psychologist, Floyd Henry Allport, who made the profound observation that: "A woman brings out the best in a man by a judicious administration of her love gifts." But to do this, she must have gifts to offer. A sexually gratified husband is always eager and willing to please the woman who has pleased him. The wife is now in a position to direct this enthusiasm and energy into channels that lead to the family's best growth and welfare. This is her secret weapon. And since women from earliest times have felt the greater responsibility for the children, it is with this weapon that she surely and easily achieves her aim of winning the father's full cooperation in raising them well. Of course, a woman, too, has her amatory needs. And she looks to her husband for their fulfillment. A true male does not fail her!

Basic to success in marriage and the best insurance against the breakup of the home, home tensions, man-woman unhappiness, with all their attendant miseries for the children, is conjugal loyalty and fulfillment. Would that this were better understood.

It is a sad fact that much husband-wife conflict can be traced to sheer ignorance, especially in the field of sex, a subject on which there is now sound knowledge available in marriage manuals such as Eustace Chesser's, *Love Without Fear;* Oliver McKinley Butterfield's *Marriage and Sexual Harmony.* No one fails to appreciate and stay with a marriage partner with whom he feels sexually fulfilled.

"Better children," said the Senate Report on Juvenile Delinquency, "can come only from better parents." But better parents, in turn, can come only from better mates. Loving each other, they naturally love and cherish the offspring of their union.

It is in the spontaneous overflow of your mutual affections that your children find the kind of love they need. It provides a secure home for them. It is warm and comforting. It teaches the valuable lesson of cooperation. Furthermore, when parents genuinely love each other, there is no urge to turn an abnormal affection on the children and so corrupt their feelings. The Oedipus and the Elektra complexes do not grow in a home of parental peace.

A well-ordered home follows a natural routine with everyone cooperating to promote everyone else's comfort and well being. The cynic or the sophist may permit himself a mocking smile at the boredom of domestic harmony, but what he wouldn't give to enjoy some of that harmony himself! The core of the home, the parent-child relationship, stems from the vital husband-wife relationship and flourishes best when governed by mutual sexual happiness, and least when lacking it.

Mankind lives and moves on an invisible sea of love. Let the waters recede and mankind sinks, as every now and then it seems in peril of doing. How priceless then, is the contribution of those fine men and women who know how to renew its failing resources by individual contributions of their own.

Every family, too, as a small world, faces this possible peril of falling apart for lack of the love to sustain it. How much of family happiness is lost when husband and wife sulk at each other—for days, for weeks, in some cases, for years.

In their homes the shadows fall. Life is harsh, gloomy, and cold; and the children come to think this is all life has to offer. They expect no more of it. They get to believe that all people are unkind and suspicious, cruel and destructive to each other. The home is their concept of a society, and they bring into the world the destructive attitudes they acquired there.

In your own home, are you the one who knows how to initiate love? Do you start the warm currents of affection and good feeling going by your ready amiability and good cheer, thus upholding the spirits of your spouse and children? And can you do all this without losing your force and effectiveness? Then you have mastered the fine art of domestic relations. You are almost certain to build a fine family with healthy and happy children.

So many people have the fifty-fifty idea of marriage—I'll do for you as much as you'll do for me. Do they realize what a petty, mean philosophy this is for all its seeming fairness? Where does your fifty end and mine begin? One could argue this endlessly—and one usually does, alas!

Total love—not fifty-fifty love—is what it takes to make a marriage.

As we give greatly in love—never counting the cost, never calling for return—we challenge our mate to do likewise. His pride will not allow him to be outdone in generosity. Our marriage then moves to a high plane of mutual generosity and good will—and will stay there as long as we maintain our attitude of being ever willing to initiate love.

The cynical will challenge this, declaring we merely tempt the other to exploit us. That may be true if our giving is patronizing. But not if it is true devotion. Everyone enjoys love, and most everyone is quick to return it, even though he may not have had heart enough to initiate it. The great of soul are those who are willing to take this first—and seemingly risky—step. But they don't lose out by this. Nearly always it wins an affectionate response plus admiration and praise.

Summary and Suggestion

Love is a tremendous energizer. No domestic task, no outside job seems difficult to those infused with its electric impulses. You will have all the energy you require for carrying out your many duties as a parent, as you replenish each other's affectional needs and add the magic pinch of romance, too. The happy lovers are the potentially effective parents. They instinctively love the product of their union, for they engendered it in joy. And they readily seek out and obtain the necessary knowledge for doing a good job of parenthood.

This wonderfully precious possession—a mutually satisfying married love—don't ever lose it! Don't let its fires dwindle and die for lack of the care to tend it. You can make many mistakes in life, and still get by. But don't make this one!

Unless you love each other, you cannot really love your children!

CHAPTER VII

Parents Are a Child's Fate:

Children Are a Parent's Fate

WHAT YOUR children most need is YOU—a happy, healthy well married YOU. His parents are a child's fate. There is no good fortune quite equal to that of being born to a sound father and a sound mother who really love each other. That is why we have begun this study of "What Your Child Needs" with an analysis of what you need—namely, your spouse's full love and devotion.

Do you who read this book enjoy that full love and devotion? If not, think hard and long of why you do not. Nothing that you will ever get out of life will equal what you are losing by its lack.

It will be natural for you to explain this lack—if such it be with you—by detailing your spouse's shortcomings. But don't give way to such thinking. No good can come of it. He (she) won't change for all your complaining.

Try rather to analyze how you might be a better lover yourself and have the heart to make the first move toward improving your marriage. Don't hold back the instinctive flow of affection now rising within you. Unexpressed love is like miser's gold. It buys nothing. It makes no one happy.

It is the sad fact of human nature that while all people long
for love and are usually quick to respond to it, not all people are
good at initiating, or renewing, it. Are you the great-hearted one
who will?

Your reward is sure.

You will at once have more energy. You'll feel big because
you have behaved big. You'll arouse new and unexpected responses in your marriage partner which you will enjoy all the
more because you paid an honest price for them.

Your happiness will spread to your children. They will suddenly show joy and enthusiasm. They will do things of their own
accord you previously couldn't make them do by force or urging: they will help in the house, study their lessons, speak courteously to each other, even "eat their spinach" without squawking.
Every now and then one of them will give you a spontaneous
hug or kiss or climb on your knee and tell you how wonderful
you are. Parenthood will become both pleasant and important.
You'll want to be good at it.

Soon you'll realize that just as you make your children's fate,
they make yours. They give your life worth and meaning.

Many are proud of having made a mint of money, and some of
having created books or music or pictures. Still others glory in
political power. But success with children is something different
again, something extra special. Some of the world's greatest suc-
cesses couldn't quite achieve it. It calls for a very particular
quality of personality and character. And because the modern
world is so troubled about its children, successful parenthood is
mightily applauded. The self within you will receive constant
nourishment from the approving words spoken of your children.

But of course that isn't all. Children are a great joy in themselves—that is, if you really join with them in happy talk and
play. They relieve the tedium of your toil, they recharge your
energies, they make you feel young again. How interesting it is
to watch them grow!

And how satisfying is their affection, uncalculating and real, often catching you when you are low in spirits and giving you just the lift you need.

Best of all, children bring, as the poet Wordsworth put it, "forward-turning thoughts." They lead you into the future. Something to do, someone to love, something to hope for, is a basic formula for happiness. Life has promise when you have children—great promise, if you have raised energetic, happy, self-confident children.

A father to admire and emulate is Theodore Roosevelt, hero president to the American boy—and girl! Here was a man who in one lifetime lived a dozen careers; cowboy, sheriff, soldier, hunter, explorer, politician, writer, historian, naturalist, police commissioner, governor, finally President. Yet for all his many activities he always found time for a romp or a frolic with his children. He read to them, played with them, talked with them. If they were away, he wrote to them. Always he was their inspiration and guide.

By contrast, how many present-day fathers protest that because of the demands of their job or business, they have no time to spend with their children!

Listen to what this great man and great father said of home and family life:

"No other form of personal success and happiness or of individual service to the State compares with that which is represented by the love of the one man for the one woman, of their joint work as homemaker and homekeeper, and of their ability to bring up the children who are theirs.

"It is exceedingly interesting and attractive to be a successful businessman, or railroad man, or farmer, or a successful lawyer or doctor; or a writer, or a President, or a ranchman, or the colonel of a fighting regiment, or to kill grizzly bears and lions. But for unflagging interest and enjoyment, a household of children, if things go reasonably well, certainly makes all other forms of success and achievement lose their importance by comparison."

*   *   *

These are inspiring words. Children need their fathers to set
them an example of courage, responsibility, force—as "Teddy"
did for his heroic sons and brilliant daughter.

You as a loving married pair will have little trouble bringing
up your children. Fulfilled in your own love life, you turn your
satisfied feelings toward your offspring. Most of the misbehavior
of children is brought on by the desire to draw attention to themselves. The beloved child has no such need. Your happiness has
made his. Such is the interacting fate of parent and child.

*   *   *

At the age of one, baby Linda looked at life and found it good.
"It's a nice world," she said in her own baby tongue. "I'm glad I
came!" And she smiled at the guests who had assembled to cele-
brate her first birthday. They smiled back at her with enthusiasm.

Why was Linda so glad to be alive on her first birthday? And
why did her parents and grandparents feel so proud and happy
about her?

Baby Linda had mastered in her first year life's most valuable lesson: the art of receiving and giving love.

Credit for this goes first of all to her mother. It was she who
gave Linda the constant loving care which is every infant's need
and turns the newly born's first wail of anger at entering the
world into a constant coo of delight. No duty of feeding, cleaning, comforting was too difficult for her. She always got there
with what was needed before the whining could begin. Lucky
Linda! Her environment was secure. She could look forward to
life with faith, not doubt. No wonder she always smiled back
when her mother smiled at her.

The father deserved a lot of credit, too. He gave his wife
through all this period such gallant assurance of being loved and
admired as a woman, she felt confident in herself and strong to
do her duty as a mother. An unhappy wife is a nervous mother.
Her bitter feelings communicate to her baby and make it fretful

and ill. Husbands who know how to love their wives assure themselves of happy and healthy progeny.

And the grandparents, too, could come in for some of the credit, the husband's mother in particular. She had released her son fully and unequivocally to her daughter-in-law's love. She praised and encouraged her and never intruded with uncalled-for advice or assistance. Linda's mother could give her full attention to her child because none of it was distracted in worry about what a critical husband or mother-in-law might be thinking and saying about her. No wonder the child turned out so well.

Summary and Suggestion

You are off to a good start in parenthood when you are sure of your affection for each other.

Life is pleasant for married lovers. Their body urges are gratified; they enjoy agreeable mental and emotional companionship; their creature comforts are provided for in a home of their own.

You should have a year or two of this sweet all-for-each-other life together before you undertake parenthood.

But don't fear parenthood. "Many children, many cares," said the old philosopher. But he was quick to add: "No children, no felicity."

For your fullest happiness, for your true growth as a man or a woman, in a word, to know life whole—you will want to be a parent. With the right knowledge and the right will, the job is pleasant, interesting and not too difficult.

Besides, in your love for your children, you will find a greater love for each other.

BOOK TWO

Acceptance

EVERY CHILD NEEDS TO BELIEVE:

that his parents like him for himself, just the way he is

that they like him all the time, and not only when he acts according to their ideas of the way a child should act

that they always accept him, even though often they may not approve of the things he does

that they will let him grow and develop in his own way

CHAPTER I

Rejection:

Tragedy of Childhood

"WHEN I was an interne and you were a student nurse," the distinguished surgeon reminisced playfully to one of the older nurses at the twenty-fifth Staff Reunion Party, "I used to come up to your floor each evening and ask you to make me some hot cocoa. Remember?—Gee, I drank a lot of hot cocoa just to get acquainted with you. But it didn't do any good."

And he smiled a wry, sad smile at the shy, gray-haired, but still pretty woman as he turned to chat with another guest.

Did she remember?

Yes, she remembered very well. Nothing lived stronger in her memory than this might-have-been romance. Why had she not been able to go after a man as other girls did and win him for her very own? A lot of lonely women ask themselves this question.

The answer is that as children they had suffered rejection. And all their life long they could never think of themselves as worthy of being accepted. The good things of life, including love, were not for them.

73

That is the tragedy of the rejected child. It isn't that he likes to suffer, as some unfeelingly say. Nobody likes to suffer. He just can't believe that anything better is coming to him. What you expect out of life, that's what you get.

So many chapters of society's ills and evils, so much of history's war, crime, vice, as well as individual grief and sorrow have been acted out by rejected children that few concepts are more important for the parent to understand than the term "rejection." Would there, for instance, ever have been a Hitler, if all parents—all people—had known how to accept and love all children? Wittingly or unwittingly, many parents reject their children with dire consequence to the child, to themselves, and to society.

A child may be said to be rejected if his parents do not like him, did not want him in the first place, do not give him the love and care he needs to feel that he belongs. Sheldon and Eleanor Glueck in their monumental studies of juvenile delinquency, "The Making of a Delinquent," "One Thousand Juvenile Delinquents," and others, point out that rejection by the parents was the major factor in impelling these children to crime.

It is characteristic of the rejected child that if he does not react to rejection by humility and submissiveness, he may give way to rebellion and aggression, leading eventually to criminality. Some authorities even go so far as to say that all social rebellion is the result of rejection. That is why the tough delinquent appears to some as a pretty pathetic figure. And in one way he is. For are not all his acts of aggression merely attempts to draw attention to his great need of love? If a love equal to his need could be given him, would he still attack society? In the few instances where such a love was afforded by social agencies, a very genuine reform was effected.

Sometimes one parent and not the other will reject the child, in which case a warring triangle may result. Sometimes rejection is due to the sex of the child, as when one parent seeking to fulfill his dreams in a child of his own gender, refuses to give his love to the child of opposite gender born to him. What folly not to freely accept whatever child God gives us! Yet many parents commit this folly because of deep inner needs of their own.

In fact, the rejecting parent may very likely himself have been a rejected child. Or he may feel rejection in his marriage. An amorous husband, for instance, who feels a distinct diminution in his wife's ardor on the arrival of a child, especially a boy child— will certainly not give that child his full acceptance and love. Similarly a woman who has been forced into a marriage she really did not want, may let out her dissatisfactions on her child. The same may happen if she had to give up a glamorous career because of an unwanted pregnancy! Even if children mean merely the sacrifice of a round of social interests, dancing, partying, some immature men and women give way to feelings of resentment toward, and rejection of, the child.

Some women—the so-called feminists in particular—reject the feminine role altogether of which the child is the living symbol. They believe that men have the best of it and consider children a burden and a nuisance. They certainly aren't going to make their children feel loved and wanted. And many men—100,000 a year in America—just walk out on marriage because they are too immature to accept the responsibility of parenthood.

Most tragic and desperate of all forms of rejection is the alcoholic's abandonment of his children to poverty and shame that he may satisfy his own inordinate craving for drink. Alcohol is the especial enemy of children. Ask any superintendent of welfare in any large city what is responsible for most cases of families on relief and he will answer alcohol. And one widely-circulated woman columnist on love and family problems has declared that according to her mail, alcohol is now the Number One menace to American family life.

"Everything has gone from this house. That is what alcohol does. When it comes into a house everything goes—love, affection, loyalty, all decent human feeling—it leaves nothing. This is its terrible curse." Thus one parent described his home after the other parent had turned alcoholic.

Here is another illustration:

"Mommy's mean to me, she's just mean to me! And it's because you drink so much."

When his beloved thirteen-year-old daughter suddenly jumped up from the piano where she had been nervously practicing under her mother's fitful criticism and cried these words hysterically into his ears, Harvey Baxter was shocked into thinking more seriously about his drinking than he had ever done before.

Fortunately he was not yet an all-gone alcoholic. And fortunately he had not yet lost the love and respect of his wife and children. But he was on the brink! Family life had frequently been made miserable by his failure to come home when expected and by his surly quarrelsomeness when he did arrive drunk.

Everything can be fine in a family until the father turns alcoholic. Then, good-night! Grief and shame overcome the children. Life for them loses hope; and what is life without hope?

If you love your children, you can't love alcohol, too. Hard-drinking fathers should take a long thoughtful look at that sentence.

Daughters especially suffer. Her father is every girl's ideal of a man—the kind she will fall in love with some day and marry. But what sort of an ideal can a drunkard be to his daughter? He is ugly in appearance and nasty in behavior. She suffers a thousand shocks each time she sees him in this sodden state. All men become hateful to her because her father has deserted her. She can have faith in none of them. Her father has killed her dream of love. And for a girl, what's left of life when you take away love?

In *Lancet*, the journal of the British medical profession, Dr. G. Gladstone Robertson traced in painstaking research the problems of alcoholics' daughters. Most of them grow up to be sexually frigid when they marry, besides developing all kinds of functional ills, indigestion and gall stones in particular. They make poor wives, of course, usually driving their husbands to drink or giving them ulcers and other physical ills. Thus alcohol goes its disastrous journey through the generations ruining all children in its progress.

How much alcohol? That's every drinker's personal problem. In moderation, alcohol relaxes and gives pleasure. It enlivens many a social gathering. It closes many a profitable business deal. But in excess, alcohol is just plain poison, an all-round misery maker, the especial enemy of children, the doom of any family whose head falls under its sway. Every true father will keep this in mind. If he finds that alcohol is getting the better of him, he will at once consult his family physician, or a specialist, on how to cure this sickness.

All these rejecting parents may not totally reject their children. Many may seemingly give them a lot of love—but always this love is forced. It fails to make the child happy.

Rejecting parents have subtle forms of expressing their rejection. Sometimes these forms are so subtle that the parents are totally unaware of what they are doing and may protest to the death that they are giving the child love. They do not persuade the child of this or fool the discerning eye of the psychologist.

They are always criticising the child or setting standards for him too high for happiness. They never praise him. They frequently compare him unfavorably with other children and express a cutting surprise when someone says something good about him. If they do attend to his wants, it is done grudgingly or with an air of martyrdom.

To propitiate the fates—as in childhood he had tried to win over the angry parent—Rejection's Child when grown up, will give things, service, humble devotion, model deportment, anything he has. But somehow nothing seems to help. Rather his abasement invites abuse. People: his spouse, his boss, political leaders—even his children if he has any—kick him around, tyrannize over him. They hurt him more than they intend, for somehow he seems to bring out the worst in them.

In desperation he gives more—he lacerates and denies himself. Still to no avail. He is mocked but not loved.

Finally he resigns himself. He is the condemned prisoner in life's jail. He serves out his time and dies. If there is such a thing as a reincarnation he prays to be born again, but this time to parents who will not reject him, who will love him as he longs to be loved. Then how different will be the history of his life!

Summary and Suggestion

X 'If love is a child's greatest need, then the lack of love is his greatest loss. Rejection is the tragedy of childhood./

The Mental Health Way—always constructive in its philosophy—puts it in positive words thus under the heading ACCEPTANCE:

"Every child needs to believe that his parents like him for himself, just the way he is . . . that they like him all the time, and not only when he acts according to their ideas of the way a child should act . . . that they *always* accept him, even though they may not approve of the things he does . . . that they will let him grow and develop in his own way."

How many children experience rejection, partial or complete, from their parents? Countless numbers. How much of the grief and evil of life, how many of its mental and moral ills are due to this one cause!

As we study various examples of rejective behavior on the part of parents and see its sad consequences, let us try to understand how happily different the story might have been if the parents had known and practiced The Mental Health Way of love and acceptance—at all times and under all circumstances.

Scrupulously search out your own conscience to see whether any of your attitudes toward your child cause him to feel rejected—outcast from your love and care. Are you taking out on him feelings of frustration you have in your relations to your mate? Are your standards too high, or are you so lax that he thinks you are indifferent? Are you unwilling to let him grow and develop in his own way? Whatever it may be, correct it. Your child has no future if he grows up feeling rejected.

CHAPTER II

Rigid Rules:

A Baby Experiences Rejection

IN A cultured American home of a quarter of a century ago, a baby's cry was heard in the middle of the night. Instinctively the mother stirred. She wanted to go to the baby, take it to her breast, feed it, then croon it back to sleep again.

But her husband, who had also heard the cry, held her back. "Don't do it, Anne. You'll never train him that way. You know what Dr. X said: 'Pick up a baby every time it cries, and you'll bring up a brat.' We have to feed him on schedule, not every time he demands food. Otherwise, you'll go crazy trying to take care of his every wish!"

Did the baby stop crying?

No, it didn't. It wept and wailed until in utter exhaustion it fell asleep. The next morning at its scheduled feeding time it seemed to have less interest in food than in sleep and had to be forcibly awakened to take its bottle. Once more it was unhappy.

The next night it howled again—only more desperately, more insistently, maddened by hunger pangs. But again the idea of training triumphed, and again the baby was denied its 2 o'clock feeding. The father and mother were intensely distressed, but remained obdurate. Their baby must be trained!

A half a world away, in a peasant hut in Okinawa, another infant cried in the night at about the same time. Instinctively the mother stirred, picked up the baby from beside her, brought it to her breast, let it suck as long as it wanted, then laid it down again. Through it all the husband snored peacefully. Soon mother and babe were asleep also, and all was contentment and quiet again in a hut in Okinawa.

Was the Okinawan mother so much wiser than the American mother? No. By their instincts both women wanted to do the same thing with their crying child.

But the American woman, like many others at that time, was in the grip of the Behaviorist theory of child training then prevalent which was all for scheduled feeding and other strict regimens. Training was imposed on the child without consideration of his physiological rhythms and natural desires. And even affection was rationed in the fear that too much of it had a weakening effect on the personality. The result was a generation of neurotic, spoiled, unhappy children who—in retaliation—grew up into egotistic, tyrannical, quarrelsome adults.

The folly of these child-training methods was brought home to army psychiatrists who followed our troops to the island of Okinawa. There they found the best behaved and least neurotic children they had ever known. And what was the explanation of their fine conduct and manners? The absolute lovingness with which their parents—particularly the mothers—raised them.

Instinctively these native mothers sensed their children's need of food, rest, affection, and supplied them, not on a fixed schedule, but on demand as the need was expressed. Gradually the demands resolved themselves into a regular routine. What American mothers fought and suffered to attain but didn't, (at what grief to the child no one can calculate), the native mothers accomplished with ease by working with and not against nature. The same was true with toilet training, a particularly vexing problem in our culture. The native children were allowed to train themselves, which they did, and just as quickly as the children of the overanxious Western mothers. But they escaped the personality distresses which forced training causes.

Of late, a change for the better has come about in this country, brought on by Mental Health teachings. The writings of the Okinawa-based American psychiatrists stirred up a lot of thought, too. We now realize that rigid rules as to eating, sleeping, toilet training represent in reality a rejection of the newborn child. He is not accepted as he is and his needs supplied. No, he must be forced into a mould of behavior that we have set for him regardless of how unnatural it is and of how he suffers in it. And how disastrous the effect may be on his later personality!

Training is fine. Set your sights for it high. But love comes before training. With love your baby will gradually adopt a reasonable schedule. If you try to force an arbitrary time for such matters as eating, sleeping, bowel movements, if you have rigid rules for behavior, you will raise a neurotic, rebellious child who will pass on to others the tyranny you imposed on him.

But the well-loved infant is stabilized in personality from the start. He flourishes on your love both physically and spiritually. He goes out to meet the world with self-confidence and carries off the prizes of success and happiness. He brings honor to the parents who raised him so wisely and so well.

Summary and Suggestion

The Good Book says that man was not made for the Sabbath; the Sabbath was made for the man. In the same way, your child was not born to illustrate rigid rules of training; training must be in accord with the child's temperament and needs. Work with your child's feelings not against them. Make sure that he is comfortable, that he is fed when he is hungry, comforted when he is hurt, that his body functions according to its natural rhythms and not by a superimposed schedule. Soon he will establish his own schedule, and both you and he can be happy in carrying it out.

Because you work with the child's physiological and emotional rhythms—and not against them—does not say you can not have high standards. Time things right, and you can lead your child to a fine pattern of behavior. But beware of rules that are rigid without being realistic; that represent the adult rather than the child's point of view.

CHAPTER III

Reject Your Child:

Reject Your Self

It was the wise American psychologist William James who said: "Energy grows with the willingness to use it." This simple but profound psychological principle can be immensely useful to parents—especially mothers—whose duties, the Lord knows, are many and arduous.

You will be agreeably surprised to find how easily you will get things done as you learn to latch on to this law. It's almost like magic. You jump up to each job with enthusiasm, finish it in no time, and sense no fatigue. And how good it feels to let out your full energies!

But, oh, how weary, flat, stale, and unprofitable life can seem if you don't like your work. To whom has each day become a burden? The rejecting parent. One reader of my newspaper column writes:

"Dear Dr. Goodman: You seem to have a knack for writing columns as though they were calculated to annoy parents—mothers mostly. Yesterday's column 'As Children Sleep' was no exception.

"You paint such a simple picture of fussing with the children during the day and pleasing hubby from the moment he steps in the door.

"Why not take a consensus of male opinion as to whether they would prefer staying at home with the little dolls, cleaning house, shopping, and preparing meals to the work they are now doing? By the time 6:30 P.M. rolls around, a mother is apt to feel like a prisoner in a monkey cage, but too worn out to attempt an escape to some civilized society.

"What with stained upholstery, hacked woodwork, finger printed walls, raided bookcases, and floors littered with toys, as well as wet diapers and more, what is less glamorous or gratifying than the life of a mother?

"That we have kept to our marriage vows is, perhaps, because we were so happy in the two years before the children came. Sometimes I feel that it is only the hope that the years will fly by till they will marry that restores my will to continue.

"There just aren't enough hours in each day to keep a home shiny and attractive, attend to the children, and do the other things a woman likes to do—like crocheting, crossword puzzles, reading. Well, how on earth is a woman to be charming and interesting each evening if her day was spent doing the same things she does the other six days of the week?"

Sounds pretty awful, doesn't it? Sad to say, there are a great number of mothers who would endorse this complaint as describing their own situation, too.

But, fortunately, there are many other parents who don't feel this way at all. They think parenthood is great fun and assume its burdens gladly.

One such, a father, writes:

"After twenty-five years of marriage and of taking care of a large family, I found out: There's no boredom, no monotony, no pessimistic fatalism. Like everybody else we love all our children. But we love each child in a different way. I am convinced that every time God sends a new baby into the world, He also sends a brand new and totally different love.

"Parental love cannot be analyzed scientifically. It must be a powerful force from above. My wife and I never had a dull moment. At times it was rugged, yes—especially in money matters. But there was rugged romance, too, with beauty and delightful variety. I'm just getting by, but certainly happily."

What a difference between these two parents!

The first has rejected parenthood. As a consequence everything about it has become difficult for her. She conveys no joy, no enthusiasm to her children. Subtly they sense her rejection of them. Therefore, they feel no real love for her, either, no obligation to be obedient. This mother has no energy for her task, for her heart isn't in it.

But she doesn't have to stay this way!

Let her accept her task, willingly, and at once life will take on different and brighter colors.

She will have more energy. And with this new found energy, plus a little careful planning of the children's activities and the wisdom to leave them alone more, things won't be so hectic. She'll be able to smile a little, laugh a little, join in the fun.

And how her children will enjoy this new attitude! And what a difference it will make in their behavior.

With a loving, accepting mother it is easy to cooperate. She hasn't rejected you and so you can't reject her. You obey much more willingly. And you become competent and strong because your mother has loved you unqualifiedly and shown faith in you.

And when hubby comes home for dinner, it won't be too difficult to be the smiling wife whose good cheer compensates for the moil and toil of his day.

You're tired, sure. And he's tired. But it's a pleasant tiredness because it is the product of a day well spent and duties proudly accepted.

You and your husband can relax through the evening in chit-chat or a game or a Hi-Fi concert together "As Children Sleep." And when you yourself retire for the night a loving embrace smoothes away the last of the day's weariness. You sleep the happy sleep of the just. And tomorrow is another day.

Summary and Suggestion

"Life is difficult," the parents declare, listing their many problems. That is true enough. Life is difficult.

But it is also true that once you accept the fact that life is difficult, it becomes less difficult. By acknowledging that this is a struggling world, a place for growth as well as enjoyment, you suddenly feel strong and able to handle your problems.

This is a very valuable idea not only for yourself but for your children. As they see you sturdily facing up to the difficulties of your daily life, they will catch the idea from you and do likewise. For them, too, life will be difficult. But enjoyable! Would you wish it otherwise?

You will save time and energy by lovingly establishing a gentle but firm sense of order in your family and daily routine. Frantic attitudes, the feeling of hostility toward life's duties and problems, will not help you to improve your situation. Say "yes" to life, and life will say "yes" to you. Accept your children, and they'll accept you—obey you, love you, develop in ways to make you proud.

CHAPTER IV

Give Love First,

Then Ask Obedience

"IF YOU want mother to love you, Henry, you must do what mother says. Now come here and promise me you will never, never tease your little brother. Promise? You've got to promise! . . . Now that's a good boy."

Only after he had promised did Mrs. R. take her six-year-old son in her arms and give him a hug and brush away the tear that was forming in his eye.

Little Henry sighed with relief and hurried off. How he enjoyed his mother's hug and kiss! But why did he always have to promise to be a good boy before he could get it?

Poor Henry! He struggled hard with that question. And he isn't the only little boy asking why he has to be good to get his mother's love. Can't she love him just the way he is? If he could be sure of that, maybe he wouldn't have to tease his little brother so much . . .

American mothers who in their ego distress feel a need to dominate over their children—using love as the instrument of power—would do well to reflect hard and long on Henry's question. Mother's withholding of love has taken the place of father's strap in the training of children. It's a subtler, crueler, more damaging weapon. The generation coming up will have many personality distresses and weaknesses if too many mothers indulge in this way of winning obedience.

"What's the difference," you might ask, "between calling for obedience and then giving love, and giving love first and then calling for obedience?"

All the difference in the world. Your whole success as a parent may depend on your understanding that difference.

The child who is loved for himself—as is—feels valued as an individual. He has been accorded the full rights of an individual when the choice, to obey or not to obey, has been left up to him. He is proud to have that choice and in his pride is glad to obey.

He has received love as a free gift, no strings attached. His obedience, therefore, is a free gift, too. This is an exchange of worth and dignity. He feels big because of your faith in him. He will always want to live up to what you see in him. Recognize the aspiring spirit in your child, and you will have a child who will aspire and grow.

Only the child who is loved for himself, as is and with no qualifying conditions, will have the self-confidence he needs for making his way in the world. Self-confidence is a child's most precious possession, more valuable than any property you may bequeath him. With it he feels sound and strong, able to do things. With it he will make his own fortune.

But the child who always has to win love, who does not receive it as his inalienable right, feels unsure of his worth and so will step out into the world lacking the vital self-confidence needed for accomplishing things. Conditioning your love is rejecting your child and may be responsible for his later poor achievement.

Now suppose Henry's mother, noting that he was continually teasing his little brother, had paused before she punished and asked herself why he was doing this. Maybe she would have realized that Henry was jealous of his little brother because the latter was getting most of the love that had formerly been all his. Then, instead of lecturing Henry, she would have lifted him up in her arms, given him some extra cuddling, taken time to play with him alone, and finally brought the little brother into the game.

Then Henry would have realized that he hadn't lost anything by the advent of another child in the family. Out of satisfaction over his mother's love—so freely given and therefore so gladly received and greatly enjoyed—he would seek out ways to continue to have it. That would, of course, include being a good friend to his little brother.

Always, first things come first. Love is first in a child's life. Give love and you'll get obedience. Demand obedience first and make your love conditional on getting it, and you'll raise a surly, disobedient child who will thwart you as much as he dares. Or a negative ninny, humbly obedient to the will of other people and accepting whatever life does to him because he feels he is entitled to no better!

Summary and Suggestion

Winning obedience through love is the supreme grace of the good parent. Do you possess that grace? If so, yours is a very special reward. Your child, in addition to being a happy, pleasant person, will gradually acquire a conscience, his instinctive guide to right and wrong. Then you won't have to be always telling him what to do. He'll know himself. And do it.

It's important to know how a child develops a conscience. Ours is a society greatly troubled by the bad behavior of its children. If we gave all children adequate love and a good example, each child would develop a conscience and we wouldn't be plagued with this problem.

CHAPTER V

The Accepted Child
Acquires A Conscience

"WHY DID they do it? Had they no conscience?"

Parents ask these questions whenever some particularly horrible story of juvenile delinquency hits the headlines. The occasions for questioning have been only too common of late. Juvenile delinquency has become America's number one social problem.

In asking these questions the parents are, of course, thinking of their own children. "Could my child do anything like that?"

The answer is: No, if through your love and acceptance of them, plus the example of your own high standards, you have helped them acquire a conscience—their own instinctive guide to right and wrong. With a true conscience, your child's behavior need no longer worry you. He will do right of his own accord.

For four years the Senate Subcommittee to Investigate Juvenile Delinquency, aided by a staff of trained research workers, went up and down the land through cities, towns and villages earnestly endeavoring to track down the causes of child crime. If they could find the cause, they might also effect the cure.

America could then build a better society on a foundation of better children.

What they discovered as to the cause was very different from what they had expected.

Poverty, poor housing, lack of recreation—all the traditional reasons for juvenile delinquency, which might possibly be remedied through proper legislation—were found to be not the real reasons. The real reason was the character of the parents, something no legislation can change.

Children turn delinquent for lack of parents with good social standards and the love that will persuade the children to accept the standards. The loved child takes on his parents' standards. "Better children," the Committee summarized, "can come only from better parents."

These findings were practically the same as those brought out some years previously by the noted sociologists Drs. Sheldon and Eleanor Glueck in their monumental work, "The Making of a Delinquent." For this study the Gluecks and their co-workers made a detailed comparison between five hundred delinquent boys in Massachusetts reform schools and their carefully matched non-delinquent counterparts, matched in age, size, intelligence quotient, physical strength, country of origin of parents, and economic status.

What did they discover to be the essential difference between the five hundred delinquents and the five hundred non-delinquents? The non-delinquents had parents who gave them affection coupled with something of a social standard.

This in essence means they helped them develop a conscience which was their defense in time of temptation.

What is this thing called conscience and how do children acquire it?

Conscience, simply defined, is that part of human personality which guides the individual in distinguishing right from wrong. Psychologists call it the super-ego or higher self. What distinguishes man from the beast is that man has a conscience. To the degree that man develops his conscience, he can build a moral order and out of this a good world for himself and his children.

Note carefully that the parent begins this creation of a conscience by loving the child. The child has to know what it is that he is in danger of losing if he misbehaves. And the parent does not actually withdraw his love when the child misbehaves; he merely shows his disapproval of the child's act. But the child fears that the love may be withdrawn, and this alone is usually enough to get him back on to the track of good behavior, because the child greatly values his parents' love and will do anything not to lose it.

Even the most hardened delinquent would probably become law abiding if our love equalled his need. His misbehavior is really nothing but a desperate bid for attention: "See how unhappy I am. Why don't you do something to help me? Why don't you give me love?" Unfortunately, by the time the delinquent reaches court, and society does begin to pay some attention to him, he is so far gone morally and emotionally, many feel that society can hardly afford to reclaim him. But how different his story would have been if he had been loved from the start!

Children whose parents have rejected them or feel cold and indifferent to them, displaced children, or children brought up by a succession of hired nurse maids and governesses, will with difficulty develop a conscience.

Furthermore, since a child acquires his conscience by the reward of love for behavior that meets with his parents' approval, it is obviously necessary that the parents themselves have standards. They must know of what to approve.

And their standards must be real; they must live them, not just talk about them. Morals, like manners, are caught not taught. You can't carry on with one set of standards in your own personal business or professional life and hope to bring up your children by another.

In the powerful social drama "God of Vengeance" by the late modern playwright Sholem Asch, the story is told of a brothel keeper in old Poland who had a beautiful daughter whom he wished above all things to keep pure and virtuous. He consults the religious leaders of the community: he arranges to buy a Biblical scroll. All to no avail. The daughter has furtively made friends with the girls of the house. And one evening returning after an enforced absence, the father discovers to his horror that his beloved and adored girl has joined the others in their trade.

Parents must realize that their own ethical principles, secret or open, pervade the home and set the standards for the children. Life is not mocked. Live below your moral level and your children can't grow. They can't acquire a conscience if you lack one.

That doesn't mean that you should set perfectionist standards for yourself or them. Perfectionist standards are a strait jacket that inhibit wholesome growth. They do more harm than good.

Children so conditioned are rarely happy. They are under constant strain to live up to the severe standards their parents have imposed upon them. Since they are unhappy, they rarely make others happy. This will include their own spouse and children when they later acquire them. Perfectionist standards may —and have!—spread harshness and unhappiness through the generations.

"The good are always the merry," said the Irish poet Yeats, a profoundly true statement. When virtue wears a stern and forbidding face, as it so often does, youth is repelled and the moral advance of Mankind retarded. "Dost thou think, because thou art virtuous," asks Shakespeare, "there shall be no more cakes and ale?"

There is no harm in cakes and ale and none in music and dancing, either. Youth is entitled to joy. Joy is its own security. You'll never sell morality to the young by making it morose and repressive.

We must show the young that there is plenty of fun left to life within the moral law, that it is, in fact, the moral law itself that makes life sweet and satisfying.

And since we cannot always be with our children to guide and direct their behavior, we must see to it that they acquire a conscience of their own and so be able to stand by themselves four square before the many temptations of life.

Summary and Suggestion

First we give love and acceptance, letting each child feel that he has a place in our home and our hearts. Then we let them know of what behavior we approve and of what behavior we disapprove—all the time setting a good example. Because they enjoy our love, they usually behave well in order to continue to receive it. In time this good behavior becomes habitual and instinctive. Our children now have a conscience and may be trusted to take care of their own moral problems.

Would this procedure be equally effective in schools? Would love and acceptance on the part of teachers plus the example of their courtesy and conscientiousness produce better pupil behavior and thus make possible higher scholarship?

That's an important question for Americans. The National Education Association has declared that pupil misbehavior is a key problem in American education, greatly limiting our scholastic achievement and making us therefore more vulnerable to our enemies. In an age when all warfare is technological, the side with the best schools will win. Are we going to allow pupils misbehavior to make us a second rate nation?

CHAPTER VI

Teachers, Too, Help Children

Acquire A Conscience

"IF EVERY teacher were like that teacher," I told the principal, "pupil misbehavior would certainly not be the big problem it is in American education." I was visiting a well known High School to study the relationship between teacher personality and student behavior.

The principal smiled in appreciation of the compliment.

"In my school we don't have much misbehavior. But, of course, this man is exceptional. I'm not claiming that all my teachers are like this teacher. But they could be. His techniques are really very simple."

The principal was obviously on a favorite topic. I let him do the talking.

"Have you noticed that in his class the children are completely absorbed in their work throughout the period, never once giving way to restlessness or star-gazing or scrapping with each other? Have you noticed, too, that at the end of the period they get up from their seats with that nice look of satisfaction on their faces which betokens the job well done? And how they keep looking back as they leave to smile at the teacher and to catch his smile? All this is Mental Health at its healing best. The most disturbed children in our society would feel at ease in that teacher's room."

"Yes, I think they would. How does he do it?"

"He makes each one of them feel valued as a person, feel important. It's an act of pure grace and charm which to him comes as easy as breathing."

"Indeed! Tell me more."

"Being an absolute gentleman himself, he treats any ragamuffin in the room as if he were an absolute gentleman, too. When he calls on a boy, he invariably smiles at him, speaks his name warmly and thanks him when he's through, thanks him and means it. Can you imagine what such courtesy does to a youngster whose own parents call him 'a dirty brat' and give him a slap or a kick at the slightest provocation?

"But that isn't all. He makes certain that each pupil is successful at learning the lesson. Did you notice how carefully he explained in advance all the difficulties in the assigned homework? Not just 'Read the next twenty pages' and the devil take those who can't understand them, but detailed explanation of how to do each part of the lesson well. As a result he will have a roomful of smiling, creative workers tomorrow and not a roomful of sullen, confused failures.

"You and I know that success is a necessity for all children and especially for the potential delinquent. What causes his antisocial behavior? The feeling of being a social outcast, a failure. It is really to attract attention to himself and his distresses that he commits his criminal acts. If we are to help him control his wayward impulses, we must see to it that his six hours in school are a time of love, peace and achievement.

"His home may be squalid and his parents cruel and neglectful, but at school, in such a classroom as this, he finds a pleasant world where a fine strong person accepts him and considers him worthy of courtesy and affection. Something happens to a disturbed child going through such an experience—something that quiets his destructive urges and gives him a more reassuring view of the world. He can latch on to life somewhere and feel that he belongs.

"But children who fail at school are all potential delinquents. Their lives in some instances run a sorry course: tiring of class attendance, they play hookey, hang around taverns and pool rooms, get caught up with bad company, and finally are involved in crime. That is why we must prevent school failure, and not by making our courses easier but by making our teaching more effective—like this man's."

As I left the school, I felt that I had found confirmation of my thesis that courtesy and consideration on the part of teachers, coupled with sound pedagogy, could turn pupils into scholars and obviate the misbehavior that was a blight on our schools.

The parents are the main force in creating a conscience in children. But teachers, too, exert an influence. Many a child from a poor home background has nevertheless achieved an honorable career and made a valuable contribution to society under the inspiring influence of some good teacher who showed belief in him and gave him affection and regard.

A touching and meaningful story of the redemptive influence of a good teacher on wayward boys was told some years ago in the pages of *Readers Digest*. It ran something like this:

A sociology professor in Johns Hopkins' University sent a team of research students into the slum area of a large city to seek out potential juvenile delinquents. He was sure he could "spot" them according to certain specific tell-tale signs which he had worked out. The idea was to check the careers of these same youngsters twenty years later to see whether these signs provided a reliable forecast. If they did, juvenile delinquency could be greatly reduced by catching the delinquents early and helping them before their behavior became unmanageable.

But when twenty years later another team of research workers went out to the same slum area to check on the findings of the first, they discovered to their surprise that the children doomed to delinquency had not gone delinquent at all, had in fact turned out quite all right both socially and morally.

What could be the explanation of this?

As the second team proceeded to seek out the reason, everywhere they went they heard mention of a certain teacher who had at one time or other taught all these boys.

It would certainly be interesting to hear from this teacher about these boys.

When they finally tracked her down in a home for retired school teachers—they found a gentle, white haired old lady:

"Those boys? Yes, I remember them well. I loved every one of them."

Summary and Suggestion

"Better teaching, less delinquency," would be a great slogan for our schools. The American teacher could become the hero of the fight on crime—our Number One social problem.

For many children the school is the only pleasant place they know, and the teacher the one fine person they meet each day. If this teacher will rise to meet his opportunities, if he will give children the courtesy and kindness they do not get at home, if he will comfort their hurt egos by providing opportunities for success experiences, he will, to a considerable degree, disarm their anger at society and call forth the desire to cooperate and serve rather than destroy.

But the largest number of rejected children in the United States is the great—and growing—army of the orphans of divorce. There are 4,000,000 of them now and the number may grow in time to 10,000,000. It's a black day in the life of a child when his parents decide to divorce.

CHAPTER VII

Orphans of Divorce: America's

Legally Rejected Children

"Daddy! my Daddy!" the little girl cried and flew across the court room to where her father sat. She gave him not one, but many kisses, repeating, "Daddy, daddy, come home!"

The mother sat stonily in her seat, surveying the scene but speaking not a word.

The judge was visibly affected. "Why don't you two try again to reconcile your differences?" he pleaded. "You're not going to ask me to divide this little girl between you, are you?

"She wants and needs both her parents together. Come back again in a week and tell me what you've done to make up.—Case adjourned."

Not even the wise Solomon knew how to divide one child between two parents. But in divorce-ridden America, judges are called on to do this all the time!

One of them, the well known Judge Julius Howard Miner of Chicago, who has presided over a very great many divorce cases, has this to say on the subject:

"I have seen first-hand the incalculable misery and degradation of the principals to the suit, and the humiliation, anguish and suffering of their children. I have granted divorce decrees and awarded custody of bewildered children whose love and affection for their parents is indivisible."

Another experienced divorce-court judge, Edward F. Waite, of Minnesota, adds this pointed observation: "Nature provides the child with two parents, each normally performing functions which the other cannot take on so well, if at all, and the two joining in much that can be done better together. When from any cause the total duties of parenthood fall upon a single parent, the child loses something valuable; but his disadvantage is plainly greater when there is a divorce than when the loss occurs through death or necessary chance, because of the psychological disturbance incident to an atmosphere of domestic discord."

The thoughtful parent recognizes from these two realistic statements, written right on the divorce battlefield, what a tragedy divorce is for children and resolves that he will resort to it only as a last desperate measure.

But weary of contending with a loveless or incompatible mate, many a fine man or woman, filled with the normal human longing to love and be loved, drifts into a new relationship, and then begins insidiously to ask:

"Would it so much matter to my child, if his parents now divorced? After all, he has seen us quarreling these many years. Wouldn't he perhaps be better off to have two separated parents who are relatively happy, or at least peaceful, than two parents who stay together but cannot love each other?"

How often do counselors and advisers hear this question. And how well they know the answer that is expected of them.

"No, it wouldn't really matter, sir, (madame). Go ahead with your divorce and marry that other woman (man) that you have already set your heart on. Your child will get over it. There are millions of children of divorce in America. Don't they all get over it—in time?"

But they don't say these words, because they know differently. They have seen too many of these children putting up a brave front of sophistication and indifference but never really losing the look of irremediable grief in their eyes.

Nothing that you can give a divorce-orphaned child of extra financial and social advantages can ever make up to him for what he has forever lost, namely, normal family life with two parents who love him and each other. The divorce-orphaned child is a second class child, lacking many rights and privileges that other children enjoy. Deep down he knows this, and many are the bitter reflections he has over it. His parents have rejected him. They did not think enough of him to try to reconcile their differences and make a marriage.

Professor Judson T. Landis, one of America's outstanding authorities in the field of marriage and the family, in a carefully documented research study of college students whose parents had been divorced, discovered:

1. Few of the students felt relieved when divorce ended open conflict in the home.

2. Most had suffered "a most traumatic experience" on learning that their home was not the happy secure place they had believed it to be.

3. Only one-third of the children reported that they had considered their homes unhappy prior to the divorce. One-third said they had regarded their homes as "very happy" up to the eve of the divorce.

4. All the students queried, including those too young to recall home conditions prior to the divorce, said they had felt handicapped in social life afterward. They reported having felt different from and inferior to other children, ashamed and embarrassed.

5. One-third said they had tried to save face and cover up the fact of divorce, some by telling friends a parent was away on a trip or dead.

One of the most evil consequences of divorce is that the children are deprived of the father influence in their lives, custody being usually awarded to the mother. The blighting effect of this arrangement on the spiritual and emotional life of children, and on the mental and moral health of society, is unfortunately not generally understood. When it is, a distinction will be drawn between divorce for childless couples and divorce where children are involved. There will be a children's advocate in every divorce court to defend the rights of the children. He may demand that in spite of all the evidence, the divorce should not be granted because there is equally valid evidence that the children love and need both the parents. "Don't the children have rights in this court?" he will ask.

The usual divorce settlement gives little thought to the needs of children and especially to their emotional needs. What it concerns itself with primarily is the property: so much to the wife for her maintenance and support and so much for the children. Then the time of the children is apportioned off, as if it, too, were property: so much visitation time to the father, the rest to the mother.

Are the children consulted in this arrangement? Are they protected against one parent's poisoning their mind against the other, against being made a football in their parents' strife? No, they are not.

The law is a most unpsychological law, and heavily do the children pay for its lack of understanding of their needs.

Just as flowers must have *both* sunshine and rain for their proper growth, so children require both a masculine and a feminine component in their development. The lack of such a balance may later cause all kinds of personality distresses in both the boys and the girls. The greatest present need of American children is to have more of father in their lives.

Put a firm but loving father at the head of every American home and let him be steadfastly present there, and how greatly would juvenile delinquency, drug addiction, homosexuality, and other social evils, decline!

In the United States where one marriage in four ends in divorce, there are a great number of broken homes. Judge Louis H. Jull of the Juvenile Court in Louisville, Ky. said to a social worker recently: "Close to ninety-five per cent of our court's business is with children whose parents are divorced or separated. As a result of the deep deprivation of the love and discipline of one or both parents, these youngsters become emotional vandals."

But this is not the worst of the story. The experts predict that within a few years one marriage in three in the United States will terminate in divorce. At present for every four divorces, three children are involved and that ratio is increasing. Orphans of divorce in this country now number over four million and may in time come to number ten million. No one who loves children, the innocent victims of divorce, can fail to feel appalled by these figures and to want to do something to reduce them.

What can we do?

We can go to the source of the problem, the American ideal of marriage, and try through education to improve it. We can teach our youth in high school and college courses on marriage and the family that a good marriage doesn't just happen; you have to work at it. One college text book on the subject, Landis & Landis *Building A Successful Marriage* has in it this sound yet noble definition: "A successful marriage is one in which two people have intelligently committed themselves to a lifetime together, in which each seeks to enrich the life of the other as well as his own."

The inculcation of such an ideal of marriage upon our youth as opposed to the fantastic Hollywood concept of impulse and passion on which the minds of our children have for all their impressionable years been nourished would go a long way towards stabilizing marriage in this country.

Another strengthening influence is the realization that divorce is not the answer when a couple starts quarreling. That is the time to take your problem to a trained Marriage Counselor who will bring to it a healing knowledge that may happily amaze you by its rehabilitating power. No parent can say he loves his children if he does not give marriage counseling at least a try before resorting to divorce.

Many a couple who have gone through counseling together find that just this is enough to reunite them. Each appreciates the effort the other is making to do right and be fair. Each sees the other as a sounder and finer person than he had thought and also more loving and lovable "for isn't he (she) doing this for me?" Soon the dying embers of their affection for each other catch a spark, old memories revive the old love, and, to the great joy and satisfaction of the children, the happy home life is restored.

Summary and Suggestion

"If I had only known before divorce what I know now," says many a divorcee, "I never would have gotten the divorce." What is it she knows now that she didn't know before? One woman put it this way:

"If I had given the thought, energy, devotion to making a success of my marriage that I now must expend in trying to make an adjustment to life for my children and myself, no divorce would have been necessary."

And that's the great truth on this much discussed subject.

In growing together, in helping each other rise above individual weaknesses, in learning to accept each other in spite of faults, in loving the whole individual and not just the qualities agreeable to us, we make a marriage. And making a marriage, we build a home of love and security for our children, insuring their future health and happiness. No child of ours, we vow, shall join the ranks of love's disinherited, the orphans of divorce.

CHAPTER VIII

Parents Without

Partners

WHILE WE greatly deplore divorce and recognize that, in the main, it represents unmitigated tragedy for children, nevertheless, it is true that there are some strong women who are capable of piloting their children, through a divorce, out of a bad home and into a better one. It should be kept in mind, however, that their experience is exceptional, just as the women themselves, no doubt, are exceptional in strength of character, feminine charm, or just plain good fortune.

❊   ❊   ❊

In her intelligent and forceful letter, one mother defended her divorce and denounced those who declared all divorce to be wrong:

"I have found quite the reverse of this stand to be true. In every case of divorce among my friends, and including myself, people who had given months and years of thought to their situations, when divorce took place, it was beneficial to the two persons directly involved and to their children.

"In my own case, as I came from a conservative and loving

family, I tried for ten years to stick to a poor marriage for the sake of my two little girls. Then, after many attempts at reconciliation, I finally got a divorce. I felt like a whole person for the first time in years, and I believe this attitude reflected on my children. We three had a happy home by ourselves and when I later remarried, my children adjusted amazingly well. Now that we have two more children, we seem to be as whole and complete a family as anyone could wish."

* * *

Such happy endings to the divorce story are rare indeed!

And all credit is due to the successful divorced mother! Furthermore, she, like others of her character, will be the most apt to happily remarry! Their very attitude of love, strength and understanding, makes them as desirable as wives or mothers. And, too, they will instinctively understand what is psychologically involved in winning the stepfather's love for their children, or, as in the case of Mrs. J., seek the knowledge and counsel necessary.

* * *

When she married her second husband (a bachelor in his early thirties), the primary consideration with Mrs. J. was that he promised to be a good father to the eight-year-old boy she had by her first marriage. But it didn't turn out that way. The new father was autocratic and cold. He made her boy's life miserable.

"Each morning the aura of our home is that of a Commanding General (my husband) issuing orders and bellowing at the lowly Private (Jimmy). 'Tie your shoelaces! Did you brush your teeth? Did you forget your handkerchief?' These may seem like nothing, but when it's a regular routine, it can be very hard on the nervous system (not just my own, but the child's, too).

"Jimmy cannot open his mouth to speak without fear of being reprimanded ('Children should be seen and not heard'.) He has almost no freedom at all, of voice or action, and I find myself at the point where I resent being the buffer between them.

"If I should comment (not in the child's presence, of course) on Tom's attitude, he gets terribly excited and says that I resent his scolding the boy because he is not his natural father. Believe me, this is far from the truth. I most certainly would have no objection to constructive criticism or disciplining the child, but the constant shouting and excitement are becoming very difficult to withstand.

"I have tried to explain to Tom that Jimmy must be given a chance. Jimmy tries very hard. He idolizes my husband, greets him on his arrival with a hug and kiss and the same when he leaves the house. He really seems anxious to have Tom like him.

"Tom, though, is from a family which does not normally make any display of feelings or emotions. But I believe that even though not accustomed to doing so, he should show some fondness or affection for the child's sake."

❉   ❉   ❉

He certainly should! A child's first need is love. Why can't the stepfather give it?

The answer to that is that he hasn't had any experience. And Mrs. J. realizes this in part, since she mentions that he came from a loveless home, remained a bachelor until past thirty, and never knew the heart-warming experience of cuddling an infant child of his own. But most important for Mrs. J's understanding, is that he has many ego distresses and a natural male jealousy of the man who knew his wife first and fathered her child.

The mother must take all this into consideration—she and the many other women struggling with the same problem. There are ways to enrich a man's emotional personality. As she builds up her husband's confidence in himself as a man by letting him feel that he is worthy of her admiration and ardor, he will have less need to be picky and critical. Out of the rich satisfactions of his relationship with her, he will gladly do his duty by her child.

This is the price a woman must pay to get a second husband to love the child of her first marriage—a something extra of passion and devotion. It should be considered a fair deal. Great numbers of unhappy stepchildren would take on smiling faces, if more of their mothers understood this.

Meanwhile, even if they do later remarry, there is always a period of time when they are single and a parent alone. And it is from these women that the counselor all too often hears these words:

"But I did divorce! Are then my children doomed and damned?"

By no means! But you and they will need help!

Since the vast majority of single parents are women (widows or divorcees), a great number of children in our society are raised without a father; without a man to model after if they are boys, or, if they are girls, a man to see as a husband ideal and protector. This is a very real psychological loss, unfortunately not sufficiently understood by our divorce-ridden and widow-surfeited society.

Unsung heroines of America are the millions of women, widows, divorcees, deserted wives, who bring up fine children without benefit of husbands, and without much help, alas, from city or state governments.

Their greatest need is faith—in themselves, in their children, in life. All people have more energy, more skill, more persistence than they think they have. Call on your inner resources, keep clear of self-pity, believe in the essential goodness of human nature, and you, like many other women alone, will raise a worthy family.

A psychological rule that can be especially helpful to you is: "One day at a time." Put all your energy into meeting the day's obligations. Do not waste any in regrets for the past or fears for the future, and you will find that somehow or other, you always manage. There's no situation so bad you can't handle it for one day.

The day well lived brings a double profit:

First, it strengthens your faith. If you do well with one day, you feel you can do well with another. And so on.

Secondly, the good days add up. Gradually, they alter circumstances. A little improvement here, a little improvement there, and the first thing you know, the whole picture is brighter.

Don't hesitate to call on your children to help you. Don't let your sympathy for them lead to overprotecting, and thus weakening them. It's their fate to be born to hardship and difficulty; they will be the finer and stronger for meeting it. One of your greatest temptations may be to patronize your children. Resist that temptation!

Another temptation, and possibly a more serious one, is to tie your children, especially your boys, too strongly to you emotionally. Children need freedom for their best growth. The mother-bound boy (so many of them have widows or divorcees for mothers!) is a kind of emotional misfit. He rarely makes good in his boy-girl relations; he sometimes has special difficulties adjusting to his job; he may develop very real personality quirks and weaknesses.

This doesn't mean that you may not give, and receive, a great deal of affection from your children. Just make sure that they feel free as they mature to turn their full romantic feelings on their own age mates of the opposite sex.

*   *   *

"Mommy, can I get into bed with you?"

When her five-year-old son first asked that, she had readily acquiesced. His daddy was gone. The boy was scared and lonely. He needed comforting. She needed comforting, too. They held each other close and slept through the night together.

But when the next night he asked to come again, she was troubled. She knew this wasn't right. She had read too much about mother-fixated boys not to know the dangers.

But she remembered, too, that as a little girl she had gone into her parents' room whenever she felt lonely or frightened and that her mother had shooed her angrily away. How bitter was the memory of it! Did that make her believe she could never be loved? Had that perhaps caused the failure of her marriage? She let him stay.

"Sometimes I cuddle him for a while, then lead him back to his bed. Other times I let him stay, since I learned it wasn't too good to make him leave. Frankly, I don't know which is the right way. Can you help me? I want to do what is best for him. Sometimes kiddingly, I'll say: 'How many beds are there in this house?' and he laughs and goes back to his bed. But I am thinking of this in the long run—how best to handle it so it won't hurt his personality in any way.

"I know in my own personal case I did the same thing as a child and my mother would get very angry and shoo me away. And I remember this and how it did me harm. So I've never gotten angry with Ken. However, with Ken, as he is a boy with his mother. . . . Isn't it . . . different . . . ? I mean . . . ?"

*   *   *

Of course, it's different! And also difficult. Which points up the trials and tribulations of a sincere and conscientious woman bringing up a boy child alone.

Her problem and that of the other women in the same situation is to make certain that their sons develop truly masculine personalities and do not become too attached or too dependent upon their mothers. Mother-bound boys have a hard time of it later in a man's world, and perhaps even more difficulty in making a good marriage.

*   *   *

If you are raising children alone, recognize that they require association with both genders for their emotional development and try to see that they get it.

The mother should seek out some male substitute for the lost father, a relative perhaps, and ask him to train the boy in masculine skills and attributes. A boy needs to learn to face up to danger and responsibility, to fight square, to speak truth, and to swear properly. A woman can't teach him all that. But a father surrogate can. So can male teachers, camp counselors, Scout Masters, or a foster father.

A boy also needs to know how to make a go of it with girls. If his mother is the whole feminine world for him, he'll never seek out girls and learn to love one and be true to her as a man should.

Keep in mind always that your boys must be masculine and girls feminine. You, as a woman, may be able to teach your girls to be as femininely charming as you are, but your boys need a man in their life. A boy doesn't learn to be a man from his mother, anymore than a girl learns to be a woman from her father. So don't hesitate to call on some relative or friend of the opposite sex to guide and lead your children into activities proper to their gender.

*   *   *

"I would like to ask some questions concerning the welfare of my own children," a divorced father said. "I want above all to do what is best for them."

His wife had been awarded custody and was, he felt, spitefully limiting his visitation rights to one afternoon a week. "I feel that my children should see their father more frequently, and that I am entitled to this as I had no guilt in the divorce. My wife divorced me on false grounds. Being the victim of well-meant but poor advice, I declined to contest the case.

"Should I try for a reconciliation with my ex-wife for the sake of the children?

"Should I marry someone else, take the custody of the children and give them a good home?

"Should I wait until my ex-wife remarries? Somehow I feel that I owe it to my children not to remarry until their mother does, so that, if reconciliation is possible, the door will be open."

*   *   *

It is admirable of this man that his first concern is the welfare of his children. He would even be willing to resume relations with his ex-wife to re-establish their original home.

This genuine concern for the children is rare amongst the recently divorced. They are usually too busy fighting and hating each other to give the children, who are the innocent victims of their quarrel, the consideration and care which is their due.

The parents should, under competent psychological guidance, try for a reconciliation. Some of the most seemingly hopeless marriages have, nevertheless, been restored to sound health when the two parties, for the sake of the children, underwent counseling.

But if reconciliation is found to be impossible, it is necessary that the children continue to have a loving relationship with each parent.

* * *

Therefore, if you must divorce, try to protect your children from its evil emotional consequences as much as possible. The children should be told: "Your mother and father no longer love each other enough to live together, but they are still good friends and will always love and care for you."

Above all, guard yourself against speaking ill of your erstwhile partner. Every child needs to believe that he comes from two fine parents, and it can only weaken his pride and self-confidence to learn that one was less than admirable or an out and out "stinker"! Your former partner will also cooperate better in providing for the children if the quarrel is not continued. Nor will the children be harassed by being made part of the quarrel.

You will save yourself later tortures of conscience if you give every consideration to the emotional as well as the material needs of your children in the face of their fatherless state.

The child, already shaken by the breakup of his home and filled with vague fears and even possible sense of blame, must not be further racked in soul by having his anger stirred against one parent whom he will still need to know, love and honor. The child should understand that the trouble is with his parents, not with him, that though they differ too much to live together any longer, they agree in their love for him and will continue to care for him.

Divorce is always tragic for a child, but its griefs can be greatly lessened if each parent will promote the child's good relations with the other. Too bad they didn't cooperate to make a go of their marriage, but may they have this saving grace, at least, to cooperate in planning the best possible future for their child.

The gain will be theirs, too. Relieved in mind, they may now turn more effectively to rebuilding their own lives!

But don't be too self-sacrificing. That can impose a heavy burden on your children's conscience. Rather have some fun yourself, live your own life. In the deepest sense, you cannot be good to others, including, of course, your own children, unless you are also good to yourself.

In spite of your own troubles and necessities, remember that children need a cheerful home, free of perfectionist standards, but disciplined in cooperativeness.

Hold a family council. Children cooperate in plans they had a share in making. Plan constructively. Make your family a circle, with everyone equally giving and receiving love. Happy at home, happy outside.

Learn to get satisfaction out of little things.

Practice through daily prayer the presence of God in your life. You'll feel protected; your life will become more orderly. And you will never need to fear that your fatherless home will be the spawning ground for future juvenile delinquents. Indeed, you would have every right to resent such a suggestion, as did one Mother Alone.

*   *   *

"I object," she wrote in a bitter letter, "to such conjectures as 'a child cannot be raised other than as a juvenile delinquent if it comes from a broken marriage.' Theories are not accurate. Since I have a 14-year-old girl who reads the paper, and I am divorced, it might lead her to think she must have a right to extreme behavior."

*   *   *

This mother's complaint certainly deserves attention. The many writers and commentators who have been emphasizing the fact that most juvenile delinquents come from broken homes, should be careful to add that this definitely does not mean that *all* children of broken homes will turn delinquent. There could be no greater error of logic and no greater injustice to the many fine women, who, divorced, nobly dedicate themselves to the task of worthily raising their children alone. For this, all the more credit is due them. And many have made an outstanding success of it.

This mother, for instance, has through periods of poverty and illness and great personal deprivation raised her daughter in the best traditions of American girlhood. "Now she is a top honor student, has a very high sense of values, is outstanding in character, reliability, initiative—according to all her teachers."

It is clear by now that this mother isn't the only woman meriting praise for raising a fine child alone.

Yet, for all their strength and competence, these women need guidance and should not be ashamed to seek it.

What can "parents without partners" do to raise wholesome normal children? A small beginning of an answer to that question is being formed in New York City. It is an organization called "Parents Without Partners." The aim is to provide a meeting ground for single parents, through which these mothers and fathers without partners can work out solutions to their many problems, the main one being to find temporary foster mothers and fathers for their children. Thus their children may receive companionship and guidance, according to their respective needs.

Summary and Suggestion

All children need a masculine as well as a feminine component in their lives. If the woman alone will steadfastly keep this in mind, she can with resolution, intelligence, good

humor and faith seek out the help she needs and success-
fully raise a boy as well as a girl child. More power to her!
Her ex-spouse has equal obligations toward his children.

When parents have turned to divorce, not lightly but
only after careful consideration of what is best for the family members, they can make the best of a bad situation by
cooperating without rancor in the care of the children,
making certain always that a good substitute is found for
whatever parental influence has been lost.

CHAPTER IX

True Stories of

Rejected Children

Do THE parents who reject their children or, to put it more kindly, fail to give them the love and acceptance they need realize the life-long damage they may be doing them?

Without a basic foundation of love and acceptance, a child cannot become stabilized in spirit ever. Such a child is always restless and disturbed. Unhappy himself, he cannot make others happy. The criminals and the neurotics, the world's maladjusted millions, were all "Rejection's Children."

Following are ten true stories of children who, under various circumstances, shared one common fate—rejection! In the summary of this chapter there will be specific suggestions as to how a counselor could have prevented each particular tragedy.

IRENE, THE GLAMOR GIRL

Pretty, 5-year-old Irene had a pretty new dress.

"See, Daddy," she cried, as she danced gaily before him.

But Daddy was absorbed in his newspaper and bore a bit of a pout besides. "Pork chops for dinner! Pork chops!" His wife knew he didn't like pork chops, but just because they were quick and easy to prepare, she would have pork chops.

"Daddy, daddy, my new dress!"

Irene smiled appealingly, pleadingly. "See my new dress!"

Daddy grunted "yes," looked up for an instant, turned on a grin, turned it off, and went back to his newspaper and his pout.

Irene grew up to be a great beauty. Strange, however, she never could believe that she was really worthy of love. Many men pursued her, but she never had any faith in their protestations of love. Men didn't really love. They might say so, but their words didn't mean much. Love? No! With them it was just vanity. Get a glamor girl and show her off to your friends!

Irene was married several times. Sometimes she married for money, sometimes for social position. She had several affairs, besides. Once, just for the fun of it, she took up with an oriental pasha. He beat her. Funny, she enjoyed it.

Weaker men, however, she liked to tyrannize over. As Aphrodite's misery maker, she ran up quite a score.

Only once was she really in love, with a sad-faced school teacher who read poetry in a way that stirred the spirit. She declared that she would be willing to live in a rat hole if he would love her, but he, funny man, preferred his homely wife.

Love! Love!! Always would she think of it, long for it. And a thousand and one romantic fantasies would rise in her imagination. But each time at their climax, they would fade away, and the same cold dream would come instead.

She was a 5-year-old girl. She had a pretty new dress.

"Daddy, daddy, see my new dress!"

But daddy was absorbed in his newspaper and bore a bit of a pout besides:

"Pork chops! Don't she know I don't like pork chops!"

SAMMY AT THE BALL GAME

On that Sunday morning little Sammy sneaked out of bed while his mother was still sleeping and hurried over to the house of his father and that "other mother" whom he had hardly gotten to know yet. Sunday, by court order, was visitation day with his father.

His real mother heard him hazily in her half-sleep but was glad he was gone. She could sleep late now. What a luxury a Sunday morning in bed can be when you have worked hard all week and been out partying hard most of Saturday night!

"Hello," cried Sammy, all bright and eager to his father and "the other mother" when they opened the door. His father answered, "Hello, Sammy," and gave him an affectionate pat on the shoulder. Sammy stared in high expectancy at the woman, but she didn't say anything, just stared back at him.

"Had your breakfast?" she asked awhile later.

"No," said Sammy.

"What does his mother give your kid for breakfast?" she called across the room to the father.

"Oh, anything. Anything. Cereal and milk and banana."

Sammy didn't eat very much.

After breakfast, he sat around looking at the funnies. Suddenly he heard his father and "the other mother" break into an argument in the other room.

"What do you mean, take him to the World Series game after dinner? Do you know what a pair of tickets cost to see a World Series game? Me you never take to anything better than a movie, and your kid has to see the World Series!"

Sammy wished he could cry, but he couldn't. His father had promised to take him to the big game, and he had told all the fellows about it. What could he tell them now?

His father, fortunately, stuck to his guns. He had promised to take his boy to the ball game, and he wasn't going to go back on his promise.

It was one of those World Series games made to order for kids—a couple of home runs, some high fielding to catch hits that might have been home runs, and a pitching duel at times tense with drama as great players swung and hit, or swung and missed!

Sammy, between hot dogs and soda pop, shouted and cheered. He was having a great time.

But about the seventh inning, he noticed that his father was hardly looking at the game anymore. He just sat there slumped in his seat, gazing off into space. Sammy began to sit still, too. Gradually, the game lost all interest for him. He never knew the final score.

"How was your father?" his mother asked on his return.

"Oh, all right," said Sammy.

"Yeah, I'll bet," said his mother.

Sammy went to his room. The desire to tell his friends about the ball game was gone. Ball game? He didn't think he'd ever care to see a ball game again.

For a long, long time he sat in his room, just sat.

"Is my daddy ever coming back?" he suddenly cried out to his mother, his voice filled with a fierce anger.

"No," his mother said. "No, your daddy's never coming back."

MARY, THE FAT GIRL

As Mary surveyed her abnormally fat body in the mirror, she shook her head in despair.

"How can I ever reduce that much?" she reflected to herself.

And as always when she felt moody and unhappy, great waves of hunger pangs suddenly beset her. She struggled with them a while, remembering well what her doctor and psychological counselor had told her. But like the alcoholic, whose urges are stronger than all his griefs, she feverishly sought the bread box, thickly buttered a half dozen sugar buns she found there, and greedily devoured them. No lover ever kissed his mistress with more passion.

Alas, poor Mary! And alas for the 25,000,000 other Americans whose daily battle is with obesity. Again and again they try to follow a diet, but in most cases go right back to the overeating that is their ruin.

Why is their struggle so unavailing? What is so hard about

adhering to a moderate diet, sensibly restricted in fats and starches but otherwise wholesome, tasty and nourishing?

The answers to these questions run deeper than you think. The overweight have profound emotional needs, usually harking back to a loveless childhood, and requiring a continuous compensation, which for them is food.

"My mother just didn't know how to love us," said Mary to her counselor. "She was a morose, silent woman absorbed in her own thoughts. She never encouraged me to make something of myself—to learn to dance, or sing, or play. My father kept away from her—and us. Even as a little girl, I would go off by myself when I was unhappy and console myself with candy or cake."

BEATRICE AT THE BALL

At the wedding party, blonde and seemingly beautiful Beatrice danced with the gayest. Charming to see was her graceful coquetry as she twirled from one dancer's arms to another's, or sat with just the right posture of casual but adoring attention at the feet of some handsome swain, meeting his attempts at clever talk with the full flattery of her rapt attention.

But all this was from a distance or for the nearsighted. When you drew closer, what did you see?—A bright-eyed girl of fine figure and chiseled features but with a skin all blotched and broken and erupted. Her defiantly-cut, low-necked dress betrayed that all of her was just the same, and what are you going to make of it?!

"You see, it's my skin," she would say directly to anyone who sat to talk with her, like the alcoholic taking the cure who knows that his only hope of salvation is to set the bottle right before him and then defy it. "It's my terribly ugly skin! But that's not going to make an introvert out of me. I'm going to live—gay and happy—with the best of them!"

With this as introduction, her talk would turn to anything you had a mind for, with ideas to match any of your moods. Particularly charming in her speech was its insistent praise of people as against the all too pervasive blame you hear in this critical world. One young girl who had incurred the enmity of some of the dowagers at the party because of her daring dress and dashing manner, she defended with special fire:

"What a fine wife she will make to any man who can tame her. What fun they'll have!"

"What a fine wife *you* will make," her conversation companion contended.

"Me! You know you don't mean that. I'll be nobody's wife, just as—as I was nobody's daughter.

"Oh, I had parents, but they disowned me. And for what?!" Her voice broke into an ironic laugh, and her skin became more livid.

"Because I wouldn't finish the course in the strict girls' college to which they had sent me. I need freedom. I couldn't stand that place. So I ran away and for that they disowned me. That's when my skin trouble really got bad.

"If I could only say 'I forgive them,' I know I'd begin to get better. But I can't! I can't forgive them . . . To take away their love for that!

"Why can't parents let their children be themselves? If you have life in you, you have to be yourself, don't you? Yourself!

"But so many parents don't want to let their children be themselves. And that can be a terrible tragedy, as you can see—from—!"

Here she again broke into a laugh, a merry laugh: "I was going to say, 'as you can see from me.' But I won't. My life's not going to be tragic. I'm going to have a lot of fun. And some of it right here and now. Shall we dance?"

DADDY WILL PLAY WITH YOU
TOMORROW NIGHT

"Daddy will play with you tomorrow night," the voice on the phone said. "Daddy has to work late today."

But tomorrow night never came. Daddy's little boy was sick.

He grew worse and died. How Daddy wished he had played with his boy—today!

A child's life is now. There is no truth of child psychology more significant than this. Your children love you and want you very much—now! All your striving to provide for their future, to give them comforts and luxuries, has little value if it deprives them of your company. They would gladly do without many things to have more of you.

Fathers, particularly, in their mad struggle for business success, neglect their children beyond all conscience. They leave them almost entirely in the care of the mother not realizing that for lack of the masculine influence in their lives they may develop unwholesome personality traits.

A boy needs a man in his life to show him how to fight hard, play fair, and swear properly—how to be a man! A girl needs a father, too, to be her first beau, to bring out those feminine graces in her with which she will later capture a good husband.

Children need more of their mothers, too, than many now receive. So many women go to work who don't really have to, leaving young children to get their own meals and find their own entertainment. That explains a lot of malnutrition and misbehavior in children. Add up the carfare, lunch money, joint tax loss, and cost of business clothes, plus wages for a once a week cleaning woman, and do you have enough left to warrant depriving your children of their mother's care?

The club woman and the social climber, forever gadding about to luncheons, teas, meetings, also neglects her children. And there are other neglectful mothers, too, who desert their children for even worse reasons.

When your school children come home, do they find you there, cheerful and chatty, serving them a warm lunch or a tasty afternoon snack and sharing their experiences of the day? What a lot of fun that is for them and you! And how dreary their house looks if you're not there.

One fine mother said: "I know my children run right out again to play the minute they come home from school. But I also know they are glad to find me home that minute."

Yes, a child's life is now. And would that an adult's were also. All through the ages wise men have warned of the folly of forever postponing our good. But we in America, with our mad search for success, sacrifice the present only too readily for a material glory that often proves disillusioning when we get it. We are nervous and strained, poor marriage partners and poor companions to our children. With a little more living in the present, we could make our children happier and lead more satisfactory lives ourselves.

CAN YOU ENCOURAGE ME?

"What I need most," the sad-faced woman told the counselor, "is someone to encourage me. Can you encourage me?"

"Can I encourage you? Well—maybe. Let's talk about it."

"You see I have a friend who lived with her aunt, 'cause her parents were dead. This aunt always encouraged her, spoke nicely to her. And my friend grew up fine. She's a—well you could call it a success. She's got a husband and they've got a business. And everything's good in her life, 'cause someone encouraged her. But me, nobody encouraged me. And I ain't got nothing.

"And I've been around to a lot of big preachers and psychologists—all those people that write the books, you know—and have asked them could they encourage me. And they talked very nice to me. Rev. Dr. X talked to me about my cosmic self and my personal self, and all that. He's such a very nice man. But he couldn't encourage me, tho' he said God would, if I believed in Him.

"Now don't ask me about my father and mother. That's all you psychologists do is ask about father and mother. I don't want to talk about my father and mother."

"You mean they didn't encourage you?"

"No, they didn't. But what's the good of talking about it?

They didn't. So they didn't. That's what I'm telling you, they didn't. But what can I do now?

"Does it mean that 'cause they didn't encourage me, nobody can encourage me? You couldn't encourage me either, huh?"

When your children grow up will they be forever seeking someone to encourage them, to lead them out of the failure in their lives? Or will you have encouraged them in the receptive early years to believe in themselves and life and so to achieve happiness in the world?

THE REJECTED CHILD REJECTS HIS COUNTRY

Of the twenty-one American G.I.'s who chose to remain in Red China at the end of the Korean War, twenty had never heard of Communism prior to enlistment, except as a "dirty word." All of them, save one, had been brought up in American towns and educated in American schools. Most of them had above average I.Q.'s. Many of them had unusual cultural inclinations: a love of classical music, devotion to good literature, unusual linquistic accomplishments, basic religious beliefs, a sense of personal neatness. A few had a natural capacity for making friends, showing kindness and sympathy. Superficially regarded, one might even speak of them as typical American boys.

What then, was this dread thing lurking in the hidden recesses of their minds that made traitors of them?

From the splendid research and reporting of Virginia Pasley's book 21 Stayed comes the answer:

In their personal family history all twenty-one of them had experienced childhood's greatest grief—Rejection. All had the feeling that they had been "put upon" by life. Sixteen came from broken homes and were reared in an atmosphere of hostility and separateness and inter-parental warfare. More specifically and significantly, nineteen of the twenty-one admitted that they had felt unwanted by their fathers or stepfathers. Psychologically, their longing for a father manifested itself in their adoption of a new country which was to them like adopting a new and ideal father.

That there was much "good stuff" in the make-up of these boys is borne out by individual examples of kindness and bravery and by the ability, however perverted, of all of them to "succeed" with the Communists. How different their lives would have been if their energy, strength and courage had been rightly channeled from childhood; if they had not been made to feel that they were unwanted outcasts whose only salvation lay in becoming extroverts, bullies and "wise guys," too smart to suffer themselves when they could use their fellow men as pawns in the battle for safety and success.

Without the loving guidance of parents who nurture his natural faith, how can any child be expected to acquire ideals? What has the rejected child to keep him away from delinquency, crime, even Communism and disloyalty?

No child can live without love. Reject him and he becomes a potential delinquent, neurotic, or enemy of society. Accept him, give him something to believe in, like him and love him for himself and not for what he does, and be becomes the happy, strong man, firm to do his duty.

IT'S A GIRL

"It's a girl!"

As the doctor made the announcement, the mother directed a swift glance toward her husband to see how he would take it. Her worst fears were realized. His face bore such an expression of repugnance and disappointment, she was overwhelmed.

All through her pregnancy he had talked of the boy he wanted, and how he would raise him to be a greater man than himself. It frightened her at times, but she reflected he couldn't really mean it. If a girl came, he would welcome it as his own and be happy with it and love it as a father should.

But he didn't!

Alas for the children who grow up rejected in their gender.

There are more of these than you would ever imagine. They have a sad destiny.

They never feel confident in their sex and therefore never make good in it. The boys do not become manly men, nor the girls womanly women. Abnormality, perversity to some degree is the inevitable fate of most of them. Trace the personal history of promiscuous women and see how many of them had been rejected as girl children. They sell themselves cheap because they have no sense of their own worth as women. And how many men accept a low level of sex life, because they don't dare meet the challenge of romantic love. That wouldn't have been their lot if they had been raised to be proud of their gender.

Why do parents commit this cruel folly of showing a preference for a child of one sex rather than another—a preference over which they have no control? The reasons are always a lack of maturity; some want to live their own lives over again and, of course, can do so only in a child of the same gender. Others want a love-object of opposite gender easier to handle than an adult love-object, one that won't argue but will always be sweet and affectionate.

Some parents have a strong preference but hide it, or pretend that it's only a joke. The damage these parents do to their children, however, is no joke. They make spiritual cripples of them.

When we are proud and happy in our own gender, and truly mature, we rejoice in parenthood itself and accept whatever children come and gladly. We don't have a set pattern for our children. They are free to unfold according to their own nature. Boys are wonderful. Girls are wonderful. Their very differentness is what is so interesting and challenging.

And what achievement of parenthood is greater than to have raised manly boys and womanly girls who will catch the torch of life from us and in turn produce and raise fine children!

A WOMAN (?) AND A WIFE (?)

"How can I be a woman and a wife," she exclaimed to the marriage counselor, "without having been a daughter first."

When she was a little girl, her mother and father were divorced. But that wasn't the worst of it. Her mother, who had received legal custody, used every scheme possible to prevent her from ever seeing her father. His letters were intercepted, his visits evaded, his support refused.

"Your father doesn't want to see you. He doesn't care for you. He's married someone else and has another little daughter whom he loves. Your father was a mean, bad man."

Years later, when she discovered the truth, it was too late. The father had remarried, was happy and at peace with his new family, and wanted only to forget the misery of his first marriage. He refused to see her when she pleaded in letter after letter to be allowed to know that she had a father. After a time, he returned her letters unopened. All her life she sought to make contact with her father but he never would let her.

Since she was a good-looking woman, she had a number of suitors. In apathy and indifference, perhaps with some glimmer of hope, she finally consented to marry the most persistent of them, but the marriage never really took. How could it? Physically she was a grown woman, but emotionally she was as one not yet born.

It is the tragedy of the rejected girl child that she can never believe that she is really loved. For that reason she cannot truly develop into a woman and a wife. The defeated women of the world: the spinsters, the promiscuous, the unhappy wives—these are all Rejection's daughters.

WHEN THE REJECTED CHILD BECOMES A PARENT

"Where," she asked, "does a person like myself, thirty-six years old, wife and mother, seek that security of love that was never established in the early years of childhood? As the months go by, yes, years, I feel more at a loss within myself. I carry such deep-rooted feelings of insecurity within me which far from help the relationship with husband, family, friends.

"I've never known a close feeling with my mother; her attitude toward me has always been hostile, nagging, and envious. I've finished a book, Harry and Bonaro Overstreets' *Mind Alive,* and at the beginning it expresses so well the forlorn feelings one gets when deprived of a secure and loving background of parents and home.

"I've had some psychiatry, but could not afford to continue it. I don't drown my troubles in alcohol, though I've had some pretty rough times and deep depressions.

"When, or can I ever, expect help, counsel? There must be help somewhere, but I don't know just where it is. All that I know is that my husband's and child's happiness depend a great deal on it."

This profoundly moving statement should make clear to parents the life-time injury they may do their children by failing to give them the love they need to feel accepted and worthy. The rejected child always hungers for love but cannot believe that he will ever get it. He expects rejection and by this very expectation invites and often receives it.

Rejection's children, when they grow up, either live alone fearsome and unhappy, or, if they do marry, fail to establish the marriage relationship fully because they cannot bring themselves to believe that they are truly loved. If they should have children they may smother their personalities in a kind of desperate possessiveness. Or they may behave coldly toward them as their own parents had done to them. The simple human act of exchanging love, which should be as natural as breathing, they never quite manage. All their life is a blind seeking and longing —and a self-frustration.

Summary and Suggestion

All these rejected children, how different might have been their fates if the parents, rising above their own distresses, had cooperated with each other to give them the love and acceptance they required!

1. If Irene's father, for instance, had made a practice of spending a small quarter of an hour each evening with his daughter in happy talk and play, speaking admiration and praise wherever he legitimately could, before settling down to his newspaper or T.V. program;

2. If Sammy's parents had taken their marriage problem to a good counselor before resorting to the desperate remedy of divorce;

3. If Mary's mother had encouraged her to get interested in music or dancing or some other prideful activity, instead of abandoning her to the one consolation of food;

4. If high spirited Beatrice could have been allowed a voice in the selection of her school;

5. If American daddies could be made to realize that their children need them more than their money and would rather have their company *now* than a fortune later;

6. If all parents would give their children constant emotional support by speaking words of praise and encouragement to them whenever they legitimately could, and by avoiding all talk of blame;

7. If all children were brought up to regard their home as a good society, with love and justice its guiding spirits;

8. If girl children were always as welcome as boy children and vice versa, with no parent committing the folly of showing a gender preference;

9. If orphans of divorce did not have their griefs multiplied by being told by the parent with custody that the other parent never cared for them;

10. If all children received constant assurances from both parents that they were well loved and accepted;

If—If—If! How simple it all seems after the event!

It was just as simple before the event, if only the parents could have understood the true needs of their children. Don't let any child of yours walk the weary road of rejection throughout his life, because you never gave him the warm assurance of being loved and accepted.

Every patriotic American will be interested in improving family life in this country. As the family so the nation. No country can be healthier, sounder, stronger than its families.

Our children are the basic strength of our country. They will form the America of the future. Let us insure that all of them will love their country and prefer its ideals to those of any alien philosophy. How? By making certain that all of them feel loved and accepted.

———

BOOK THREE

Security

EVERY CHILD NEEDS TO KNOW:

*that his home is a good safe place he can
feel sure about*

*that his parents will always be on hand,
especially in times of crisis when he needs
them most*

*that he belongs to a family or group; that
there is a place where he fits in*

CHAPTER I

Love, Not Things, Make

the Secure Home

WHEN THEY look back upon their childhood, what will your children remember of their home? What of joy, what of sorrow?

In a recently conducted research study, Professor Judson T. Landis of the University of California, author (with his wife Mary Landis) of the popular text *Building a Successful Marriage,* asked 150 university students first to make a list of the specific home circumstances which brought greatest happiness to them when they were between the ages of five and twelve. The same students were then asked to make a second list of specific factors which caused greatest unhappiness in their lives as children.

It would be enlightening, perhaps a bit shocking, to some parents to see the report of this study.

Heading the first list, that of pleasant home circumstances, was "Happiness of parents," followed immediately by "Parental expression of love for me."

Other happy memories were: "Sense of the family's interest in me"; "Sense of parents' trust"; "Family unity and fellowship"; "Meals always on time and house always clean."

Not until ninth on the list do we come to, "Family able to provide adequate financial means."

In other words, your children remember and honor you for your spiritual qualities, your ability to build a home for them of love, order and security. They are grateful for your financial support, to be sure; but they place it low on their list of happy home circumstances.

The parents in our American society, and especially the fathers —knocking themselves out to provide their children with every possible luxury and comfort—would do well to revise their thinking on what their children really want of them.

Believe it or not, your children want YOU more than they want your money and what it can buy. They are perfectly willing to live in modest circumstances if they can have more of your companionship. And they especially enjoy seeing you happy with each other. They know their home is secure when you are secure in each other's love.

What gives them grief, as the second list showed, is to see you quarreling with each other, or to feel that you fail to understand them. They also are unhappy if there is quarreling of brothers and sisters in the home, or if they are compared disadvantageously with other children. An especially troubling fear is that parents will separate. Sometimes they feel a great loneliness in their own homes.

But absolutely last on the list of circumstances which cause them unhappiness is "Lack of adequate finances."

The significant truth is that our children have a great capacity to endure material hardship and discomfort, much more than we give them credit for. But they can't get along without our love.

The renowned Norwegian playwright Ibsen, whose dour dramas of family life (*A Doll's House, Ghosts*) shocked and depressed his generation, was once questioned by one of his readers:

"Why do you always portray the seamy side of family life?

Aren't there some good parents as well as bad parents just as there are some good potatoes and some rotten potatoes?"

"Only the rotten potatoes have come under my observation," snapped back the author.

In the same way many present-day psychologists and sociologists—yes, and many newspaper columnists—harass parents by continually harping on the subject of juvenile delinquency and imputing the fault to parents. An example is that terrible and unjust sentence so frequently written and spoken: "There are no delinquent children; there are only delinquent parents." The present generation of youngsters is portrayed as doomed, and parents are made to seem the cause of it.

This, of course, is a false and one-sided picture. The writers who set forth these views are probably so very sensitive to the evils of life, they can't see the good. They feel that our society won't advance until these evils are done away with.

True enough, there is a vast amount of divorce, mental illness, and delinquency in the United States, which means there must be many examples of poor family life. The spawning ground of most neuroses is in the disordered and divided home.

But it is also true that there are a great number of fine families in American life. An observation of their joys and satisfactions can be just as instructive as the previous chapter's presentation of the miserable lives of the rejected. In the happy families we notice always that it is the rich but unpossessive love of the parents that is responsible for the good spirits of the children, their sound behavior, and finally their high achievement.

And why can such parents love their children and yet judiciously let them alone? Because they find fulfillment in each other. It is the spontaneous overflow of their own mutual affection that envelops the children, gladdening their hearts but in no way striving to possess them. In love and freedom the children enjoy their childhood and develop into happy and healthy adults.

One such family that I had the great satisfaction to observe— and, may I add, the even greater satisfaction of being accepted

by as a sometime fellow member and friend—comprised Peter
and Mary F. and their seven children, ages twenty-two months
to fourteen years.

Peter and Mary are a relatively young couple, in their middle
thirties, who have a large family purely out of choice, nothing
in their religion forbidding birth control. They just love children
and can't have too many of them, even though they must work
hard to support and maintain them.

I shall never forget my first visit to their home, a large rambl-
ing old house set in woods on the outskirts of a pleasant suburban
community. I had been invited to lecture before the local P.T.A.
and Peter, whom I had known only professionally on an editor
to writer basis, had asked me "to have dinner with Mary and
the children" before the meeting.

When I arrived, I was greeted by the most joyous group of
children I had ever seen, yet well-poised and mannerly for all
their high spirits and lively talk. The younger ones clambered
all over me, hugging and kissing me and chattering away in all
directions at once, but never once demanding more attention
than I could give. The older ones, two boys, talked of their
studies and sports in genuine enjoyment of an intellectual exchange. The middle two, girls seven and nine, sat with me in a
large armchair, one on each knee, before the fire. For a father
whose progeny were already grown, it was renewing the joys
of parenthood to be so enthusiastically accepted by these wonderfully live and natural children.

How does a mother manage with seven children, a large
house, and no servants? She manages by teaching the children
to help themselves—and each other. Children love to feel needed
and will do more than you'd imagine if you ask them right.

The two eldest, though boys, assisted in getting the dinner
ready, made the fire, set the table, while Mary with great com-
posure chatted with her guest. She knew she could rely on them.

Seven o'clock was the younger ones' bedtime. The mother
took care of the infant, but the elder girl aged nine or ten played
the little mother by putting the other three to bed, reading a

story before tucking them in. Then she joined the older people at the dinner table. You heard nary a cry or a whine from any of them.

Charming to note at the table was the reverend dignity with which grace was spoken by one of the children, not just a rush of words to get to the food, but a sincere expression of thanks to God for "our daily bread."

The liveliest table talk followed. The two boys were greatly interested in rockets, space satellites, and all the newer trends in science, and spoke with authority and fluency about them. They were able to relate scientific progress to the political issues of the day. The father sat at the head of the table, the figure of authority, dispensing the food and directing the conversation, but always giving the children their chance to speak. The mother at the other end smiled and monitored the table manners. Everybody ate heartily and expressed appreciation for each tasty dish. When we got up from the table, all of us felt well nourished in both body and mind.

It was interesting to note both before and after dinner that as the children played, there was little conflict or rivalry among them. They enjoyed their toys and games wholeheartedly but shared them without quarreling.

One of the girls had a big black cat which was her special pet and which she carried over to show me with great pride. "This cat," said the father, "will come to you when called, though cats usually keep aloof. She has been so well loved, she likes to be with people."

And love it was—an easy, graceful natural love that pervaded the whole home. This love had its source in the great man-woman love that the father and mother felt for each other. But it overflowed, enveloping all the children. Everyone was related to every one else in a true family circle, with each one equally giving and receiving love. And yet each one was an independent free spirit, allowed all the rights of individuality.

The sight of such a family is very heartening to a student of American family life. It shows that with love family life is easy and full of satisfactions, regardless of how many children there are or how limited the circumstances.

The dutiful parent, though encouraging self-reliance, is always lovingly present in a child's life, ready to provide help and comfort if called on. But not all parents are dutiful. Some of the saddest tragedies of childhood may occur just because the parents were away when the child most needed him. Take John's case for instance.

John was a nice, normal high school senior, having the usual adolescent conflict between his body urges and his conscience. His parents were well-to-do, social minded people who cared a great deal for their son but were much too busy socially and professionally to give him much attention.

One Saturday evening John found himself entirely alone in their large suburban home. His mother had gone to a resort place for a week of fun with some friends. The father had promised to take care of the boy, but on Saturday night was inveigled into an all night poker game at the club house with some business cronies.

"I'm sure you can take care of yourself, John," the father called up to him as he hurried out.

Johnny answered: "Sure, sure. Go ahead, dad, I'll be allright." But within himself he felt a vague misgiving.

In his restlessness, and knowing his father's poker hours, John called various high school friends, hoping to be invited to a party. Several social groups were forming, but when "the gang" heard that Johnny had the whole house to himself, some of the bolder ones insisted on holding the party at his place.

And so they did!

The record cabinet was well stacked with rock-and-roll records; the liquor closet well stocked with rye, scotch, and gin. What a set-up for a party, especially as there were no adults around. Flaming youth could have an uninhibited fling.

Which is exactly what flaming youth had. But with disastrous consequences! As always, liquor let the barriers of social convention down. Wild dancing was followed by heavy petting.

One or other of the young couples wandered off to the bed-
rooms. Johnny, too, got involved with a sophisticated older girl
who was known to have had several affairs.

When the party broke up well toward morning, Johnny's head
was reeling with confusion, doubt, remorse, and fear. What if
one of the girls should get pregnant? What if! There were a
thousand and one "what if's" to be worried about. He felt that
the whole blame belonged to him.

But did it?

An extraordinary number of parents in our society cannot
seem to learn how unsafe an empty house is for children or
adolescents. While Johnny was going through this miserable
initiation into vice—shattering to young love's dream—his mother
was dancing with strangers in a resort casino and his father was
sitting in a smoke-filled room lost to everything but his hand of
cards.

Summary and Suggestion

The good society, let us always remember, begins in the
home. Wise parents can create a pattern of a non-aggressive
way of life in the home, with the children considerate of
each other and cooperating for the family's general welfare.
Such children, because they are happy at home, will later
carry over the same ideals into the world outside, gradually
establishing ideals of creativeness and cooperation among
its members and discouraging techniques of domination
and aggression.

The first rules of mental health are to give children love
and security. When you do, you will be happily amazed to
find how easy it is to raise them right and set them off on the
path of building fine families of their own.

In a home dominated by spiritual ideals the child feels
secure and safe. The parents are kind and dutiful. They are
always present, ready to give help or comfort where needed.

The family is a circle with everyone equally giving and receiving love. In such a family a child develops a strong sense of *belonging*. There is always a place where he fits in. That's what the Mental Health people mean by security—the security felt by the well-loved child in a well-ordered and happy home.

————————

CHAPTER II

Discipline Gives Your

Child Security

Typical of American parents is the remark: "I want my child to have an easier life than I had." Many of us have undergone a pioneering experience. We faced up to new and difficult experiences. We struggled and overcame. But the going was tough at times, and so we say—with satisfaction: "Thank God, my Johnny or Jane won't need to struggle as I did." Perhaps there is a touch of vanity in the thought: "Because I was strong enough to accomplish what I did, they won't have to work so hard."

But this is a deceptive kind of reasoning. A harsh and dangerous world confronts our children. We have enemies within and without that threaten to destroy us. These enemies have to be met and overcome. There is no use trying to make life easier for our children than it was for us. All signs indicate it won't be easier; it will be harder. Their best security is their own strength developed through their own self-discipline. "In schools and colleges, in fleet and army, in home and nation, discipline means success and lack of discipline means failure." This wise thought of the philosopher-historian, James Anthony Froude, should

143

give us pause. It is not a pleasing thought for comfort-loving American children, but it's exactly appropriate to our present situation.

How will our children acquire discipline, the training of their physical, mental and moral powers that will enable them to accept responsibility, to enjoy hard work, to persist in their endeavors, to think a problem through, to hold out in a fight until they win?

Discipline comes from conscience. We have explained in a previous chapter that children acquire a conscience out of a desire to keep their parents' love. The loved child is obedient— that is to such standards as the parent sets before him. By systematically setting before his child good standards and patiently insisting that they be followed, the sound parent disciplines his child.

Instinctively the loved child wants to do right in reciprocation for his dear parents' love. But children also have many wayward impulses of pleasure and self-indulgence that they will want to satisfy also, if you let them. The point is not to let them, at least not to any immoderate degree.

All people—and that includes our children, of course—are as good as they can be and as bad as they can get away with. This may sound like a cynical statement, but it isn't. It's just a rewording in popular terms of the age old truth that in all people there is the struggle between good and evil. By giving our children a conscience and strengthening it through discipline, we make it easier for them to choose the good, and thus to make a better life for themselves. None are so secure in this world of trial and trouble as those with a well-disciplined conscience.

So when you next see your Johnny or Jane struggling with a moral issue, such as helping with the dishes instead of idly looking at T.V., or tackling a tough subject in school that it would be so very relieving to drop, you must stand on the side of conscience and discipline, and lovingly but firmly insist that the better thing be done. Don't be tempted to say: "All right Jane, you can go. I'll do the dishes myself."—or—"All right Johnny,

I'll see the principal and ask him to let you drop the subject."
You're deciding in favor of Johnny's weaker self and destroying
his discipline.

The truth is Johnny wants to do the right, the strong thing,
as much as he wants to do the wrong, the weak thing. Both instincts are struggling within him. Here's where you come in. By
your steadfast insistence that he do the right thing you encourage his instinctive aspirational endeavors and make certain that
he acts as he ought, always careful of course to make your demands reasonable.

The rest is practice.

If you have ever gone in for regular body building gymnastics,
you know what a joy it is to use your muscles, to feel the surge
and lift of your well-trained torso. It's good to be physically
strong. You move fast, you catch and carry, you make and do and
it's all easy, a pleasure.

It's also good to be morally strong. You are at peace within
yourself. And you triumph over circumstances through the application of principle. All this you can give to your children.

Believe me, your children really prefer high standards and
are proud of the parents who set them for them, provided, of
course, that you are sincere and do not ask them to do what you
wouldn't do yourself. Beware of hypocrisy; it befouls all moral
issues.

Beware also of perfectionist standards which act as a strait-
jacket and do more harm than good. Remember always that
the good are the merry. A sour and sombre virtue has no merit.
But you can always ask of your children a little more than they
can easily do. That's what growth means. Your children want
to grow!

Your children know that you genuinely care for them, if you
take the time and trouble to train them. They like that. It gives
them a sense of their own worth. Our heroic Theodore Roosevelt, one of history's finest examples of a father and a man, said
of his father:

"My father was the best man I ever knew." And when the

father died, Teddy spoke this eulogy of him: "I have lost the only human being to whom I told everything, never failing to get loving advice and sweet sympathy in return."

This shows how a fine son appreciates a father who gives him guidance and ideals, the security of a built-in conscience. Will your son say the same of you?

Summary and Suggestion

For the harsh realities of the world that now face us, your child will need all the strength he can get. The wise parent knows that discipline gives strength.

This doesn't mean that he sets up strict rules and insists that they be obeyed, come what may. No, there is a more natural way to discipline. Discipline derives from a child's conscience. The parent who has through love and a good example helped his child acquire a conscience makes it easier for a child to accept discipline. The child wants to do right to please the beloved parent.

The rest is training. By steadfastly, cheerfully insisting that your child abide by the high standards you have set for him—and which you illustrate by your own behavior— your child becomes a strong, well-disciplined person.

CHAPTER III

Courtesy of Parents Promotes Children's Happiness and Sense of Security

WHEN HIS children came down for breakfast in the morning, Harry Gordon did not greet them with a mere "Good morning," but would say "Good morning, George," or "Good morning, Joan," speaking the name clearly and cordially. The children liked that. To a child, as to an adult, there is no sound so sweet as the sound of his own name. When you are called by name, you are given recognition as an individual.

At the breakfast or dinner table, food was passed from parent to child with a pleasant, "Will you have some cereal, or milk, or vegetable, or meat?"—or whatever the dish was. There was none of that nagging and urging to eat which children find so offensive, and which have made a shambles of so many a family meal. Nor was there any talk of table manners. It was taken for granted that the children would behave well. So they always did.

147

Talk at table was lively but contained. The children were allowed their full say on any subject and were listened to by the parents attentively and patiently. If a child made a particularly apt remark, he was complimented for his cleverness. Neither parent would think of interrupting a child just because he was a child, or of terminating the discussion by rising from the table before the child had made his point.

All this was typical of the courtesy that prevailed in the Gordon household. It paid off. Their life was gracious, easy, and interesting. The children enjoyed home and were happy to be there. Even in adolescence, when most youngsters are forever gadding about to the great worriment of their parents, home was a base for the Gordon clan. They enjoyed family games and sociables or just sitting around and chatting or reading together.

To be courteously treated by his parents makes a child feel sure of his own worth. That's important to his all-around sense of security and self-confidence. It is with his self-confidence that a child makes his way in the world. That is the great endowment we bestow upon our children. Without it all other gifts are worthless.

The psychology of courtesy runs deep. It is no mere surface gloss to human behavior, as some mistakenly believe. Courtesy is kindness and love. It sustains such civilization as mankind has yet attained. In our competitive and complex society, with everyone so harried and driven and so uncertain of his status, it satisfies the almost desperate need of the individual for recognition and acceptance.

Courtesy is caught, not taught. You can tell your children a hundred times to be polite, to say "thank you," to pay attention when others are talking; but if they don't see their parents doing these things—to each other, to strangers, and to them—they won't do them either. What you are speaks much louder than what you say.

There's always time for courtesy. In fact, courtesy saves time. When you consider the endless hours some households waste in petty wrangling, you realize how much time and energy might have been saved if all its members had been just reasonably polite to one another.

Especially, if you are concerned for your children's future success in the world, should you make certain to train them in a positive, creative courtesy. Courtesy opens doors. Many a youth with great gifts has achieved very little because of his lack of skill in getting along with people. And conversely many with limited talents have made a very fine place for themselves by their grace and charm of manner. One of the most liked and respected men of my home town, and quite well to do besides, is a shoe repair man whom the whole town patronizes because it's such a pleasure to be greeted by his cheery chit-chat and warm smile. Business executives agree that the ability to get along with people is the quality for which they will pay the highest salary.

But courtesy goes deeper in its aims than worldly success. In its essence it is a spiritual quality betokening reverence and regard for the individual. The first commandment is that we should love God and one another. Behind all the rules of courtesy, sincere courtesy, is this spirit of love.

Why then do many parents not practice this family courtesy that could be so profitable to them and their children? Irritability is the answer. Many a man who could be king of his household, many a woman who could be treated as a queen, becomes a mere object of fear and dislike to the children by the constant exhibition of irritability, the so-called vice of the virtuous.

What is your irritability quotient? Some of the so-called best parents make a bad score.

And so do some of the best teachers!

A school teacher's life is not a very easy one, nor does he often enjoy the gratification of success for his labors. But he could lead both an easier and more successful life, if he would learn to lower his irritability quotient.

Irritability, as has been said, is the vice of the virtuous. Good people, struggling to maintain high standards of self-discipline and labor, perhaps too high for comfort, are hard on themselves and tend therefore to be hard on others. Their frequent outbursts of ill temper undo more than their virtue accomplishes.

In a certain well-populated private preparatory school, there was a teacher of English whose every lesson was a model of pedagogy. In addition, she had an exquisitely expressive voice, a deep understanding of literature, and a precise, almost encyclopedic knowledge of grammar and rhetoric. Yet as a teacher she was a failure. Why? Her irritability quotient was too high.

She expected perfection of her pupils and would accept nothing less. If a youngster misbehaved, she considered his action a personal affront. Her grades were always much lower than those of other teachers. Her pupils were in a continuous state of strain. Every one feared he would fail or be subjected to withering criticism. Very few mastered the subject. All of this teacher's great abilities were of no avail because of her lack of human warmth and appreciation. Pupils would not learn from her, and without learning there is no teaching.

By contrast with her, there was a teacher of foreign languages in the same school whose manner was so very relaxed and friendly that his every class lesson was productive of progress and fun. Foreign languages study is not exactly the favorite subject of high school kids, but in this school it was.

The principal once observed a minor case of misbehavior in his room—a boy teasing a pretty girl student by pulling a ribbon off her hair. Instead of giving an irritable outcry at this interruption, the teacher merely stopped, fixed an amused smile on the boy until he desisted, and then went on with the explanation he was making as if nothing at all had happened. The girl reached out her hand for the ribbon without taking her eyes off the teacher, and soon the boy, too, yielded to the larger lure of the lesson. Here you have the master teacher, too serene within to give way to irritation without.

All teachers should know that kids are quick to sense an opening for getting power over them. Irritability is a dead giveaway of weakness. At the first sign of it, the kids chortle wtih unholy glee, knowing they have one teacher whom they can dominate. Don't let it happen to you.

Teachers are sometimes impatient that their students are slow to answer or seemingly pay no attention. Instead of getting excited over this, why not realize that it is natural? The subject that seems so important to you does not necessarily appeal to the youngsters; their inattention to you is not a mortal sin. Your exclaiming upon it, however, often makes a tragic situation out of what could be a simple incident. As a corrective to this, try reciting to yourself Richard Armour's cute jingle, which appeared in the *Guidance Newsletter:*

> "A mind? yes, he has one of those
> It comes, however, and it goes,
> And if, when it is called upon,
> It mostly happens to be gone,
> Don't fret, don't shout, don't curse the lack:
> Just wait awhile—it will be back!"

Your child's mental health is sustained and strengthened by his teacher's inner poise and warmth. If he has such a teacher, be sure to bless her in your prayers and vote yes on any question of raising her salary.

If, on the other hand, your child's teacher seems to have a high irritability quotient, you might ask the school's principal to discuss the subject at a faculty meeting.

First be sure of your own poise and self-confidence.

If love is the supreme gift of the parent to the child, irritability is the base destroyer of that gift.

In many discordant families, with each member seemingly hopelessly hostile to every other, a general touchiness of temper is basically all that is wrong. Everyone is so quick to get offended. A mood of irascibility pervades the home. Nobody is happy. And why? Ego pin-pricks is the answer.

All of us know the type of high-minded, generous, hard-work-ing, devoted parent whose virtue is marred by his sensitiveness. Nobody dares say a word for fear of giving him hurt. What good are all his moral qualities? One show of ill temper and their work is undone.

Such a father may take time to teach his boy games, but if the latter acts clumsily, being but a learner, he considers it an affront to his instruction and cries angrily: "Didn't I tell you to hold the bat this way, or stop a grounder that way?!" He monitors his children in good table manners, but if one of them should back-slide into the old way of slurping his soup, or biting his bread from the whole slice, he exclaims: "All my trouble to show you good manners, and you eat like an animal!"

Mothers have their way of showing irritability, too. A weary mother may give way to angry exclamations when children break up a housekeeping routine—leaving muddied rubbers in the center of the hall, failing to put their clothes away, not answer-ing her call to dinner, and other annoyances. Such exclamations are natural enough; it's making these simple acts of childish care-less appear as intentional affronts to the parent that overwhelms and disconcerts the children: "I work like a dog all day, and look what you do to me!"

One of the worst acts of parental irritability is the sudden slapping of a child's face. A whack on the buttocks, yes, even a couple of them, but slapping a child's face degrades him. No child, big or little, fails to resent this.

Every parent should realize that ill temper is a very real sin. It unspiritualizes the whole personality.

Furthermore, it may doom you to failure as a parent. The temper-tossed home does not function effectively. The children become cranky, resistant, incompetent. They do poor work at school. They make enemies in the playground. They fail in all their human relations. Consciously or unconsciously, they blame you and dislike you for it.

The root of all irritability is ego-distress. If we had a more secure sense of our own worth, we would not flare up so quickly at every little affront to our dignity.

The cure for ill temper is not necessarily will power or self control. The bottled up temper is dangerous. Frequently it bursts forth in a wildly destructive blast.

There are flank attacks on temper. We have to understand ourselves, come to terms with our inferiority distress. Accepting ourselves, we more readily accept others. This self-understanding is a big help.

But the best remedy of all is to bring God's love into our lives. When we relax and are receptive to the Divine Beneficence, it floods our whole being. We then feel secure and strong, and go about our business free of hurt feelings because we don't admit them into our consciousness.

All parents should have a quiet time with God each day. In their meditations and prayers they should ask:

"From irritability, dear Lord, preserve me. When I give love to my children, let me never take it back by ill-temper."

Summary and Suggestion

Courtesy with children brings its own reward. The youngsters respond in kind, creating an orderly and pleasant household.

Discourtesy to a child is a mistake, and habitual irritability a great mistake. It creates an unhappy, disorganized home.

Children expect to be corrected for their mistakes and misdeeds. But, please, don't make it personal. Your child is then hurt more than he deserves, and you lose some of your force and effectiveness as a parent.

He can't admire you as he would like to, when you show yourself so petty. He may even take advantage of your weakness and behave worse than ever.

So, for your own dignity and self-respect, don't give way

to irritability. Keep your poise as a parent. Remember always that your child is a child and you are an adult.

The well-mannered adult is a joy and inspiration to his children.

CHAPTER IV

Home is a

Comfortable Place

"Yes, I remember my mother used to bake whole wheat bread twice a week. Gee, it was good! I can still see her bending over the oven to take the loaves out and us kids standing around her enjoying the smell. There's nothing nicer than the smell of freshly baked bread. And I remember. . . ."

Prick up your ears at a social gathering and notice in the conversation with what satisfaction grownups recall to mind some of the creature comforts enjoyed in childhood—especially of food and dress provided by a loving and thoughtful mother or of sports and games organized by a manly and interested father. Important as are the spiritual ideals that pervade a home, to a young child the proof of a parent's love lies largely in the care and attention given to his physical needs. It takes a lot of forethought and energy to supply these needs, but to the devoted parent it is all a labor of love.

Having a room of his own furnished especially for his comfort and pleasure is a great satisfaction to a child. It gives him individuality. The room can be small and the furniture plain, but it is all his. He is king in his own castle. If you want your child to have a strong, well-defined personality, to feel secure in his self, try to give him a room of his own. If he must share his room, let it be with another child.

There is much that a parent can do to make a child's room safe, comfortable, and interesting. Certain furniture is basic: a crib or bed, a low table and a chair or two to match, low shelves or boxes for keeping books and toys, a chest of drawers for intimate clothes and a closet with low hanging hooks for coats, shoes, etc. All furniture, wall coverings, etc. should be attractively colored and made of durable and washable materials. Articles that are easily soiled or that could possibly hurt or injure should be kept out of a child's room. A play pen and a toilet chair are indispensable for the young chlid.

The wise selection of toys and play materials is an important duty of parents. A child's first learnings are with his toys. Interesting constructive toys help a child become both creative and self-confident.

The best all-around toy for children is a big box of blocks. This gives opportunity for endless making and doing according to the imagination's dictates. My own children had two of them with a hundred varied pieces in each. Starting with simple structures they learned in time to copy, in blocks, the cathedrals and castles pictured in the encyclopedia article on Architecture. Blocks also give an agreeable, and harmless, outlet to a child's desire to demolish and destroy. Toppling over a huge temple of blocks gives them a satisfying sense of power.

An excess of toys should be avoided. Children who surfeit don't dream. What is life without a dream? Children who surfeit also fail to create.

In a former generation many children made their own toys of bits of wood, string, cloth, rubber bands, discarded baby carriage wheels, etc. I can still remember the rubber band paddle boats I made and floated in the bathtub as well as the rubber band fiddles and a complete chess game carved out of my mother's discarded spools. In later years, we kids made very serviceable wagons of wooden boxes and baby carriage wheels and raced down hill with them. It was great fun.

Present-day kids have no such inventiveness. Their plenteous toys are all ready-made and therefore the more quickly tired of. Nor do they seem to have the skill to make up games and have fun by themselves without the direction of playground teachers and scout leaders. You are wise to encourage your children to create their own fun. Creativeness grows by what it feeds on.

An internationally known newspaper correspondent tells this story of his children's experience with toys:

On a resident assignment in tense, but quiet pre-war China, he was accompanied by his wife and his five and seven year old girl and boy. The couple took a house far from the capital and from the "white settlement." They moved into this somewhat isolated section with only a few belongings, awaiting the arrival of the freighter that was to bring their household goods for the long stay, and also the children's many American toys. Soon afterwards, word came that the ship had been sunk in a storm. Meanwhile, the children had made friends with the children of their rather poor Chinese neighbors. Nevertheless, and despite the real disappointment in losing the household goods, the mother was most concerned about the loss of the children's toys.

"What will they do without them? All those toys and games!" she remarked to her husband as they sat on the verandah.

He was looking out on the terraced yard below. The children were happily playing, all chattering without awareness of any language barrier.

"Come here and look," he answered, taking her hand.

They gazed long and with increasing astonishment at what they saw. The yard held an assortment of toys of unique types, strange shapes and fantasies. Much originality and not a little artistry had gone into their making. Taught by their small Chinese friends, the American children had learned to make their own toys. There were dolls of straw, bound with string, crayoned features, dressed in bright scraps of material. There were fiery red horses made from empty firecracker cartridges, complete with sweeping straw tails and splinter-like legs. There were lopsided clay animals, all colored by careful selections from the nearby red and yellow clay. There were several Chinese houses made of multicolored pebbles stuck into straw-matted, sun-hardened clay. These last had the curved and upsweeping cornered roofs of the houses of old China, made from the father's pipe tobacco tins.

The children were excitedly playing some inexplicable game with small sticks, the rules of which were apparently a mystery to all, except that they involved the pet duck. Either as a fine, or perhaps, as a token of winning, one of the avid contestants would break off to race to the four corners of the yard, followed by the duck! Then the play was resumed and another contestant made the rounds.

The wife spoke in awed surprise: "I never realized . . . ! How busy they are! And this box here in the corner, it is full of things they have collected, but I never realized that they had made them, too! All I know is that it is so cherished that I have to promise several times a day not to disturb their ' box.' "

"Well dear, we certainly don't have to worry about the loss of those fancy toys from home," her husband laughed. "They obviously have more fun making their own. I must say, I never realized that Sally and Rob were so ingenious!"

She joined his quiet laughter: "They do look a bit odd! But you know, some of them are quite clever, and actually artistic!"

When this family returned to the USA, the children continued making more grown-up toys as their years increased. The neighborhood children also took up the idea with delight. It was plain that their products were individual to each child, for no two toys were alike, just as no two creative impulses are alike.

Children can make their own toys—if we let them. And what a stimulus that will be to their creativeness. Every child must create to be happy.

The success of Robert Paul Smith's two best sellers: *Where Did You Go? Out. What Did You Do? Nothing.* And its sequel *How to Do Nothing, All By Yourself, Alone,* is indicative of the

American parent's growing understanding of the American child's need for simplicity and self-direction in amusements.

Group play and activities, cooperative home, school and sports participation are essential. Equally essential is a certain amount of occupied aloneness for every child, whether this kind of aloneness is spent in complete absorption of watching cloud formations, or in running across a field because "you are a horse" or, in doing "a lot of nothing," as Mr. Smith phrases it.

"We did a lot of nothing. And let's face it, we still do it, all of us grown-ups and kids. But now, for some reason, we're ashamed of it. I'll leave the grown-ups out, but take a kid these days, standing or sitting or lying down all by himself, not actively engaged in any recognizable, by grown-ups, socially acceptable activity. We want to know what's the matter. That's because *we* don't know how to do 'nothing' any more. Kids have got enough sense to roll with the punch, to give in and be a slack-jawed idiot when boredom is afoot, but we can't let them alone. It's the old business of the reformed drunk: we can't do that any more, so we won't let them."

It is important for children to have fresh air and sunshine and outdoor space in which to play. How many of the trials and tribulations of present-day children—and how much of the vexation and grief they cause their parents—is due to nothing but the fact that in our overcrowded towns and cities they have no place to play. Many a municipality, hungry for tax sources allows the real estate interests to build up all the land, with no thought of the children's need of parks and playgrounds. Soon it is too late. There is no land left. And wan, sad-faced children, disinherited of their place in the sun, sit on stoops or doorsteps gazing blankly before them with nothing to do and no one to play with. The bolder ones may dash across traffic-laden streets to their peril. And some slink off to the dark alleys of delinquency and crime. What a world for children!

The move to the suburbs, with every family having its own back yard has seemed the best solution to this problem. But it has caused another problem. Father now has to spend an hour each way commuting back and forth from work. He leaves before the children are up; he returns when they are ready for bed. On weekends he is so weary he must go off on some recreation of his own like golfing. What time is there left for him to be with his children? Very little. They are raised almost exclusively by their mother, the lack of male gender influence causing an imbalance in their emotional development. Boys—and girls!—need a man as well as a woman in their life. Are grass and trees and private play space more important than father's company? Many sociologists say "no" and are sadly troubled about the whole problem.

Indeed the physical care of children in our crowded, complex and rapidly changing society is a problem to tax the energies of the most resourceful parent. But the good parent accepts the challenge. He finds ways to provide many interesting activities for them. He tactfully refrains from intruding in their play with other children, but he also organizes a lot of family fun; picnics, games, chorus singing, discussion of books and magazines.

Family meals are the most important means of uniting the family and keeping the lines of communication open between its members. Busy fathers, especially, should make a point to be always present at the dinner table and mothers should be sure to prepare a hot, nourishing breakfast. Nothing gives a child such a sense of security and satisfaction in his home as cheerful family meals. Eating together is an act of love. That family is sure of a sound development whose mealtime hour is one of affection and good cheer.

Summary and Suggestion

Home is a comfortable place to be recalled in later years with pleasure. The food we ate, the uniquely delicious dishes that only our mother could make, the games we played with dad and each other, the cozy room we lived in, the toys bought or of our own manufacture—how dear are these memories of childhood.

The child has been aptly defined as a savage—with a soul. He is full of physical needs, but he has a deep spiritual appreciation of them. Your dutiful attention to your child's needs, the comfortable, pleasant home you provide for him, is your way of assuring him in his early years of your love.

But what contributes more than things to the comfort and security of the home is your consistent use of the good word. It is the good word that makes the good home.

CHAPTER V

The Good Word Makes

the Good Home

"POOR JANEY," the mother exclaimed, stroking her adolescent daughter's tear stained cheek, "she always gets the worst of it."

"Why do you always say 'poor Janey'" the neighbor asked. "It's wrong to talk that way."

"But she is 'poor Janey.' The other kids take advantage of her. They borrow her prettiest things and never think of returning them. They abuse and embarrass her in class and at social gatherings. They—I'll bet when she marries, her husband will take advantage of her, too."

"Keep on betting," the neighbor declared with a wry smile. "Then you can be sure it will happen."

That neighbor was right. Would that parents understood how their words are continuously weaving the fate of their children. Say "poor Janey" often enough, and poor Janey it will be.

Negative words fill the household with depression and doubt. Your continuous discontent wears away your children's self-reliance, leaving them defenseless against the ills and evils of life. Without courage a child is nothing. Without courage a child

162

can't make his way in the world. Who robbed your children of their courage? You did with your negative words.

Positive words, on the other hand, give life and power to the individual. Watch what happens to your children when you use cheerful exclamations like: "Atta boy! Good for you! That's great!" How they swell with self-confidence and pride! They take strength from your belief in them. The good word makes the good, the secure, home.

In truth, what happens to us in life is usually nothing more than the outpicturing of our words and thoughts. When we deal in nothing but sick, sad, and sorrowful words, let us not be too surprised if sickness, sadness and tragedy overwhelm us.

It is the glory of the human soul that it is allowed a choice. You don't have to use negative words of fear, hate, sickness, loss: "Poor me! Never had a break! People are no damn good." You can train yourself to use positive words and to have positive thoughts. You will be very agreeably surprised to find how much less of fear, hate, sickness, loss you will have in your life, if you don't call them forth with your words. "In the beginning was the Word," says the profound Biblical verse, implying the great truth that everything comes from the word—evil from the evil word, and good from the good word. Steadfastly use warm, cheerful, hopeful words and watch your family develop in health and happiness.

Above all, let no words of self-pity be heard in your home. There is no poison so deadly as self-pity. As soon as you feel sorry for yourself, you're sunk. As soon as your children feel sorry for themselves, they're sunk. How can they, or you, ever rise above your own low estimate of yourselves?

Rather, teach your children by precept and example to assert their own positive good health at all times, to declare their faith in God and people, to praise all right actions they may observe, to use the good word.

In school, as in the home, the good word works wonders.

"Hello, John, glad to see you back!"

It was Mr. Thompson, John's first-period teacher, greeting him on his return to school after a week's absence for illness. John looked at his warmly smiling face and smiled happily back. Gee, it was good to be in school again!

But John's second-period teacher was different. He growled: "Been out again, huh? How'll you ever make up all the work that you've missed?"

The same boy, the same school—but two different teachers and two different remarks. And what a difference to John!

The weary, oppressed, nerve-strained teacher, who thinks at times that his job is impossibly difficult, can at once lighten his load by cheer-charging his language. The good word leads to the good thought; the good thought leads to the good act. Teachers set in motion a happy chain reaction among the children when they dedicate themselves to the use of the good word.

Alas, that so few teachers realize this! There is hardly a school problem that will not be resolved happily with the right word and unhappily with the wrong.

The cranky, petulant word that comes up so frequently in the classroom is a blight upon teaching. It reflects the present-day teacher's lack of pride in his profession, his ego-unhappiness. If he could discipline himself always to use the good word, he would rescue himself alive from most of his classroom distresses. He would enjoy his work and be more successful at it. Who knows but he might also ultimately win thereby the higher salary scale that is his due.

It is not enough for teachers to avoid using querulous, critical words (accentuating the negative); they must actively seek opportunities sincerely to express cheering, sustaining, uplifting words.

The greatest aid to classroom happiness and the advancement of learning is the spirit of appreciation. Praise whenever you legitimately can; overlook faults that are minor; criticize constructively. If Johnny makes twenty spelling errors in a test of one hundred words emphasize that there were eighty right rather than that there were twenty wrong.

Captious criticism is fatal. There are a score of things that one can find fault with in the classroom if one wants to: gum chewing, side whispering, slouching, paper rustling. The wise teacher, however, does not attack disorder; he outwits it by directing student participation in the lesson and making the lesson so interesting that students attend eagerly. The child with whom one always finds fault is quick to say: "What's the use?" and gives up trying. The warm-hearted appreciative teacher will bring out the best in his pupils and earn their respect and affection, besides.

But appreciation is a two-way street. Teachers, too, are people and need appreciation. If your child speaks enthusiastically of his teachers, tell him to show his appreciation of them by courteous speech and action. He, too, must learn to use the good word in the classroom.

And here's a hint for parents, also. Why don't you send a letter of appreciation to your child's teacher? That would be your good word in the classroom. As the popular verse puts it:

"If you know that praise is due him,
    Now's the time to slip it to him,
'Cause he cannot read his tombstone when he's dead."

Don't let talk of sickness get into your home.

"Did you make up this morning with a dull headache? Did you wake up this morning with the first sniffles of a cold?"

These are typical radio and television patent medicine commercials, and far from the worst. In patent-medicine America they keep coming into the home all day long and late into the night. The harm they do to your good health and that of your children is immeasurable.

The truth is many people wake up in the morning both with and without a headache. Keep on repeating the sick thought, however, and it won't be long before you do have the headache. They've talked a sickness into you and made it very real. And they'll talk a sickness into your children, too, if you don't protect them with more positive ideas of good health.

The whine of invalidism runs like a cold wind through millions of American homes. Does it run through yours? Fussing, fretting, patronizing parents and patent medicine propaganda have put it there. Only sound thinking can get it out. An interesting modern writer on health puts it this way:

"When Johnny cuts his finger at play, we should never help fear to enter his mind by saying: 'What a nasty cut! If you aren't careful it will become infected and you might lose that finger.' Instead we should build up his protective, healing consciousness by telling him: 'See, it's already starting to heal. If we keep it clean and guard it from bumps, it will soon be as good as new.'

"If Jane starts to sniffle and sneeze, we should not invite sickness by chiding her with: 'You're getting a bad cold again. If you don't wrap up when you go out of doors, you're likely to have pneumonia.' How much better it is to ward off sickness with a positive healing statement, such as: 'Those sniffles are reminders, Jane. They're to remind you to wear warm clothing when you go out to play, so you'll keep yourself strong and healthy!' "

Parents who fuss a lot about sickness tempt their children to use invalidism as a bid for attention and power. In a way, the parents' desire to patronize is in secret collusion with the child's desire to be coddled. Both attitudes are unwholesome and spiritually destructive. Be vigilant ever that invalidism does not become your child's path to power.

When your child is sick, give him care but no coddling. Do what has to be done, and then let him alone, severely alone. Let no premium be placed on invalidism.

Health is the natural condition of every child of God. In this sense, you should take your child's health for granted. Sustain it by your faith; don't destroy it by your doubts. And don't let others destroy it, either. Keep him away from the poisonous gossip of hypochondriac minds, who get a perverse pleasure from talking about their ills.

Parents can do a great deal to promote in their children sound attitudes toward health. A cheerful disposition, free of all whining and complaining, sets the health tone for the whole household. If you happen to incur some physical disability, keep it as much as possible private. See a good doctor and follow his advice. Don't lament about it in front of your children. Don't encourage your children to invalidism by the example of your own continuous concern with it.

Invalid-prone children don't succeed in life, nor later in the workaday world. Save your children from the blight of invalidism by shutting out the all too catching talk of sickness from your home.

Summary and Suggestion

Words are living realities. They don't die when spoken; they go forth actively making or remaking the world, your world, your children's world. They are the architects of your fate. If you and your children consistently choose and use the good word, you and your children will have a happy home—a good life.

The use of the good word can be learned by prayer and practice. First we have to believe in it. "In the beginning was the Word" says the most profound of the gospels, implying the great truth that everything comes from the word—evil from the evil word, and good from the good word. Steadfastly use warm, cheerful, hopeful words, and watch your family develop in health and happiness.

I would like to ask all parents to make this experiment in their own homes. For one whole week, whenever you turn to address your children, use the most positive and encouraging words that you can, and avoid as much as possible all expressions of fear or blame. Express praise for any worthy act of theirs, however small, give assurance of health and prosperity if they inquire about the affairs of the household, tell the good side of any person they happen to mention. Whatever winds blow, that weather is agreeable; whatever task is to be done, that work is interesting; whatever stranger passes by, he is worthy and lovable; whatever church is nearest is a good place in which to worship. Every day is the best day in the year.

Try it for a week.

If at the end of the week, you find that your children are generally more vigorous and cheerful, more active at work and play, healthier and happier—then you'll know you have learned the use of the good word. Don't ever give it up!

———————

BOOK FOUR

Protection

EVERY CHILD NEEDS TO FEEL:

*that his parents will keep him safe
from harm*

*that they will help him when he
must face strange, unknown and
frightening situations*

Independence

EVERY CHILD NEEDS TO KNOW:

*that his parents want him to grow up
and that they encourage him to try
new things*

*that they have confidence in him and in
his ability to do things for himself and by
himself*

CHAPTER I

Protection Precedes

Independence

EVERY PARENT is proud of the child who has achieved independence, who knows how to make and do things on his own, who faces up to new experiences with a bold spirit. How proudly does a parent remark: "My kid went off to school all by himself the first day. Didn't need me to stand by him. He just loves school." Another says with similar pride: "My boy has a lot of friends. Everybody likes him. He's the leader of his gang. He can take care of himself in a fight or a frolic."

But what many parents do not understand is that before a child can achieve this fine spirit of independence, he must feel absolutely protected and secure. His self-confidence comes from the assurance of your love. A father may say to his boy who has run in frightened because another fellow attacked him: "Aw, you big sissy! Why don't you go back and fight him yourself?" The reason could very well be that the boy doesn't feel secure with his father, that his own father has made him feel generally fearsome and unsure of himself.

It takes a nice parental touch to distinguish between overprotecting a child and throwing him into independent behavior too soon.

A good example is seen at the beach as parents try to teach their younger children how to swim. Some swashbuckling father who is a good swimmer himself, may think it smart to throw his boy into the water and tell him, half jokingly, of course, "Now sink or swim!" To the child, however, it's no joke. Being suddenly dropped unsupported into uncertain depths, even with the father standing by, is a terrifying experience and may make him fearsome of the water ever after.

Tensely holding on to the boy and quickly pulling him back at the first approach of a wave, is no good either. Again the child is made to fear the water. Gradual but firm stepping forth into the water, plus patient and steadfast instruction in the motions of swimming, using encouraging words all the while, will do the trick. The lad will soon happily cry: "O.K. dad, I can go by myself now."

Sometimes a vain mother may urge a socially bashful daughter to act more boldly with the boys, telling her: "Don't be a wallflower! Throw your charms about. No boy will notice you unless you use glamor." The girl, however, may interpret this to mean that the mother does not think she is charming at all and may shrink back more shyly than ever.

But if the mother had first provided her daughter with all the prerequisites of charm, good grooming, a beautiful and becoming costume, plus training in the social graces, and then said warmly: "You look lovely, dear. Have a good time," her faith would have communicated. The daughter would have stepped forth on the dance floor with the self-assurance that always attracts the boys.

Only when a child feels absolutely secure in his parents' love, knowing that they will always protect him and keep him safe from harm, is he ready to develop a fearless and independent spirit. He learns to feel safe in the universe as he had always felt safe in his parents' home.

A striking example of this was presented to the American psychiatrists who followed our troops to the bomb-torn island of Okinawa in World War II. There they found the most extraordinarily fearless, poised, and unneurotic children they had ever seen, and this after many months of bombardment and deprivation. What could be the explanation of this fine behavior of the Okinawan children? That question greatly intrigued the American observers. They were not long in finding the answer.

As they observed the way the Okinawan mothers and fathers handled their children, they soon realized that it was the atmosphere of love and security in the home that gave these children their free spirit. These children could always count on their parents to provide promptly for their needs and to keep them safe from harm. At the same time, these parents were wise enough to send them off to independent behavior as soon as they felt they were ready for it. Without first feeling protected and secure, a child is not ready to adventure and struggle with new experiences.

The wise parent maintains a nice balance between protection and independence. If you protect your child too much, if you keep him in leading strings too long, he is likely to become a weakling. But if you throw him off into independent behavior too early, telling him to sink or swim, he may become hysterically fearsome and feel afraid all his life. You can't rush these steps in growth. The child must feel protected first and then be gently led step by step into independent action.

"See you later, alligator," the young mother rhymed playfully to twenty months old Linda, as she set off for an evening out with her husband. The child smiled back and waved "bye" to the parents, then turned to the baby sitter and soon engaged in a merry game of roll-the-ball with her.

The same sort of easy exchange occurred at bedtime. "Nighty-night," the mother would say, depositing Linda in her crib and giving her a last snuggle and kiss. She then closed the door. Linda might play with her dolly a bit, or with her big stuffed panda, or she might go right off to sleep. The mother heard nary a cry or call from her.

Other mothers who have to use all kinds of tricks and stratagems to get away from a wailing child for an evening out—or whose bedtime hour is a shambles of demands, outcries and ultimate punishment—might well wonder how Linda's mother had established so happy and fear-free a relationship with her child.

The answer is she earned it. Earned it by complete dutifulness in her care of the child. Linda had no doubts of her mother's love and devotion. Never once had it been lacking—or even late. Every need of the child was supplied definitely and on time and always with the gayest willingness. Mother and child had a perfect understanding between them. The little girl was entirely secure and happy; her health was good; she led a pleasant and interesting life. She was protected and yet permitted her small independencies in her own private sphere. Why should she wail?

From this we see that dutiful parenthood pays off. Your child is easy to handle, charming to be with. And all the time he (she) is growing into that fine person of whom you will later be so proud.

Better still, it is this child who feels so protected and safe in his (her) parents' love, who later steps forth into the world with courage and self-confidence and wins a good place there. He is free of nervous distresses; he is sure of his own worth. He expects good of life, having always received it. What he expects, he usually gets, for his faith draws it to him.

But even from the earliest years while lovingly caring for your children, you can encourage them to little acts of independence and growth. As the twig is inclined, so the tree will grow.

While you are always lovingly present, watching and guarding your young children, you do not restrain their first steps toward freedom. In fact you encourage them. In the long run the bold are safer than the timid and certainly more successful in life.

———

Summary and Suggestion

Some readers may think there is a contradiction in the statements that what children most need is protection and what children most need is independence.

But there isn't!

The wise parent allows his child a great deal of independence to grow and develop according to the needs of his inner nature. He does not impose the burden of his adult emotions upon him. Above all, he does not interfere in his creativeness; he does not rob him of his tasks. As Gladys Andrews so aptly phrased it, the child has a . . .

"Bill of Rights

Let me grow as I be
And try to understand why I want to grow like me,
Not like my Mom wants me to be
Nor like my Dad hopes I'll be
Or my teacher thinks I should be
Please try to understand and help me grow
Just like me!"

———————

CHAPTER II

First Steps in Attaining

Courage and Independence

As THE butterfly struggled to break through the cocoon, the pseudo-naturalist slit an opening to help it out. That was a mistake. The butterfly that emerged never developed strong wings or brilliant coloring. It never knew the joys of flight as other butterflies did. It died before its day.

Do you allow your children to get out of their own cocoons? Or, are you a parent who does for his children what they can very well do for themselves, thus preventing their proper growth and development?

It was the wise Emerson who said: "We take unto ourselves the strength of that which we have overcome." If you want your children to develop competence and self-reliance, you must let them do a lot of overcoming.

How admirable are those children who act and move on their own, who feed and dress themselves, keep their playthings in order, clean up if they have made a mess, finish a school assignment without help! If you send them on an errand, they go—and come back directly, without asking a dozen questions first of how and when and why.

By contrast, there are the weak, whining, wish-washy children who always have to be helped—to eat, to dress, to put their room in order, to finish their homework. They have no talent for getting things done. How did they become that way? Their parents did for them what they could very well do for themselves.

Why does a parent act so unwisely?

Out of his ego-distresses the parent is driven to assert his strength. He likes to think that the child needs him. Whenever the child is in difficulty the "strong" parent comes forward to help him out. But if the parent were wise as well as strong, he would pause and wait to let the child work his own way out of the difficulty. Then the child, too, would become strong.

When the toddling infant falls, the sound parent lets him pick himself up. When he begins to speak, he lets him have his talk out. He doesn't shush his child. He doesn't put words into his mouth.

When he starts handling his own knife and fork and spoon, he lets him finish his meal by himself. He never urges food on him. The child is master of his own meal.

When he starts school, he lets him go alone or with his gang. He doesn't lead him by the hand. He doesn't do his homework for him.

When the child is old enough to know what money is, he gives him a monthly allowance for his personal needs and lets him manage it entirely himself. If he spends wisely, fine. But if he spends foolishly, that's his hard luck. Neither begging nor whining will get him another penny.

The adolescent especially must be allowed to be more and more on his own—to choose his own friends, build his own social life, pick his own career. You advise, if he asks you. You stand by, if he gets into trouble. And always you cheer him on by words of encouragement and faith. But the main decisions you let him make himself. Attaining adulthood is his business.

Children are forever grateful to the parents who allowed them to grow. They know to whose wise guidance they owe their success in life. And the world honors you, too, for their achievements and character because the world knows that the apple doesn't fall very far from the tree.

Therefore:

1. Never do for a child what a child can do for himself.

2. Never interfere with what a child is doing—unless it is dangerous or destructive.

On these two simple principles you can build in your child his most valuable qualities for making a success of life: independence, courage, creativeness, self-reliance. You can't begin too early to apply them to the training of your child.

Even in early childhood, children may be taught to behave independently and courageously.

*   *   *

"There's Linda climbing those stairs again! Stop her, stop her before she falls back and gets hurt!"

But grandma (who had the week-end care of her) had different ideas. It's good for little children to climb, to adventure, to go forward without fear. That was her philosophy. So she didn't restrain her thirteen-month-old grandchild, but smilingly followed behind her, ready to catch her if she fell.

Up, up, scrambled Linda on her hands and knees, gurgling with glee at each mastered step. Oh, the triumph of it when she reached the top! She laughed, she chortled; her eyes gleamed with pleasure. "Look at me," she seemed to say. "I'm Linda, I'm big enough to climb stairs!"

Would you have allowed Linda to climb those stairs? Do you believe that it's good for children to climb, to adventure, to go forward without fear? Or are you one to overprotect your children, establishing fearsome attitudes in their young souls to plague them all their lives?

The shy, the timid have a sad fate. Whether it be job or marriage-partner, they rarely get what they deserve. For one defect of character, they face continual frustration and defeat. Would that their parents had instilled in them more courage.

How?

1. Let your children move about freely while keeping a watchful eye on them. Hold off the restraining hand. Unless they are in real danger, don't interfere with what they are doing.

2. Introduce them early to other children in playgrounds, parks, backyards and let them mingle freely with them. Don't let your child become an "isolate." The isolate of childhood becomes the shy adult, also an isolate. There is no sadder fate.

3. Don't interfere in your children's friendships. In the give and take of friendships freely formed, children acquire social self-confidence, understanding of character, skill in handling people. All valuable life time assets.

4. If they get into a fight or argument with other children, let them handle it on their own. A kid must fight his own battles. None are so wounded as those who run away.

5. But if, by chance, one of your children has become frightened, don't mock or blame. That only confirms his feeling of inferiority. Start all over again with loving patience to teach him to face up to the trials and difficulties of his young life. Remember always, love drives out fear.

Of course, there are risks in teaching your children to be bold. Sometimes Linda might climb stairs with no grandma around and fall and really hurt herself. You've got to think of that. But there are also risks, perhaps greater risks, in overcautiousness. Always guiding and protecting our children, holding them back from new experiences forbids their developing the strong personalities with which they can later handle whatever difficulties or dangers may arise in their lives. In the long run, the bold are safer than the timid and certainly more successful in life.

*　　*　　*

"Don't help her! She doesn't like being helped," said the father good naturedly to the house guest who had reached out his hand to assist 18-month-old Carole down the high step from the terrace to the lawn.

The guest drew back and amusedly watched the little toddler

work out the engineering of this (for her) great feat. Twice
Carole came to the brink and gingerly put half a foot forward
as her eye measured the distance.

No, she couldn't make it, her baby judgment told her. She'd
surely go boomps on her head. And little Carole didn't like to
go boomps on her head. For a minute she hesitated.

Then she turned around, walked back a pace or two, got on
her hands and knees and made the descent backwards.

"Easy, see!" her smiling face said to the two men watching
her. They grinned, and little Carole ran off in happy self-confidence to join the other children on the lawn.

*   *   *

The Mental Health authorities consider the spirit of independence a primary need of children to be encouraged from the
very start of their lives. In *What Every Child Needs,* they state
it this way:

"Every child needs to know that his parents want him to grow
up and that they encourage him to try new things; that they
have confidence in him and in his ability to do things for himself and by himself."

Little Carole was lucky to have a father and mother who instinctively understood this and made it a guiding principle in
the rearing of their child. But many other parents—aided and
abetted by visiting guests and relatives—are forever helping
children do what they can very well do for themselves, thus undermining their strength at its source. Or they intrude in children's activities, killing their creativeness.

*   *   *

Self-confidence grows by what it feeds on. The more your
children carry out individual tasks, the more they act and move
and do on their own, adventuring forth into the world and accepting its challenges, the surer they feel that they can handle
whatever comes up. And how they enjoy this sense of power in
themselves.

Therefore, make it a rule not to overparent your child. Set

an example of constructiveness and courage, get him good schooling, cheer him on in all his endeavors. But otherwise let him be. You will bring out more of his great potential by what you forebear to do than by what you actually do for him. It cannot too often be repeated that children get strong only through their own doing.

*   *   *

"Let go, Daddy!" little David cried, gleeful and proud. "I can ride it myself, now."

Someone had presented five-and-one-half-year-old David with a regular two-wheeler. His mother was a bit fearsome about his riding a bike at that age and suggested that maybe the side training wheels be attached first to take away the danger of his falling and hurting himself.

"Aw, gee, Ma," little David remonstrated, "I don't want them trainers. You'd think I was a sissy."

So little David's dad took him out for his first bike ride, steadying him from behind. They hadn't gone far before David got the hang of it and declared he could go it alone. And away he went like a whiz and forever after rode a bike all by himself. He learned to ice skate the same way, and swim, and dive, and ride a horse. Also to box and wrestle.

Little David had nerve, and his parents were the last ones to try to kill it in him.

But some parents always act fearsome and protective toward their children, not realizing that by destroying their nerve they are also destroying their chances of having a rich, interesting, exciting and successful life.

It becomes a boy to be bold, to face danger and difficulty, to stand up to an opponent; above all, not to run. Run from one danger and soon you're running from another, and another—and from life!

Mothers particularly should pause to think what they are doing to their sons by overprotecting them—as so many mothers do. Such boys grow up to be weak, shy, ineffectual males. They don't know how to fight for their rights and so suffer a lot of abuse from their companions, overseers, bosses. They are un-attractive to women and have to take second best in the marriage market. Under threat of some real danger, they may become panic-stricken and develop real personality defects. Dr. Edward Adam Strecker, chief psychiatrist of the Armed Forces in World War II, wrote of the boys who broke under the rigors of military life as *Their Mothers' Sons*.

Of the letters that come to my column, you'd be surprised how many ask for advice on correcting timidity in children, obviously an all-too-common fault in our all-too-protective society.

Better than correcting timidity is not allowing it to form. Children are born with few real fears. If not repressed by their over-anxious or tyrannical parents they would have a natural courage that would sustain them throughout life.

However, if you know that your child is fearsome and want to make him courageous, don't go to extremes by abruptly throwing him into danger. He may become hysterically frightened and never get over his fears.

You have to build his self-confidence first. Help him to become skillful at sports, outgoing and friendly with people. Show him a lot of love and express praise whenever you legitimately can. Never, but never, think to shame him into overcoming his fears by calling him "sissy," or "baby," or any other derogatory term. Keep him from repeated failure or too severe competition, especially in the beginning of his training. Help him gradually to become less dependent on adults.

If by your tact and warm assurances you succeed in making him feel self-confident, he will overcome his fears. In time as he meets more and more dangers and difficulties on his own, he may become positively courageous. Courage increases as fears are conquered.

In the long run—we repeat—the bold are safer than the timid. And certainly more successful in life.

*   *   *

The bigger fellow was obviously cheating the smaller kids in the game.

"Hey, that's not fair!" a young boy cried from among the by-standers.

"What's that to you?" the big fellow shouted. "Shut up or I'll bust yuh one!"

In a minute they were fighting.

The father of the young boy hurried over to see what was the matter.

Should he interfere? The bigger boy was more than a bit bigger and tough and mean. His boy might take an awful beating. It wouldn't be unfair to step in considering the great difference in their ages. But then again, here was a wonderful opportunity to see what his boy could do against dangerous olds.

He waited.

How proud he was to find that his boy did all right. After a while the older fellow was willing enough to quit. Would you have waited?

"Be bold," reads the mystic inscription on the gates of Busy-rane, a fabled region described by Edmund Spenser in "The Faerie Queene." "Be bold, be bold, and evermore be bold"; and then again at the third gate—"Be not too bold."

Kids have a natural courage, but in our society get few chances to show it. Some day their daring may be greatly needed, for our country faces a perilous future.

Why do present-day American kids like to read comic books, and the bloodier the better? Because there is no danger in their lives. Comic books supply a substitute thrill. Children miss the zest of danger in their too sheltered lives.

Much that we call juvenile delinquency, too, is nothing more than the "don't fence me in" outbreak of vigorous youth cramped by the barriers of civilization.

One parent wonders whether her child is not too bold:

"We live in a quiet section at a dead-end street, and the homes in this end of town provide a large open area for playing. I have noticed, however, that in crossing streets, or standing

near precarious edges, our eight-year-old son has a sort of
abandon for his own safety. School is over a mile away but he
walks there alone. Is this unconsciousness of danger a phase
which all children go through, or is there something that should
be explained more thoroughly to him? We have often spoken of
the rules of safety, etc."

These parents should rejoice that so far their son is free of the
fears that weaken personality. We need boys like that.

Summary and Suggestion

How attractive are those children, girls as well as boys,
who have a bold, courageous manner! Who are not readily
outfaced by the bully or the braggart, who instantly leap
forward to undertake the dangerous and the difficult!

Of course there is such a thing as foolhardiness, which
the third gate at Busyrane warns against. But most of our
concern should be the other way around. Will our kids have
the courage to stand up to life, to meet its demands steadfastly and without flinching?

That's up to us, the parents. Don't overprotect your child;
don't interfere when he faces danger. Let him fight his own
battles.

Even the handicapped can, with courage, make a good
life for themselves by concentrating on what they have left
of body and mind and developing that, rather than be-
moaning their loss.

CHAPTER III

Teach Handicapped Child

to be Self-Reliant

THE HANDICAPPED child, does he need consolation or inspiration? He needs inspiration. And wise is that parent who rises above pity and stirs up his handicapped, or failing, child not to think of what he lacks but to concentrate on what he has and with this make a life. The great and noble example of this is Helen Keller.

The first instinct of a parent whose child is, or has become, physically crippled or otherwise handicapped is to express all love and sympathy, to hover over, to caress, to hurry to satisfy every wish.

Obviously this can only lead the child to believe that he is a pitiful creature, so weak and helpless that he needs constant care and comforting. This won't inspire him to rally his remaining resources of body and mind to still make something of himself. Rather he will think that resignation and acceptance of his sad lot is the best he can hope for.

But it isn't.

Many a handicapped child has, through parental encouragement and the proper training, more than compensated for his

185

initial handicap and made a fine, strong adjustment to life—including some contribution to society as a whole.

Take Paul for instance:

Paul is a little blind boy in the nursery school of the non-sectarian New York Guild for the Jewish Blind. His class of four-year-olds is taking a singing lesson. The sweet-voiced teacher strums a guitar and sings out a greeting, first to the group as a whole and then to each child individually. Her enthusiasm is infectious. The children answer her in song.

Everybody sings! And everybody acts out the little games that go with the songs, like this one of the rocking horses:

"Here we are together; we're rocking on the floor."

And the little children sit down on the floor, hold their knees in their hands, and rock up and down like little rocking horses. Then they go on a bus and each plays and sings a part. One is the driver, one rings the bell, one sounds the horn, one collects the money "klinkety klunk."

You had come with a heart full of pity for the little blind children, but you forgot the pity quickly enough as you watched their merry play.

There were seven children in the room. Six were quite gay. One was sad faced, occasionally giving way to tears.

She was a new girl. She didn't know yet that you could be blind and happy, too. But gradually, as the others went singing along, a bit of a smile came to her face, too.

"Will she get to take on the lively manner of the other children?" I asked.

"Sure she will," my guide told me. "It takes time and training; but they all do. These blind children come to feel just like other children. We don't cater to the grief in their lives. We stir them up to be strong and self-reliant. The aim isn't to have them philosophically accept a segregated life. Oh, no! We get them ready to join the classes in the regular schools for sighted children. They learn to stand on their own two feet. Later they will make their own living, even contribute to society, maybe more than many a sighted one will."

Her words had the same heroic ring as the speech I had heard a few nights before at the Annual Report Dinner of the Guild at the Waldorf. The speaker was the eloquent Colonel Edwin A. Baker, Managing Director of the Canadian National Institute for the Blind, himself a blinded war veteran. Thousands of blind people through the length and breadth of Canada had been rescued from a life of self-pitying uselessness to one of proud usefulness through his inspiring guidance and sound training.

"It's not what you have lost," Colonel Baker declared. "It's what you still have. When we realize this we rise above our handicap."

All parents with handicapped children should work to impress this idea upon them. But some parents, out of their own ego needs, emphasize a child's weaknesses rather than his strengths.

*　*　*

"This is my son Robert," her loud voice proclaimed. "He flunked algebra. I want him to repeat it in your summer school."

"Glad to meet you, Robert," said the principal, flashing his usual warm smile. "Did you fail both terms of algebra or just the second half?"

"Oh, Robert flunked the whole subject," interposed the mother. "He doesn't know a thing about algebra. He should take the whole course over again."

Just as the principal was beginning to wonder whether the boy had a tongue or not, Robert murmured something about a job he had for the summer, and could he possibly take the course in the evening session? It was an interesting job and he wanted very much to try it out. The mother interrupted with emphasis:

"You know you're not the one to go to work during the day and to school at night. Why, you can hardly pass just going to school, much less working."

Then turning to the principal she went on: "All I care about

is his passing. Next to his health I worry most about his schooling. I keep on talking to him, but it doesn't seem to help."

"No, madame, it doesn't help." That's what the principal
would have liked to tell her. Instead, he just smiled sadly to himself and had the boy registered for algebra first and second term
in the day session.

The office of a summer high school I have discovered is a fasci-
nating laboratory for the study of human failure. Most of the
youngsters who apply for admission have to repeat a subject or
two in which they have failed. Why did they fail in the first
place, and is the habit of failure already established in their
lives? These are interesting questions. Particularly pathetic are
those whose parents think they have to come along to help in
the ultra-simple procedure of registration.

Why can't parents understand that if they do all the talking,
all the arguing, all the planning, they're going to bring up ninnies
for children?

You literally choke your children off from their needed growth
and development every time you do for them what they can and
should do for themselves. Children learn only from their own
doing. And children acquire the habit of success only from their
own achievements in the line of their aspirations and dreams.

As children repeat the experience of failure, many patronizing
parents develop a second pernicious practice, that of gently dep-
recating and disparaging them (just as Robert's mother did)—
always with the best intentions, of course. All they really want,
they say, is to shake them out of their lethargy, get them to do
something.

Do you do this, too? The actual results of such action will be
the exact opposite of your professed intentions and hopes. Your
children will accept themselves at your own low estimate of
them. Keep on belittling them and they'll keep on failing until
they are totally lost in a miserable spiral of defeat and despair.
And you did it by your lack of belief in them.

Over-solicitous as well as dominating mothers (usually unhappily married) make their children fail. Parent and child

re in unconscious collusion—the one to remain dependent, the other to patronize on the claim that the child needs her. The over-solicitous mother tempts the child to cultivate his weaknesses to keep her constant care and devotion. The dominating mother makes a child feel so helpless and dependent that he has no confidence in his own abilities and no courage to use them. No wonder that these children fail.

The truly feminine mother, however, has no need to feel strong at the expense of her children's weakness. Happy in her husband's love, she is serenely self-confident as a woman. She also has a lot of confidence in her children. She lets them do their own doing. As a result they grow up to be both amiable and self-reliant, the happy product of her faith in them.

Are your children failing in school and on the playground? Why? You should do some searching questioning on that subject. Could the reason be you? The habit of failure is a crippling handicap.

So is the unwillingness to grow.

"There comes a time in everyone's life when he must leave father and mother, and he must leave not only in body but in mind. Those who do not are the future neurotics."

With these words Otto Rank, one of the noted early psychoanalysts described the great spiritual need of the individual, namely, to grow from childhood to maturity and have an independent life of his own. It is a sad fact that millions never accomplish this basic evolutionary task. They reach adulthood in years but do not attain adulthood in spirit.

Why?

Possessiveness!

Their patronizing parents never let them grow. If there is such thing as a primary sin of parenthood, possessiveness is it. In a poignant letter, revealing years of desperate soul struggle, one woman writes:

"I am thirty-one and the youngest of four children, married, and have three children of my own. As best I can size myself up,

I am the baby, anxious to please and have allowed myself to be possessed by my mother beyond normal maturity. My mother is sixty-five, has been an active clubwoman and contributed generously, beyond all call of duty, to raising her family. At the same time I think her efforts toward perfectionist standards have been deeply motivated by her own need for power.

"When she and my father visit us, I try in every way that I know, including prayer, to give her the love I should, but each time succeed less well than I did the time before. The friction, from my point of view, comes when she criticizes our friends for being overweight, messy, or generally inadequate: the minister's vestments are dirty, smelly; the children's playmates are bullies, their bikes are second-hand; my equipment in the kitchen is poor; I need this and that; I use fat (margarine) on bread; my husband's mother is no good, and so on ad infinitum.

"Now this reads in a way that is laughable. But when she comes it seems like our life is a half orange and she applies it with gusto to the orange squeezer."

Note how this mature woman of thirty-one is completely overcome by the petty criticisms of her tyrannical old mother. She knows all this is nonsense. But she has been so accustomed to submitting to her mother's opinions, she cannot now throw them off. And without intense psychotherapy, she probably never will. What a tragedy!

How about your children? Do you so completely dominate their lives, doing things for them that they can very well do for themselves, that they become so dependent on you they will never be able to attain a true individuality and maturity of their own?

Don't!

Not only will this mean your failure as a parent, your inability to rear and raise children of enough character and personality to stand on their own two feet and contribute to the welfare of the world, but you will be unhappy yourself as every slaveholder is tied to the other end of the chain that binds another's behavior.

your life is so involved with another's, you have no independence either.

The great mystic Kahlil Gibran in his profound work *The Prophet* put it this way:

"Your children are not your children. They are the sons and daughters of Life's longing for itself. . . . You may strive to be like them, but seek not to make them like you. For life goes not backward nor tarries with yesterday."

Parents who succeed in grasping this spiritual message may be assured of a very special reward. God loves all children. But he also loves and will ever bless the parents who let them grow.

Sometimes your faith in your child may be a matter of life or death to him.

*   *   *

"These children will live," the ward doctor said, "and those will die."

"How do you know?" I asked.

"These children have met their disaster with a smile. They are just as crippled as the other children. They have just as much to be sad about. But something within them says 'I want to live,' and so they smile—and live. The sad-faced ones don't have that inner something. They are overcome by their disaster. They don't face it and fight. They don't smile. And so they die."

If disaster as of a crippling illness should strike your child would he smile and live? Or would he droop and die? The answer may depend on the spiritual strength you give him.

One mother writes:

"Our four-and-one-half-year-old daughter, we have just been told, is a victim of X-disease. We are doing everything that is medically possible for her. But we are deeply concerned about her beginning awareness of her illness and how she differs from most children in appearance (thinness and size), her frequent and sometimes violent coughing, the large amount of medicine she takes daily, her frequent and regular trips to the doctor, the abruptness with which we must remove her from the company of children who have the least suspicion of a cold, and so on and on.

"We dread the time when she can read and may run across literature that explains how her life expectancy is limited. We realize we can't shelter her unduly from facts. But how can we best handle the situation at her present age of four and one half her approaching school experiences, and on into the future?"

This mother isn't the only one who has wrestled with the profound problem of how to have faith when your whole world seems to be tumbling about you. Some of the greatest literature ever written is devoted to this theme: George Eliot's *Silas Marner*, Alfred Tennyson's "In Memoriam," Oscar Wilde's "De Profundis," and most moving of all, the tremendous book of the Bible, "Job." What is the conclusion to which all these authors come? The time to have faith is when disaster strikes.

Take a look around. Note the number of blind, crippled, deprived children who nevertheless carry a rare radiance on their faces. They decided to smile and live. Somehow or other God makes it up to them.

God will make it up to this child, too. But first she must decide to smile and live. And this her parents must help her to do by smiling themselves and going on living.

Summary and Suggestion

The parents of handicapped or invalid children should concentrate not on what the children have lost but on what they still have—physically, mentally, spiritually—and with this make life as nearly like that of other children as possible. Of course, this life will have some limitations. But that doesn't say it cannot have many satisfactions and ultimately an especial worth and meaning of its own.

When sorrow comes it's all right to grieve for a time, but not for long! Life is still here, precious and wonderful. However limited, we want to live it—as long as we can, as well as we can. The handicapped do too, and we—parents, counselors and friends—can help them, by accentuating the positive of what is still theirs to develop and eliminating the negative of moody reflections on what they have lost.

———————

BOOK FIVE

Faith

EVERY CHILD NEEDS TO HAVE:

a set of moral standards to live by

*a belief in the human values—kindness, courage,
honesty, generosity and justice*

CHAPTER I

Your Child's Faith

Depends on Yours

"WHAT DO you mean '*spiritual*'?"

The class had been studying Shakespeare's great tragedy, *Macbeth*, and the teacher had tried to explain that Macbeth, though outwardly successful in his crime, was inwardly unhappy because his disturbed conscience prevented his enjoyment of the kingship that was now his. The material gain did not make up for the spiritual loss.

It was at this point that one of the students raised his hand to ask: "What do you mean, 'spiritual'?"

Suppose you were the teacher. Could you have explained to the class what the word spiritual meant? Or suppose as a parent you were asked by one of your own children what the word spiritual meant, could you explain it satisfactorily?

The teacher in question had a very difficult time of it.

Some of the youngsters thought that spiritual was similar to ghost-like, or unearthly, or mysterious. One grinning fellow said that spiritual was the opposite of practical and that in this sense spiritual people were rather silly.

197

"The practical people get along," he said, "and the spiritual people get left." A lot of the kids laughed at this.

One student cried out:

"Spiritual means doing what God said, like Jesus did."

There was a hush at this, and the teacher took the opportunity to try again to explain what the word meant. Using the boy's statement that spiritual was doing what God said, he declared that all people seem to have something within them that tells them what is right and what is wrong. How it came there we can't know, but it is just as well to say that it is God speaking in us. And what God tells us makes sense in the long run, though it may not seem to in the short run. Macbeth thought he was going to be very happy when he murdered to gain the royal power, but God had commanded: "Thou shalt not kill," and in the long run, he was miserable.

With that the teacher quit, hoping that at least some of the students would understand him. Would your child have understood him?

Parents have a very distinct responsibility to cultivate a deeper spiritual comprehension in their children. Teachers are only a part time influence, and especially so in ethical and moral matters.

But to do so, parents must have a real faith in spiritual values themselves. We Americans are so success-crazed that in our striving for worldly wealth and power, we are not always too careful to keep in concord with our best beliefs. The result is frequently emotionally disastrous for us and our children.

We are nervous, irritable, and unstable, and we don't know why. The why is in us. There is no objection to success itself, in God's law or man's. But it has to be success gained in a moral way. Play the game according to the rules and then your success will mean something.

In addition to your own inner poise and self-confidence, you will have a much sweeter relationship with your children. Why? They will look up to you as a worthwhile ideal, and you can talk to them about your beliefs without the distress of hypocrisy.

That's a very nice relationship!

And much more satisfying than the patronizing parent-child relationship, in which a man works desperately and perhaps a little unscrupulously to make the money to give his children every social advantage, only to find that they grow up to be selfish brats, ungrateful, and maybe even hating him for having reduced them to an inferior dependent position.

In the long run, the ego wants to stand on its own. In the long run, the ego wants to be in harmony with something bigger than itself. In the long run, each person is a spiritual self!

For the ultimate truth of life is that it is governed by principle. Behind the world of appearances, with all its strife and discord, there is the orderly world of truth, the moral law that governs all existence. Those who align themselves with it live at ease in the universe, because they are in tune with its purpose. They enjoy vigorous health, adequate prosperity, friendly relations with people. They accomplish much useful work; they found good families of their own; they love and are loved. It's a sweet, dear life you have if you know how to live by principles.

Vaguely, most parents perceive that this is indeed true and wish to give its benefits to their children, even though they themselves may have missed the boat, spiritually speaking. For instance many parents send their children to Sunday School, provide for their religious instruction and have them confirmed even though they themselves do not go to church or temple. Faith may not be for them, but they have enough faith in faith to wish it for their children.

* * *

If you asked me to name the nicest guy in the world, I would at once answer "Tom." I don't know too much about him: it's not what he's done; it's what he is. He's the sort of fellow who makes everybody feel good just because he's in the room.

Tom is a fortunate man. He illustrates my pet theory about life: we draw unto ourselves the good of all that we appreciate. Tom appreciates women, children, flowers, music, literature, and people. He has a really wonderful wife, three charming children, a beautiful garden, a great library of records and books, and a host of friends.

But Tom has a secret sorrow: he has never been able to reach God. And that distresses him more than I can say.

In this he has the usual difficulty of the intellectual: his logic is too keen for his faith. "There ought to be a church," said Oscar Wilde, "for those who cannot believe." And Tom has followed through on this idea by organizing in his mind a new theology which he, smiling a bit wanly, calls "The True Church of Tom."

The True Church of Tom is an Abou Ben Adhem kind of religion: If you can't love God, love people. You remember Leigh Hunt's famous poem? Abou asks the recording angel in his room what he is writing and is told: "The names of those who love the Lord."

> "And is mine one?" said Abou. "Nay, not so,"
> Replied the angel. Abou spoke more low,
> But cheerily still; and said, "I pray thee, then,
> Write me as one that loves his fellow-men."

Now that's a very beautiful thought, but it isn't quite enough. We need to know and love God, as well as know and love people. Then our spiritual well-being will be complete.

Parents, especially, need to bring the presence of God into their homes. Sending your children to Sunday School, having them confirmed, won't do it. You have to believe, yourself. You're the most important person in the world to your children. They'll follow you. If you believe, they'll believe. If you don't believe, it is very doubtful whether they ever really will.

That is what is bothering Tom. He loves his children with a kind of total devotion: he wants to do his total duty toward them. He thinks that if there is a God, it's his duty to make Him known to his children. But he just can't believe.

Tom has tried going to various churches of different denominations. And he has had long and earnest talks with several ministers. To no avail. I'm afraid you don't reach God through argument. Certainly Tom didn't.

In this present generation of parents there are many fathers like Tom. Previous generations of parents had been tyrannically oppressive in the matter of religion, forcing their children into rituals and observances and church attendance without proper consideration of their thoughts and feeling. Inner rebellion, aggravated by revolutionary concepts in science and philosophy (Darwinism, etc.) produced a succeeding generation of ag-nostics—unhappy agnostics.

It would be nice if the unhappy agnostics would start all over again in a new search for God. First they should forgive their parents for having made religion so harsh and unpalatable to them. Their parents couldn't help it.

The next step is a purely pragmatic one. Since to believe is, in your mind, better than not to believe, why not boldly declare that you do believe, and then seek to support your position rather than analyze it?

Where will the support come from?

From the great religious literature of the world and especially the Bible.

Which brings me to my final suggestion to Tom and all other unsatisfied agnostics. Take a literary pilgrimage through the Bible. It's a wonderful book. You know you always meant to read it, anyhow. Well read it. Read it all the way through, quietly, thoughtfully, by yourself alone. It may take you as much as a year. Then read it again. Read it once every year, two or three pages a day. By the third or fourth time around you'll have no more trouble believing. You will have saturated yourself with God consciousness from the example of other believers.

The True Church of Tom will then include the love of God as well as the love of people. And my ninety-five per cent happy Tom will be more nearly one hundred per cent happy. For in the total love he has for his children, he can now include the gift of getting them to know God and God's love for them.

So can you. Greater minds than yours or mine see and accept a spiritual basis to life. Why shouldn't we?

It was the great German philosopher Kant who declared "Two things fill me with ever renewed awe and admiration, the starry Heavens above and the Moral Law within."

To many of us, unfortunately, the moral law seems something distant and remote, a fit subject for discussion among philosophers and preachers, but not very immediate to our own lives! It was issued from lofty mountain tops in the dim and distant past by great prophets who had it direct from God. We must obey it for the good of society as a whole and for our eternal salvation, and we had better obey it or God will punish us hereafter. Only occasionally in modern writings is it made clear that the real reason for obeying it is to improve our own state of being here and now.

Yet a sound psychological analysis of the moral law shows us that it is in the most immediate relationship to our daily lives. That following it brings happiness in the very things that most people want, and disobeying it certain disasters. That Heaven and Hell are eternally now. How important it is to teach that to our children!

Mankind has through ages of trial and error discovered that some things help and other things hurt and stored away this experience in the deep unconscious memory of the race.

Certain great minds, prophets and teachers, have with God-inspired intuition, telescoped the experience of ages in one summary view and drawn from it the principles that make for human happiness and development. With impressive words they have set forth these principles in the great religious books of the world. They constitute the moral law.

Always it must be remembered that what the moral law emphasizes is the long range view. With our human, short range understanding, we foolishly seek the advantage of the temporary good, when the real advantage lies in the long-range good.

How can we present the moral code to our children in a way that will win its acceptance?

We have to show them, as the Irish poet Yeats so felicitously phrased it, that "The good are always the merry."

Too often is morality presented as a grim necessity, something we ought to do but which we won't find pleasant. This is the fatal error of most professional moralists and religious teachers, and more than anything else is responsible for morality's slow progress.

Fortunately, it isn't at all true. Morality, rightly understood, is the agreeable way to live and can be so taught to youth.

People with industry, sincerity, and good will can easily make a living in our society. Integrity, the luxury of a few, might just as well be enjoyed by all. The price is not too high.

Best of all, morality gives power. When you play the game according to the rules, you develop strength and competence, which the moral weaklings lose every time they cheat. No one can rise above his own estimate of himself. Believe that you can't win without cheating and you can't. But, believe that it's fun to win "on the square," and what a happy, successful life you'll have!

Morality, furthermore, when free of priggishness, makes you attractive. You have a frank, self-assured face and manner that wins friends and influences people.

"Always take the long range view!" That's the point we have to emphasize and re-emphasize in talking morality to our children. Cheating may give a temporary advantage, but what good is it if we lose out in the end? The real victory is with the moral law which is always operative.

This is the wisdom available to every parent in the religious lore of Mankind. If he will in quietness and reflection completely assimilate it himself, he will be able to convey it to his children. Nothing else that he can give them has more value.

The deeper we get into the study, the more truly do we see that the moral law is simply the accumulated God-inspired wisdom of the human race on the best way to live in the long run. That accepting it means survival for the human race, and rejecting it the destruction of life.

Unfortunately, generation by generation, Mankind goes through the experience of running counter to the moral law and meeting disaster thereby—waging wars whose only profit is death and economic depression, indulging in vices that bring on enfeeblement and loathing of the flesh, practicing greed that loses the love of family and friends. But the next generation does the same thing over again, probably for lack of proper instruction from its parents. We may have hope, however, as more and more people get a realistic conception of what the moral law truly is and learn the advantages to be gained from regulating their day by day lives in accordance with it, Mankind as a whole may advance.

Follow the moral law and all the good things of life will come to you *in due time*. Disregard the moral law and *sooner or later* you'll meet disaster. This is a truth that is derived directly from human experience as well as religious instruction. This is the truth we must teach our children.

*   *   *

The big, strong man was crying. Right out in court in front of the Commissioner and all his own fellow officials! What was he crying about? He had sold his honor for money and now he was caught.

The folly of it! Between his sobs he punched his head with his open palms as if to push the memory of it out of his mind. He had had a good position, in fact an office of great power in the big city department. His salary had been adequate for all his reasonable needs. Why? Why had he sold the dearest thing he owned for a handful of silver?

His job had called for physical courage of a high order. And physical courage had never failed him. Many a time he had risked his life in his thirty years' service to save another's. But moral courage was another matter. When the easy bribes were offered, he just didn't have the spiritual guts to say no.

Why didn't he?

That's a pretty important question for American parents to

ponder over. For that official isn't the only one who has sold his honor for money. Bribery and corruption are common enough in American political life, as recurring investigating committees have so dramatically demonstrated. And so are crooked business deals. American children are growing up in a society infected by the idea of the "fast buck." Would that their parents had taught them that there is a perfectly sound dollar to be made in American business. You don't have to be crooked to get rich. And the sound dollar can be soundly enjoyed and spent with the pleasure of a clear conscience.

So many times we seem to see the wicked triumphant and the righteous forsaken that we waver in our faith and ask: Should I obey the moral law if others do not? The answer is sure and certain. The advantages of the moral law are all individual and will accrue regardless of whether others follow it or not, that is, if we will but assume the long-range and not the short-range view.

Take for example the general ethical dictum: "It is more blessed to give than to receive." From the point of view of short-range wisdom, this simply makes no sense. "What do you mean 'give'?" asks the wordly wiseman. "Get, don't give! You're a fool if you give, because others will take and you'll be left without." So much for short range wisdom.

Now let us consider the long range wisdom of the matter:

A simple survey of the people around us shows that those that are always on the receiving end of generosity, like indulged children and "doll" wives, are usually weak and cranky. Always receiving and never giving, they have very little need to exercise their powers, which for lack of exercise do not develop. The individuals remain weak. As weaklings they are despised and disregarded by those engaged in the great and real activities of life. Within themselves they feel a vague and nameless shame, depressing and wearying. The final result is frustration and discontent.

The generous, on the other hand, have to create in order to produce the means for being generous. In creating they develop their powers and soon are so strong that they can produce not only enough with which to be generous, but plenty extra for themselves.

This is the dynamics of human growth. We all have great powers within us, but they have to be exercised to come into their full usefulness. The generous souls get exercise and so develop; the ungenerous ones do not. Therefore, purely from the point of view of the individual's own benefit, it really is more blessed to give than to receive.

The great enemy of the individual is self-centeredness, limiting not only his enjoyment of life but also his achievement. It is only in the objective attitude, in devotion to our task and service to people, that we find real satisfaction. This is pointedly expressed in the religious dictum: "If you lose your life, you find it," probably the greatest bit of wisdom ever given for the guidance of man. Let us analyze its application to ourselves—and through us to our children.

As we observe human beings who are very self-centered, we observe that they are in a continuous stew of fret and fear. Everything hurts them. When it is hot, they feel so very hot; when it is cold, they say they're freezing. In their relations with people, any word is a slight, every slight is an insult, every exchange is an injustice. They always feel mistreated, and so argue and fight continuously to get what they think is theirs. Their job is always too hard for them, their pay too small; the working hours are too long, the vacations too short; their employer is particularly mean, just to them. If married, they declare their partner to be unfair —an unloving and unlovable person. Life is for them a fevered parry and thrust of self-protection. And they are obviously not very happy. They have no power to lose themselves in their work or human relations, and so are subject to what Shakespeare called "the thousand shocks that flesh is heir to."

The spiritually evolved are not so. They are usually lost in some task or cause outside of themselves and so absorbed in it that they have no opportunity to attend to themselves. They don't care very much whether it is hot or cold, whether the hours are long or short, whether people are fair to them or not. They have their work to do and tend to that rather than to themselves. As a result, they escape "the thousand shocks that flesh is heir to," because they have no predisposition to feel them, and rise furthermore to a height of personality that is widely admired. In losing themselves in a cause, they find a new and happier self, a new and happier way of living.

The two most integrated personalities whom the author knows are a woman psychoanalyst and a man physician. It is astounding the amount of work each of these is capable of doing in a day, the number of patients they can see, the distresses they can minister to, the healings they can effect: and yet each at the end of the day is fresh and smiling, and if need be, ready for more work. Nor is their manner the least bit severe, as might be expected of those so heavily burdened: each can laugh heartily at the slightest provocation and tell a witty story with the best rogue living.

The physician once performed a tonsil operation, under the author's observation, on a little old woman who was in mortal terror of the pain and possibly disastrous consequences. It was like observing a miracle to note the effect of the man's strong and loving spirit upon the old woman's fears, the gradual assuagement of the hysteria, and the final easy accomplishment of the needed surgery. Here was a true triumph of personality.

And in the office of the psychoanalyst, each hour of the long day brought its patient with his burden of mental distress, and each patient laid down his burden and left the office refreshed. And yet for the assumption of these many burdens, the psychoanalyst was never wearied nor distraught, giving endlessly of love and care and attention, and always finding plenty more at the source.

Of course, these are people of exceptional culture and training, but others can be found in all walks of life. They show the advantage of losing ourselves in our duty.

Contrast these with the whining, puling weaklings we see all around us, the self-pitiers, the parasites, the fake invalids, the cheaters, and the hypocrites, all with their eternal moan and lament, and we can realize the health that comes from creative activity and the death that derives from inactivity and self-centeredness. Truly there is no curse like self-centeredness, and no blessing like true altruism.

For one thing, duty is definite. Each moment there is a specific and inescapable something to be done, and in doing it the personality integrates and so enjoys the blessed satisfaction of being at one with itself and free of doubt. Furthermore, doing one's duty gives the ego the satisfaction of participating in the creative work of the world. If our ego is satisfied, we can't be very unhappy. We belong and know it.

The disadvantage of living for self-indulgence is that it leaves one quickly bored and humiliated. The human capacity for pleasure is strictly limited; soon we lose appetite, and then where are we? Furthermore, a life of self-indulgence plays havoc with the ego. We feel deep down that we don't belong, that we are not really participating in the creative work of the world, and so are ashamed.

Of course in living for duty, let us not make the mistake of being over-conscientious and doing not only our duty, but also that of other people. This is moral patronizing, and, like all extremes, bad. The reasonable duty that is expected of us in the world is usually not too difficult and allows in most cases for an adequate amount of pleasure in life. Duty and the happy day go very well together. The moral law is our friend, not our taskmaster.

These are truths that we will want to teach our children, not necessarily for immediate use, for children are only children, but as the ideal of their maturity. If we send them into life with a firm faith in moral values, we can feel certain that they will get along and be generally loved, beside.

Their virtue is their strength. By it they have learned to play the game only according to the rules. They have no need for craft or deceit, the tools of the weakling and the coward. And in playing the game according to the rules, they develop their powers and so become stronger and stronger.

And if you also teach them to wear their virtue with a grace, not to boast of it or to appear self-righteous, they will also be well-liked. They give love freely and on their own initiative and get it back with interest. They create and serve others with the product of their labors. So they always live in a world of good will and interesting activity with plenty of friends and a dear, devoted family.

Summary and Suggestion

Parents who think through the problem of faith in a doubting world will want to give their children the stability and strength which only those know who live their lives by principle.

Many see faith as something mystic or unreal. It isn't. It's a very real, a very practical force.

Every action is an expression of faith!

By our actions we show what we really believe in. If we didn't believe in what we were doing, could we act at all? No. We act because we believe. And after action we believe still more because we have acted. Faith and action continually influence each other.

How then can we ever raise the level of our faith and act better because we believe better?

The answer is by throwing ourselves into a right course of action. Act right, and the first thing you know you'll feel right, and have faith that you always can.

But act!

Don't mope. Don't whine. Act! The right action always brings on the right mood. The right action wipes out our doubts. Keep on acting right and soon you will have all the faith you need for carrying out your highest duties as a parent.

The old patriarchs' barns were always full. Your children too, will attain plenty in due time as they build their business or their professional careers—by ethical principles.

And all the while they will know the sweet content of living in harmony with themselves and the universe.

———

CHAPTER II

Moral Trials and

Triumphs of Children

"Was it so very wrong what Ellen did?" the mother asked, with a kind of plaintive look, hoping, no doubt, to hear: "No, not really."

Ellen had lied to her teacher about assistance she had received in answering the questions on a routine school examination. The fact that several of the other girls had received similar assistance and that cribbing was fairly general in that high school (as it is indeed, in many others) constituted what the mother called extenuating circumstances. She had supported Ellen in her argument with the teacher and was even preparing to corroborate certain items in the story that she knew were definitely not so in order to save her favorite daughter from getting into trouble.

But the situation obviously bothered her conscience. She kept repeating the question: "Was it so very wrong?"

Didn't the mother know that it was wrong to cheat and lie? Of course she did. But Ellen had a fair chance of being admitted to one of the socially preferred colleges, and wouldn't it be a shame to kill that chance now by a prissy insistence on truth-telling in what was, after all, a minor matter?

What this mother failed to realize was that standards, moral standards, give children strength, strength that they desperately need to carry them through the long range battle of life.

That doesn't mean that we should set up perfectionist goals. Children aren't born angels and shouldn't be expected to behave as if they were. Morality is something that they achieve. But parents, from their adult point of view, should know the worth of moral values and aim to inculcate them at every opportunity for the very real good they will do their children in later life.

When a child cheats, he confesses that by himself he cannot accomplish what he set out to do and what other children seem able to do. Forever after he is incompetent. He has taken himself at a low estimate and will never be able to rise above it. Cheating has deprived him of his strength.

Kids who play the game four-square, however, assert to themselves that they have the strength to meet the issues of life as they really exist and will forever after be strong enough to do so. Honor is power.

To set up such ideals in our own families requires of us parents a very sincere belief in them. If our own standards have been, shall we say flexible, we'd better not preach. Hypocrisy doesn't sit well on a parent's face.

Maybe what we most need to do is just to think the subject through. Instead of using the words "right" or "wrong," we might say "wise" and "unwise." Plain common sense soon lets us know that "wrong" is also "unwise."

Take Ellen, for instance. Of what profit will it be to her to enter a good college, if she lacks the strength to continue there or make anything of the education that will be offered her?

"Was what Ellen did so very wrong?" the mother kept on asking.

Yes, it was wrong. It was also unwise. Would that the mother had had the sense to tell her daughter so.

❖   ❖   ❖

It was one of those situations which gives a hard, cunning man a peculiar satisfaction. He had tricked the other fellow out of his whole fortune, and yet every step had been strictly legal. That was the fun of it.

The winner smiled at his own cleverness and even indulged in the luxury of a bit of commiseration for the loser: a nice guy but such a dub! How desperately chagrined and unhappy he looked. Well, if people are fools they must pay for their folly.

When he reached home his wife handed him an envelope. It contained a special delivery letter from the dean of the college his elder son attended. It read:

"We regret to advise you that your son has been suspended from all class privileges for flagrant cheating in examinations."

When they met the next day the father bitterly assailed his son: Why have you brought this disgrace upon our family? All my life I have struggled to give our family position and standing in this town and now you do this! Why? Why?

But his son only looked at him desperately chagrined and unhappy: "I don't know why, father. Yes, I did it, but I don't know why."

His eyes seemed plaintively to ask: "Do you know why, father?"

The father perceived the question in sudden amazement and horror. Do you know why, father? Do you know why, father? The question echoed and re-echoed through his brain.

Why, Why? Because he himself was a cheat! That was it. He had cheated the other fellow of his fortune and his children's fortune. He had cheated many people. Now life had caught him and given him a son that was a cheat.

Parents must realize that their own ethical principles, secret or open, pervade the home and set the standards for their children. Life is not mocked. Live below your moral level and your children can't grow.

Nor may we delude ourselves that we can keep a separate set of values for out in the world and for the home. When we talk to our children, they know. How well they know!

"What you are," says Emerson, "speaks so much louder than what you say, that I don't hear what you say."

How can we assure that sound moral integrity in our children that will see them through life's trials and dilemmas? By living that way ourselves.

And how can we assure that America will some day lift itself out of the moral morass in which it now finds itself, with crime statistics, soaring higher every year? By each citizen's raising his own ethical standards.

Adult crime and juvenile delinquency rest on a deep foundation of connivance and acceptance by the mass of our population. If they truly aroused our moral indignation we would find some way of lessening them. But our prosperity has dulled our spiritual sensibilities. We worship success too highly and are not too finicky about how we achieve it.

If we want to leave our children a more moral America to live and grow up in, let each one of us remember: "Righteousness exalteth a nation, but sin is a reproach to any people."

*   *   *

They don't think it's wrong!

College and high school students according to a recent survey, don't think lying and cheating wrong. A great number can see nothing too bad in stealing, and some even condone sex violations.

Some 2,500 students in twenty-seven high schools and an additional 1,000 college students were questioned by a survey crew under the direction of Warren L. Duncan of Fairleigh Dickinson College, Rutherford. The purpose of this junior Kinsey survey was to determine the cause, effect, and responsibility for juvenile delinquency.

Only 19% felt lying was wrong and all but 25% excused the practice of cheating on examinations. Some 15% of the high school students and over 20% of the college students saw no delinquency in sex violations. Over 10% felt that stealing was not a delinquent act, either, if you could get away with it.

"Three-quarters of our high school children cheat in tests," one of the teen-agers declared. To which another added: "How many would graduate without cheating?" Still another one put in this cynical remark: "The law is lenient with wise guys."

Where did American youth get these ideas, what implications have they for the welfare of our country, and what can American parents do to give their children more wholesome moral concepts? These are serious questions and worthy of a parent's deepest pondering.

"When children see and hear of police and politicians taking graft, parents fixing tickets or doctoring up their tax reports, friends smuggling perfume across the border, they feel that they too can do something and get away with it," one of the teen-agers explained. That's a significant statement.

The whole atmosphere of American life is tainted with a fundamental and growing lawlessness often glorified in film and fiction. No wonder our children catch it, in fact think it smart and daring. "Don't be chicken" is a teen-age phrase, often used to taunt a youngster into an act of delinquency.

But the warning finger of history writes that when a people lose their moral standards they also lose their essential vitality and fall a ready prey to any rougher, tougher invader. Such an invader is already knocking at the gates. If our present cold war with Russia ever turns hot, and it may any minute, will our spiritually debilitated youth have the moral stamina to stand up to the enemy?

Why have American parents been so unsuccessful in selling the moral law to their children? Can the reason be that they themselves do not really believe in it? Perhaps if they studied it a little harder they would come to believe in it.

The moral law is more than a mystic directive from God which we must obey to secure salvation in some future life. The moral law is the experience of the human race on what helps and what hurts right here and now. The moral law is the individual's best friend: it insures his basic good health and well-being. Breaking it always leads to personal disaster in the long run.

For example, the youngster who habitually cheats on examinations seals his doom as a scholar. He tells himself that on his own abilities he can't master the subject. That's the estimate he has of himself and on that estimate he will live his school life. If you have no confidence in your ability, then you have no ability. Your ability dies. That's the price you pay for cheating on examinations. Did you ever think of it that way? Did you ever explain it to your children that way?

"What do you mean moral?" your children may ask you. If you can convince them that moral means strong, healthy, happy— you will have done them your greatest service as a parent.

*   *   *

As a reward for graduation from high school, Richard's father bought him an automobile. This was a sad mistake. A great many American fathers each June make the same mistake.

When you give a child an excessive reward for doing what he should do anyhow, will he ever after do, by himself, all that he should? The parents of America's over-privileged children should take a long hard look at that question.

You're no friend to your child when you undercut his endeavors by intruding with your over-large rewards. Whom are you fooling? It was not Richard who graduated from high school. It was Father and his automobile.

The very fact that the father had to offer such a heavy inducement to arouse in his son enough effort to accomplish this ordinary task has its own significance. There must have been a long history of similar bribery. Soon the patronized child can achieve little by himself.

What, you might now ask, should prosperous parents do to arouse in their children the zeal that prompts poor kids to struggle to rise above poverty? They must substitute a spiritual for the no longer needed material aim.

As a step in this direction, prosperous parents might relent a little in their own mad rush to pile up the money. Should you get ulcers so your kids can get complexes? Why? Learn to live a little yourself. There's a lot more to life than the woolen glove and mitten business and the money it can make. Believe it or not, your children really care for your company more than they do for your money. Add a little culture, a little travel, a little philosophy, and you make your company more agreeable to them and yourself more admirable. Imitating that admirable you, may arouse in them a greater endeavor than all your gifts of money.

By giving your child ideals instead of things you stir up his energies and arouse in him a very satisfying self-confidence. You show that you believe in him, and he will ever after want to live up to that belief.

The patronized child, on the other hand, instinctively feels belittled and humiliated. Your insistent material support keeps on telling him that by himself he doesn't amount to much. Nobody can be much better than his belief in himself.

A dream conceived in youth and carried out in maturity is the formula for a truly happy life. It is the tragedy of America's overprivileged child that, given everything, he has nothing to hang a dream on. The surfeited do not dream.

That's your problem, Mr. Prosperous American Businessman. You must refrain from a conspicuous display of your wealth, letting your children see that money isn't everything in life. What counts is good and useful work, especially if it serves society.

If you succeed in inculcating this ideal, you will lift the curse, the potential curse, that threatens every family fortune. Your children, having lived lean, will grow up strong. And you will still have your fortune which, since you made it, you may as well spend on yourself or on such social causes as you believe in.

*　　*　　*

The discipline was wonderful in that school. And it wasn't only that the boys obeyed all the rules. The significant thing was that they behaved well out of inner conviction, not fear. They did what was right primarily because they believed it was right.

How did they get that way?

That's what The Evaluating Committee of the Middle States Association—of which I was a member—wanted to find out. They had come to evaluate this school for its ten-year renewal of membership, and also, if possible, to learn something from it. The committee was made up of teachers and school principals. In several of their own schools, discipline problems were quite prevalent. The issue, in fact, was acute in the whole school world of America because of the ever-growing menace of juvenile delinquency. Just read the newspapers! A United States Senator had publicly declared that the country was losing the battle with juvenile delinquency, and that no answer to the problem had yet been found. The public, seeking a scapegoat, had put much of the blame on the schools. Could it be that this school had the answer?

One member of the committee declared: "You can't take this school as an example. In the first place it is a private school with a carefully selected student body, admission being determined by competitive examination. Only one in five of the applicants is admitted to the freshman class. In the second place, it is church affiliated; the children enjoy the advantage of continuous religious guidance. In the third place—."

But here one of the other members interrupted him: "There isn't one of the factors governing discipline in this school that couldn't just as well be adopted in any other school, public or private. But the staff would have to believe in discipline as sincerely and conscientiously as this staff does. And, of course, they would also have to practice it themselves.

"The kids here take discipline and guidance from their teachers, because they see in them spiritually well-poised individuals, serenely self-confident about their way of life, and not acting out of irritability or pique or emotional distress, as we so often act when we try to discipline. The teachers here set very high standards for the youngsters but they also set very high standards for themselves. The dress, manners, speech of the boys are reflections of the dress, manners, speech of the masters.

"And that isn't all: the discipline here may be severe, but it is scrupulously fair. The rules are set down in advance; no exceptions are allowed. The boys know exactly where they stand.

"But most important of all, these boys are made to recognize that discipline is to their advantage. Discipline has given them a superior school. They enjoy a rich, full, interesting life here, nicely balanced between studies and extra-curricular activities and sports, only because they are well disciplined. They also know that their graduates are readily admitted to the best colleges. Discipline, as they see it, is thus all to the good. It gives them more power and more real enjoyment.

"Contrast this with the confusion, discontent and aimlessness characteristic of many public schools, and you realize what we lose because we fail to understand that children really like discipline and will accept it readily from parents and teachers who are themselves well-disciplined and friendly and fair.

"Do you know whom the old grads go to see first when they come back to visit this school? It's Principal X, who is also prefect of discipline. He took no nonsense and they knew it. They also knew that he loved them. I wish we had a Principal X in every school in America. Then, maybe, there wouldn't be so much juvenile delinquency in the land."

*   *   *

When the choir boy committed murder and the story of his crime was flashed via radio, TV and newspaper into every home in the land, many a parent began to wonder: "Could my nice boy do anything like that?"

The answer is "no." Nice boys don't commit murder.

But sometimes seemingly nice boys are in reality greatly disturbed boys. Parents and teachers must be on the lookout for signs of emotional distress in their children that could erupt in an act of violence. Here are some of them: Moodiness, withdrawal, bad temper, lack of interest in school and play, extreme religiosity.

Don't think, as many parents unfortunately do, that quiet children are necessarily good children. There's always something suspicious about a too-quiet child. Noise is natural to children. Healthy, happy children are usually full of the old Nick. They are always letting off steam in rough and tumble play and

shouting. Be glad if yours is like that. And don't try to make
your boy a "goody-goody." It's not good for a boy to be a
"goody-goody."

The Canadian Mental Health Association in their illuminating
text "How to Know Your Child" uses as its main theme this interesting and significant statement: "There's no such thing as a 'bad'
child. There's no such thing as a 'good' child either. There are
only happy children and unhappy children, healthy children and
unhealthy children." Again we see the truth in the profound
aphorism of Yeats: "The good are always the merry."

Parents would do well to build their philosophy of child rearing around this idea. If your kids are healthy, happy, merry—
and this, of course, doesn't call for indulging them—you can be
pretty certain that they are in sound moral condition also. Beyond an occasional act of playful mischief or some unintentional
destructiveness, they are not likely to do anything very bad.

The happy home makes the happy child. Parents who are in
love with each other are in a good position to make a happy
home for their children. But merely loving and satisfying each
other isn't enough. They must also devote themselves to the
happiness of their children.

"Know thyself" was the ancient Greek adage. To which we
should add "Know your child," if you want to be successful as a
parent. And one of the main things to know about children is the
close relationship between "bad" and "unhappy."

* * *

"How could my son ever have committed so horrible a crime?"
the accused boy's father lamented. "I did everything the books
say a father should do for his boy."

The social worker assigned to the case found it difficult to
answer the distraught father's question. He had met this problem before of conscientious parents who strangely enough had
raised delinquent children. On the other hand, he also had seen
casual, seemingly careless parents, who used no rules to speak of
but whose children turned out good as gold.

How do you explain that?

The answer is that child-care is more an art than a science. It isn't the rules; it's the feeling behind the rules. If your heart is in the right place, if you know how to make your children feel that you really love them and enjoy them, you can pilot them to a safe moral harbor on most any reasonable code of conduct and on a minimum of preaching. But if you can't communicate affection and good will, all your moralizing won't help you.

In fact, your excessive conscientiousness may arouse resistance and create the very faults you seek to avoid. Perfectionist standards are a kind of straight jacket from which the child may desperately seek to break forth. It's a mistake to regard the world as a moral gymnasium for the development of moral muscles. It isn't. It's a place to enjoy and be happy in.

Children aren't born to illustrate rules of conduct. Children are born to be loved and cared for and gradually guided into good social behavior. They don't come into the world with a conscience; they acquire one out of your love and sound example. They have to be happy before they can be good.

Keep your mind on making your children healthy and happy, maintain your own reasonable standards, and your child's moral development will take care of itself.

And don't worry too much about delinquency. It doesn't happen in the home of love and decency. Discipline with love is the supreme grace of the good parent. Do you have that grace?

*　　*　　*

It's the sad fact of our teaching of morality to the young that it is based on fear. "Don't do this! Don't do that!" we warn them. "You'll get into trouble."

Youth is naturally rebellious. The more we warn them, the more it is their pride to defy us. No wonder delinquency just grows and grows.

How different the story might be if we used a more positive approach and tried to sell morality to young people on its merits as productive of a pleasanter way of life for them. This appeal to their intelligence, in contrast to the usual dire warnings, could not fail to win some attention.

For instance:

"Don't pet!" a mother warns her daughter. "You know what happens to girls who do!" Such an admonition might make a timorous girl more cautious. (And in later married life more frigid.) But a high-spirited girl might very well just laugh to herself: "Those old-fashioned mothers! What do they know about love?!"

But suppose the mother had said: "Girls who combine character with charm are doubly attractive to men. They are the kind men want to marry." Her daughter would think that one over. That's an idea that has some sense to it. It isn't just a threat.

Do other moral ideas also make sense to you and through you to your children?

Is honesty the best policy in your book? Or do you believe one has to "pull a fast one" occasionally to get ahead?

Do those who keep their marriage vows enjoy as satisfying a sex life as those who have "affairs?"

Should you be helpful to people in trouble, or say: "They made their own mess; let them get out of it!"?

What's your sincere point of view on these questions? How would you answer your children if they questioned you about them? Have you thought through the meaning of the moral law as not only God's word but also the actual experience of the human race on what helps and what hurts?

More is at stake in this matter than you realize.

Children who learn from their parents that morals make sense, who really know that the moral way is the better way to live, have a tremendous advantage over those not so tutored.

Their lives are steadfast because governed by principle. They know what they are doing and do it directly. They are not plagued with doubt.

They enjoy life's natural pleasures, and especially love, in a wholesome, balanced way and to a great old age. They get fun out of working and so are usually successful in their careers.

They like people and people like them. Thus they live a meaningful, interesting, full life.

And all this they achieve, because you taught them the common sense of morals.

* * *

The discordant, distressed, unhappy family, cast down by problems, material and spiritual, and seeking some way out of its many difficulties (alas, how many American families does this describe!) should rally around the wise, old, never failing guidance rule: WORK, LOVE, AND RELIGION HEAL.

You may see no solution to your troubles at this moment, but that does not say that you can't begin attacking them. Don't mope; don't whine; do something!

Start anywhere. Tackle the first job at hand, and soon, absorbed in your task, you will find that you feel better. Work is the great healer.

Why?

Because with your mind on your work, you can't have your mind on your troubles. And what a relief that is!

If you feel too depressed to attack your work with vigor, there is a psychological law (first put forth by the great American psychologist, William James) that can be of real help to you: "Energy grows with the willingness to use it." The most tiresome tasks, dishwashing, floor scrubbing, diaper changing, all the weary round of household duties, are readily accomplished if you accept your position as wife and mother and gladly do what you know you must do.

Many women complain: "I work so hard, but my work is not appreciated. For all that I have done for them, my children are ungrateful."

It is a fatal error of parents to couple their generous and loving acts toward their children with the demand (silent or expressed) that they be appreciated.

Your call for appreciation takes all the grace out of your gift of love. Your children want to be loved for themselves, with ap-

preciation their privilege, not their obligation. Give love freely
with no thought of getting it back, and you nearly always do
get it back. But love at a price is no love at all, and don't be surprised that it's not appreciated.

When we are really at our best selves, we know that love itself is the pleasantest of all emotions and are grateful that there
are those (especially our children) who need our love.

A great many of our troubles are due to the fact that we are
still emotionally dependent, in memory at least, on our parents
many of whom had their own unwholesome complexes and
brought us up badly because of them.

If we will now, in our adulthood, give up this weak depend
ence on our parents and transfer it to a strong dependence on
God and an orderly universe, we will find a new serenity and a
new self-confidence.

Things work out when we have faith that they will. The
parent who begins each day with prayer, who learns to "let go
and let God," will certainly find his load lightened. The spiritual
laws that govern life are ours to use anytime we're ready to use
them.

WORK, LOVE, AND RELIGION HEAL.

This is no saying for cynics or sophisticates. But if you have
an open mind, make use of this wise old guidance rule, con
taining, as it does, the very essence of The Mental Health Way
In time it will bring you and your family, though lost in a sea of
troubles, to a safe harbor.

Summary and Suggestion

Morality for children is a matter of gradual growth.

It is a mistake to ask the very young to share, to yield
place, to turn the other cheek. Like primitive man, children
are little savages: they grab, they fight, they hold on to their
own.

Your best bet with the little imps is to concentrate on making them healthy and happy. In time, out of their good health and happiness, they try to do what you ask of them because they want to retain their parents' love.

Step by step—by both your example and your teaching —you show them what you and society demand of them. You don't set too high a mark because perfectionist standards are a strait jacket that holds in the personality, that can be more effective by being free.

In time, however, you can establish quite high standards of morality and decency, provided always you practice what you preach. Your children aren't likely to be any better than you are; so, don't ask them to be.

But they *do* want to be disciplined—even the most wayward ones—and they like the parents who set high standards. It shows you care, and believe in them, when you take the trouble to train them.

Don't despair for the moral welfare of your children. Rather act, intelligently and on time, to show them that they can have a lot of fun in life and yet be good people.

CHAPTER III

Only You Can Give Your
Child a Sound Sex Ideal

IN POPULAR language the word morality is frequently limited to sexual morality as in the statement, a girl (boy) of good morals. This is unfortunate, because morality applies to all phases of life, and sex is only one phase of it. The Lord gave us Ten Commandments and not one. However, in a sense, this emphasis on sex morality may show a deeper understanding than we would at first presume. "Sex is the man," says Havelock Ellis, meaning thereby that a man's sex life shows his true character. If it is clean, wholesome, and strong, he is likely to be a clean, wholesome, and strong character. If it is in any way weak or perverted, he is likely to be a weak and perverted character.

But this is not the only point that interests us. We have been saying that the moral law works for the benefit of the individual. Does the sex code likewise work for the benefit of the individual? If we play the sex game according to the rules, will we really have a fuller, happier sex life?

Down through the ages, Mankind has slowly and painfully evolved a code governing the relationship of men and women to each other. This code is simply the experience of the human race as to how men and women may derive the most satisfaction —physical, mental, emotional—from relationship with each other. The basis of this code is monogamy, as expressed in an enduring marriage between one man and one woman, who, forsaking all others, agree to share their lives for better or for worse, until death do them part. This is the ideal we should aim to teach our children, teach convincingly by both instruction and example. A sound sex ideal is something a child can get only from his parents.

Now it is a common practice for sophisticates to laugh at monogamy as a code suitable for keeping the masses in order, but not applicable to them—the sexually elite—who, for their exceptional knowledge, are entitled to exceptional privileges; a little "playing around" outside the rules.

However, even a superficial observation of our society shows that of all people, the sophisticates are sexually the least happy. The thing that they are looking for, a sexual thrill, somehow or other always eludes them. And the proof that it has eluded them is seen not only in their general expression of cynicism and satiety, but in the fact that they keep on changing sexual partners: if they were sexually happy, would they want to change?

Some simple man and woman, on the other hand, who have worked out an easy sexual rhythm with each other, waiting for the natural onset of desire without in any way forcing it, expressing it deeply and fully with each other, and then in easy loyalty waiting for the next natural resurgence of desire, and coming together again with accumulated and intensified love for each other because of the satisfactions of the previous union, know a sexual happiness that the sophisticate can only long for but never attain. And they know it not transiently as the sophisticate does, but for a long and happy lifetime together. Perhaps ultimately they may come to experience that almost unendurably exquisite joy of complete man-woman oneness reserved especially by Heaven for the immaculate lovers. You are not playing for small stakes when you study the problem of sexual happiness. If you are sexually happy you're happy all over, while if you are sexually unhappy, you live a dead, dreary life.

It is in a sense embarrassing to talk about sex, because in this field we are all so imperfect, bound as we are to behavior patterns carried over from the frustrations and misunderstandings of early childhood—the "ghosts" that we each brought into the marriage. None of us dare throw a stone at another. Let imperfection, however, not grieve us too much. Out of imperfection comes growth. If we were already perfect, there would be no opportunity to grow. Growth, not perfection, is the right aim in life.

From this point of view, in the field of sex, it might be helpful not to use the words "right" or "wrong" at all, but rather the words "wise" and "unwise." Nearly all expressions of sex are in a sense expressions of love. Unfortunately some of them are not very wise expressions of love in that they do not produce happiness. Let us see whether with a little more understanding, we may not so direct our sex energy that we derive happiness from it rather than unhappiness, that in the game of love we win Cupid's prize and not a mess of pottage. The one can be as surely ours as the other, if we have the right understanding.

Nearly all adults remember from experience some expression of sex that brought a glow of physical, mental, and spiritual delight lighting up and warming every cell of being with a long-lasting aftermath of all-over comfort and satisfaction; and some other expression of sex that brought nothing but depression, disquietude, and even disgust, and only the most trivial moment of pleasure. What caused the difference? Why was the one gold and the other dross? Might not the answer to this question contain the solution to our whole problem?

If we will search earnestly within ourselves, we will probably discover that that expression of sex was right, or rather, wise, where the love partner was one whom we had freely chosen as matching the image of the ideal mate we had built up in our mind, and where we had reason to feel that we, too, represented a free choice based on an ideal. Furthermore, that at the moment each had let go of himself and was absorbed in the image of the other, with thought only to please the other, that there was no intrusion of any other image, no haste, and no withholding sense of social wrong or even impropriety.

To produce such ideal conditions of love and marriage is of course a large order, but who shall say that it is impossible? Some fall into them as naturally as they breathe, and all of us with care and effort can at least approach the ideal, escaping the garish adulteries and social-climbing marriages that are but specious counterfeits of the golden coinage in the treasury of sexual love.

For young unmarried people who have perhaps been frightened into believing that sexual restraint is a terrible burden, the best authorities give the following advice: Continence, with the prospect of an early marriage, is far from insufferable and has innumerable advantages over its alternative, promiscuous indulgence. Nearly every phase of promiscuous relationship is fraught with social difficulty and frequently ends in disillusionment and disgust. Sex can be the most tremendous experience in life, but it can also be the most trivial or the most treacherous!

* * *

"The back seat of an automobile was our bridal chamber," the young woman declared with hysterical bitterness to the marriage counselor. "We had to get married—but it wasn't for love."

Her experience is typical. The younger generation in America today is going through a mass orgy of loose sexual indulgence. As one college boy put it, "I would like to marry a virgin, but I don't expect to," and nothing is more obvious than that the general reaction is one of unfulfillment. The smarter young people are pulling out of this mess and quietly subscribing to the ideal of "No sex without love; and if it's love, it might as well be marriage."

Indeed, why could not the general practice of early marriage be the solution to our young people's sexual dilemma? Why should not the young Isaac sleep with the good and lovely Rebecca rather than with the coarse and vulgar harlot? Didn't the wise Abraham send his servant to find a bride for his beloved firstborn rather than a mistress, which is what some of our too, too sophisticated modern fathers recommend to their too, too sophisticated sons?

Married and unmarried alike should know that all the so-called laws for sexual morality really have for their purpose the rescue of the individual from a dividing of his sex energy, because the unifying of it is for his own greater pleasure and happiness. When we are told, "Thou shalt not commit adultery," it is more for our own good than for the good of God or society. A married person who commits adultery also commits a division in the expression of his sex energy. For him sex divided is sex subtracted. He no longer can summon his full libido, or love-energy, for the relationship with the marriage partner; therefore, that relationship will probably become weak and unsatisfactory; and, in the new relationship, there will be a stealth and shame and hurried, furtive quality that will likewise prohibit true satisfaction. So he is left hanging on a limb with true satisfaction nowhere. Similarly, when we covet our neighbor's wife or husband, we bring about a division in our sexual consciousness: the image of the mate we have is mixed with the image of the mate we would like to have, with the result that the marriage relationship is weakened, while the supposedly ideal relationship is only a fantasy. And a real mate, even with faults, is worth a hundred fantasies, however perfect.

"For he that lives more lives than one, more deaths than one must die." This aphorism of Oscar Wilde applies with particular aptness to sexual promiscuity. When you enter such a relationship you also have to get out of it some day. And with what pain and grief!

We get as much out of a sexual experience as we are capable of feeling. If we don't feel much love for the sexual partner, we won't get much pleasure or happiness out of the relationship, no matter how far it is carried. It is up to us, therefore, to use the law of appreciation to increase our sexual happiness. If we will concentrate all our thoughts on the charms and graces of the marriage partner, the libido will unite around his or her image; the love emotion, being united, will be strong; and the expression of it will prove a thrilling joy.

"Love," as the old saying goes, "is really in the lover," and if our love-life is not very satisfactory, it is probably our own fault. Just as we might say that beauty is what the artist brings to the picture—so, the much-coveted sexual thrill is what the lover brings to the marriage bed.

From all of this discussion we can see that the sexual code, far from being harsh or repressive, is a true blessing to the individual, fostering sexual health and promoting sexual happiness. However, sex is no game for the egotistic, the weak, or the malicious; here, all their deviousness leads only to frustration. The ingenuous, however, strange to say, take strength from their innocence, and barring entrapment by the vicious, carry off the prize of happiness.

This is no argument, however, for asceticism or repression.

There have been neurotic reformers, who struggling against an inner moral inferiority, have "over-compensated" by perverting the sexual code into asceticism. Fortunately, the psychological perversion involved in the philosophy of asceticism has been exposed to the world, so that nowadays not repression but normality is considered the moral ideal.

The folly of asceticism is probably responsible for much of our sexual confusion and for much of our sexual misery. Youth with its warm natural impulses resents the doctrine of asceticism and repression, and perhaps even turns away from religion altogether, with which it otherwise would have no quarrel, because of this unwise doctrine. And rightfully so!

The great religious leaders did not denounce sex per se. They merely denounced its unwise expression, and particularly any sexual act in which we have been unfair to another person. True sexual love brings out some of the noblest and happiest aspects of human personality. It can be the purest joy of our mortal sojourn, and there is no reason in God's law or man's why young people should not regard it so. Religious teachers make a great mistake to concentrate on mere self-control as the solution to this problem of the young. They should offer a more positive treatment of the problem, with real prospect of happiness for wise behavior rather than merely the threat of pain for unwise behavior.

Far better than sexual "don'ts" might be a code of sexual "do's":

Do be very determined to be sexually happy, and not for a short period of your life but for all of it.

Do be very certain to keep your sexual innocence before marriage. Vice at first view is always revolting; it is not really hard to avoid it if we just won't and don't begin.

Do try hard to make of yourself an attractive representative of your sex, a manly man or a womanly woman, that you may naturally draw to yourself a desirable sexual partner.

Do plan to marry young and permanently. In marriage, contrary to the sophisticate's opinion, is to be found love's depth and infinite variety; while sex outside of marriage really has the shallowness and monotony.

Do choose a marriage partner for love's sake only—not money, not social position, not pity, even. If you marry for love, you'll be sexually happy; if you marry for any other reason, you won't.

Do keep your marriage vows in letter and in spirit. Sex grows in depth and strength with every immaculate expression of it, while love divided is love subtracted. We get as much out of a sexual relation as we are able to feel.

If we love greatly, we will experience sex greatly. The way to be deeply and enduringly happy in our sex life is to be deeply and enduringly devoted to our marriage partner. In sex, especially, "if you lose your life, you find it."

Summary and Suggestion

"Today for most people the man-woman relationship is decisive. It can lead to the discovery of self, neighbor, and

God, or it can lead to hopeless entanglement and inner ruin. This is as true of the unmarried as it is of the married, and the answer is the same in both cases: it is that love should govern the whole field of sexuality, and that God should govern the whole field of love."

This wise and beautiful statement is taken from Theodore Bovet's *Love, Skill and Mystery, a Handbook to Marriage.* It summarizes what every man and woman should think of sex and what he should aim to teach his children.

Sex outside of love can be either a trivial or a treacherous experience, debasing and exhausting. But sex within the framework of married love is beautiful and inspiring—basic to our physical and spiritual health and happiness.

As you illustrate this ideal in your own day-by-day marriage, your children will instinctively seek to repeat your happy experience in their own lives.

CHAPTER IV

Sex Instruction

Can Be Easy

ARE YOU a good or a bad influence on the sexual behavior of your children?

Dr. Edward A. Strecker, chairman of the Department of Psychiatry at the University of Pennsylvania and author of noted works on parent-child relations, has a significant sex catechism for parents that will help you resolve this question. It consists of nine points. To the extent that you answer "yes" to them, your children's chances for sexual happiness are not good. Here they are:

"1. Do you think it unwise to kiss your mate and speak affectionately in front of the children?

"2. Do you have an understanding in your family that mother will raise the girls and the boys will be father's responsibility?

"3. When ill or blue do you complain to your children and demand their sympathy?

"4. When you are angry with your husband or wife, do you rant against marriage and the opposite sex?

"5. When your child is playing in his room with a friend, do

234

you make them keep the door open because you fear they may
be experimenting sexually?

"6. Are you disturbed if your child sees you disrobed and does
it make you and the child feel ashamed?

"7. Do you feel that you should have complete control over
your child's choice of friends?

"8. Are you hurt, openly or secretly, when your children go
off cheerfully on visits away from home and do not appear to
miss you?

"9. When you discuss the facts-of-life with your child, do you
fail to convey the idea that sex can be both beautiful and gratifying?"

These are pertinent and meaningful questions. Parents should
study them for all they are worth. They emphasize that to the
degree you are disappointed in your own love life, you tend to
poison the minds of your children against sex in general and the
opposite sex in particular. At the same time you drain their affections to draw from them the love you failed to elicit from your
marriage partner. That is what many parents do. Are you one of
them?

"Life," said the poet Browning, "is just the chance of finding
love." Because you lost out in the game of love, is it right that
you should make your children lose out also?

Nearly all the abnormality, perversity, criminality, mental illness in the world can be traced to wrong attitudes on the subject
of sex and the subsequent wrong sexual behavior. What kind of
attitudes are your children learning from you?

Are they learning romantic and idealistic attitudes toward the
opposite sex that lead to love and an enduringly happy marriage?
If so, that is a tribute to your own sexual normality and whole-
someness, qualities that have enabled you to build a happy home
for them. But if they are learning cynical and hostile attitudes
toward the opposite sex, you have something to be concerned
about.

Parents who find that they are giving the wrong answer to

some of the questions may realize the imperfections in their marriage and strive to correct them. Out of realization comes growth.

Any marriage can become more perfect as the individuals work to make it so. The first step is to look at the opposite sex with eyes of appreciation. There is a profound psychological law behind appreciation: you draw to yourself the good of all that you appreciate. Try it on your marriage partner.

Your reward will be double. You will not only improve your own marital relations and thus increase your personal happiness, but you will also cease to be a bad influence on the love life of your children.

*   *   *

"I was not swept away to Heaven," the young college girl commented, as she ruefully reflected on the sexual experience that had promised so much and yielded so little of satisfaction or delight.

Her case is typical. The younger generation in America today are rushing into life's experience prematurely and finding, alas, that green apples don't have too much flavor. By fifteen they smoke, by seventeen they drink, by eighteen many have exchanged love's young dream for a sexual mess of pottage.

How did they get that way?

The contemporary English philosopher, Cyril E. M. Joad comes up with an interesting comment, none too flattering to American parents:

" 'Children must have fun' seems to be the slogan of American parents, which being interpreted, means they must never be repressed, never to be denied anything they happen to want, and be universally spoiled. Poor little brutes! Eating their cake too early, they will get through it too quickly. How uniformly uninteresting will be their middle-age!"

These are wise words and American parents would do well to ponder them deeply. What to do about it is another matter.

If your children are still young, (lucky you) there is a great deal that you can do about it. Determine now not to overindulge them. Let 'em live lean, and they'll grow up strong, and clean, and sound. You are doing your children no favor when you buy them an excess of sweets or toys or fancy garments. Children who have everything, have nothing, because they don't enjoy what they have. No wonder such children are fretful and peevish. What is life without a desire, without something to hang a dream on? Those who surfeit don't dream.

If your children are still young (lucky you again!), give them clear, honest answers to their questions on sex, and let them always see in their parents' marriage a sweet picture of domestic content. Let them learn from you how much pleasure and satisfaction a husband and wife can give each other so that they will instinctively look only to wedlock as the way to sexual happiness.

If your children are teen-agers and more pleasure bound than you consider right, you have more of a problem. Don't start solving that problem by arguing with your children. It's much too late for that. Slowly, patiently, however, you can reconstitute your willful child's philosophy of life, if you will work at it.

First, you must make a friend of your problem teen-ager. Modest courteous speech, always allowing him (or her) to talk as much as you do, and giving real consideration to his opinions, will help a lot.

Secondly, avoid all expression of blame; praise whenever you honestly can. You don't rebuild a sick ego on a diet of blame. Your prodigal must always feel that he is his father's beloved son. If you are sincere in your love, ultimately he will reciprocate.

Third, set a good example.

And there will come a quiet hour when you and he can sit down and talk things over. If you'll remember to let him do most of the talking, your appreciative look alone will be enough to move him to reconstitute his life's values.

Every self has an ideal. *Your problem teen-ager has an ideal, too.* By believing in his ideal, you'll help him find it.

Young people who have found themselves don't rush around wasting themselves.

*   *   *

"This is terrible!" the mother murmured to herself as she read *The Readers Digest* article depicting the widespread prevalence of venereal disease among teen-agers. "Why do youngsters let themselves go like that?!" And she began to wonder and worry about her own boy.

This isn't the only mother of a teen-age boy or girl who is wondering and worrying. Sexual morals seem much looser today than they were in our parents' times.

What can parents do about this?

They will have to do more than wondering and worrying. The problem isn't simple. It requires constructive thinking and action.

As Kinsey pointed out in his famous *Sexual Behavior in the Human Male,* eighteen is the age when the male is at his sexual peak. A boy of eighteen who is alive at all, isn't living peacefully with his sexual urges. At times they seem to be tearing him apart.

Girls, fortunately, don't have the same biological difficulty. Besides, girls may look forward to marrying at a much earlier age than boys and can, therefore, be expected to wait more willingly until marriage. Still there seem to be plenty of impatient virgins among the girls, too.

In Sweden, they solve this problem on a purely sociological basis. Religion is ruled out as the arbiter of sexual morals. Children are given full instruction in sex in school. When they are old enough to fall in love, they are considered old enough to have sexual relations. Pre-marital sex is common in Sweden and is not frowned upon by society. Parents accept it as a fact of life for their maturing children and even condone it as natural and free of hypocrisy. "We believe in love," say the Swedes, "and not in prostitution."

Americans with their strong religious traditions could never accept this point of view. Even the more liberal-minded declare: "It may be all right for the Swedes, but it won't do for us."

What then will do for us?

Here are the choices:

1. Premarital sex on the lovers' basis as in Sweden or on the prostitution basis (licensed or illegal) as in most of the rest of the world.

2. Early marriage.

3. Self control and sublimation of sexual urges in creative work until the youth is really ready for marriage.

If we ban the first as immoral and the second as foolish because young people marry on impulse and frequently make a poor choice, we are left with the third.

The high-minded parent who wants to persuade his son of the third way, the moral way, has no easy task. It will take a deal of direct and straightforward talk. Beware of hypocrisy! Youth sees through that at once. But if you can really mean it, and have lived that way yourself, you can tell your boy the following:

"Sublimation of the sexual urge in creative work is difficult but not impossible. You escape many evils by this solution of your problem. And when you do marry, you will know the joy of pure love which will be compensation enough for your previous self control."

❖   ❖   ❖

Those people do best with marriage who (1) had a religious upbringing, and (2) received instruction in sex from their parents.

These two significant facts are drawn from the Chesser Report—the British equivalent of our Kinsey Reports on sex and marriage.

Here are some Chesser statistics for parents to reflect upon:

"Almost half of all girls who were tempted into a husband-wife relationship with a man before marriage, were girls who learned about sex from other children. BUT the figure was only one in six for girls taught by their parents.

"More than three-quarters of girls and women, who looked back on their childhood as exceptionally happy or very happy said they learned about sex from their mothers and fathers.

"Of those who heard about the facts from Mom and Dad, only one in fifty said they had unhappy childhood homes.

"Overwhelmingly (eighty-two per cent), the girls and women said they thought that instruction about sex should be given by parents."

As to the influence of a religious upbringing on love, sex, and marriage, both Kinsey and Chesser agree that: "Girls who have had this long-term advantage are the best and happiest wives."

Also that: "The incidence of girls who give themselves physically to a man before marriage is as low as ten per cent among REGULAR church goers, and as high as forty-two per cent among those who NEVER go to church."

What does the sound thinking parent make of these statistics? He determines that his children will have a true religious upbringing; and he undertakes the instruction of his children in the facts and ideals of sex himself.

Many parents shrink before these tasks, but they shouldn't. There is nothing too difficult about them.

(1) Children are born believers. You don't have to teach religion to a child. All you have to do is sustain his faith, which is easy if you are yourself spiritual-minded. There may be a short period of difficulty in adolescence when youngsters are naturally rebellious. But if you hold steady, you can influence your adolescent to keep his faith also.

The religious faith you give your children establishes positive attitudes in their mind—makes them feel life is worth living—and saves them from the undermining influence of the negativism and nihilism that pervade and poison the atmosphere of present day society.

(2) Giving instruction in matters of sex is a difficulty for those parents who remember how taboo the subject was in their own

childhood. But if they will reflect that their own child comes to the subject with a fresh, clean mind, they can realize that clear, orderly information can produce no embarrassment, if only they themselves will not feel any. It's easy if you are easy.

More important than information on sex, however, is attitudes. If the married life your girls observe at home is happy, you can be pretty sure that their instinctive feeling about sex will be that it is something good and beautiful, to be reserved for marriage and not wasted in promiscuity.

❂   ❂   ❂

"Mother, I can't tell you!"

When fourteen-year-old Nancy, who for her full-blown figure might be considered fifteen or sixteen, returned home from her Saturday night date, she looked greatly troubled. To all her mother's importunings to reveal the cause of her distress, the girl turned a deaf ear. So the mother suggested that she write to the child guidance columnist in the local paper "to get it off her chest."

Nancy did.

The mother wrote, too, describing her worry over Nancy and asking: "Do you think she needs a psychiatrist?"

No, Nancy did not need a psychiatrist, as her very sound and sensible letter indicated.

But she certainly could have used more of a mother's guiding hand in her personal affairs. For, like millions of other young American girls, she was rushing life's experiences and indulging in heavy petting at an age when love should still be just a wonder and a dream—"the worship of something afar"—and not a sordid physical experience:

"As the evening progressed, he kept trying, and I kept pushing him away. Then we had a long talk. He seemed to realize just about everything I'd been thinking. Well, his little doozey of a speech just about convinced me. I was very tired, I had a slight cold. I never should have gone out. But, nevertheless, there's no excuse for what I did.

"Yes, I did pet with him. It's really hard to say those couple of words. I knew exactly what I was doing and at the time didn't give it a second thought. Well, yes I did, but I wasn't worried.

"The next morning I woke with a scare, realizing what I had done and praying that it was just a nightmare—but it wasn't!

"Right now my conscience is killing me, and I'm almost scared to go out with another boy."

This eloquent letter reveals the essential moral idealism of youth. But this idealism needs fostering and protection, and from whom else but the parents?

A mother can instruct her daughter in the beauty and worth of married love and, with the father's gallant cooperation, so build up her confidence in herself as a girl, that she won't sell herself cheap.

And if mothers did the same for their sons, instead of draining off their romantic idealism by their own affectional demands, then boys would not act exploitively toward girls, but would be happy just to be with them, exchanging thought for thought, and satisfied just to hold hands and at most have a mild goodby kiss.

Adolescents should know: love is an energy, a tremendous creative force. You can tell whether you're really in love by the fact that you feel inspired to do great things. But after a session of heavy petting you're just tired and depressed. Whom are you cheating? Mainly yourself.

*   *   *

The Case Against Sex Freedom was the title of the magazine article, and the author was the world famous sociologist Dr. Pitrim A. Sorokin. Its theme was later more fully developed in the same author's *The American Sex Revolution.* If you missed reading it, you might ask your public library, or book store, to get it for you. You'll find it well worth your earnest study. A wiser or a sounder treatment of this vital subject I have not seen.

"Immorality," says Dr. Sorokin, "has helped to ruin many a

great nation in past centuries. Today it threatens the United States. Can we wake up in time to survive?"

He then goes on to explain that a sexually loose society like ours is not able to summon the backbone to resist in the face of war or to endure the austerity program that may be needed to salvage an overblown economy in time of peace. Russia, our arch enemy, has shrewdly turned right about face in her revolutionary attitude of freedom in regard to sex. Divorce in Russia is now almost impossible to obtain. Pre-marital chastity and marital fidelity are highly extolled in all official propaganda. (See the two Kinsey Reports for our side of the same story.) "And one great strength of Russia," warns Sorokin, "is that the family as far as we can observe, is as stable and monogamous as it was in Victorian England." History shows that nations are usually as strong as their family ties.

We Americans, by contrast are the most divorce-ridden country in the world. Our family life is unstable. We glorify sex and seem to be almost constantly pre-occupied with it. Statistics show that every nine minutes an American may be faced with some form of sexual stimulation in what he sees, hears or reads.

How can we change all this? Only by re-education of our people on the subject of sex, a re-education that will demonstrate that the real sexual happiness is obtainable only in an enduring marriage and not outside of it. Youth, especially, must be shown that by adhering to the moral code in his sex life, he will have a richer, fuller enjoyment of sex and concomitantly a richer, fuller life. Not repression, not asceticism should be our ideal. That's the negative approach that youth resents. The sexual education of our youth should be made up of sexual "do's" and not "don'ts" as indicated in the previous chapter.

If we can teach such sex ideals to our people, America will be strong in its family life, strong as a nation. And the American people will be sexually happy, as they certainly are not now.

✽   ✽   ✽

"Dad," she cried on the telephone. "Oh, Dad, I'm in trouble, terrible trouble. I want to come home—to you."

She didn't need to mention what it was. He had a premonition. He knew that if trouble came to his little girl, it would be love or sex trouble. That had been the trouble with his own life. Everything else he had been able to manage fairly well—his studies, his profession, his money. But sex? He had been in confusion about that ever since his adolescence.

He thought of his many affairs, all sex-centered and all unsatisfactory, and finally of the foolish marriage into which he had been trapped by the sex-cunning, but otherwise stupid girl, who had so unerringly found his blind side and used it to ruin him.

The marriage he had endured as long as he could for the sake of the daughter whom he adored, but finally it broke up. Of course, his cunning wife had the evidence and won custody plus a fat alimony. With what misguidance she had brought up their child he now understood. Had she perhaps even pushed the girl into this unseemly affair to get a fierce and final revenge on him?

Bitterly he reflected on the errors of his own life that had now culminated in the mistake his daughter had made, and from which, alas, he had not been able to protect her. What could he have taught her that might have saved her from this disaster? What could his parents have taught him that might have prevented the foolish waste of his powers in a sex life that led to nothing but disenchantment and enervation. Yes, what can parents teach their children about sex, over and above the mere biological facts, so that it may be a creative force and a source of joy, and not the misery-maker it is for so many millions. Look into the life of the unhappy and what is wrong with most of them. They are living a sorry sex life.

Out of the tangle of taboos, misrepresentations, prejudices and fantasies that most people have built into their conception of sex, it is necessary to abstract a wholesome and usable ideal leading to human happiness. From whom can children acquire such an ideal? Only from their parents and only from parents who are themselves happy with each other.

*　　*　　*

"Do you know the facts of life, Rollo?"

"Yes, father, what information would you like?"

This popular parable, really no joke, points up the ineptness of the typical American father in giving his son information on sex. Many a man will postpone this until his boy reaches adolescence. Then, remembering the moral trials and difficulties of his own youth, he rushes in to supply the basic facts, only to find that his youngster is already quite well informed, even a bit blasé, on the whole subject. All the time that his son has been picking up information—and misinformation—from his school mates and street companions, the father could have been giving him not only the true facts but those sound and wholesome attitudes toward sex which hold a lad steady in time of temptation.

Mothers have similar difficulties with their daughters. One woman writes:

"I am a mother with a girl sixteen years old who has been asking me about sex life and what is intercourse. She said she heard girls in school talking about it. I don't know how to answer without blushing. Please, could you send me a book on what a girl her age should know. Please help me out."

If this mother, overcoming her inherited inhibitions, had from the earliest years answered the questions which all children ask, she would have established a relationship of confidence and trust with her daughter that would permit her to discuss freely with her those subjects which are now considered too delicate and difficult. Her daughter would be thoroughly informed on the facts of a woman's love life and strongly fortified as to its ideals. Significant are the findings of both the Kinsey Report in America and the Chesser Report in England that those girls who learned the facts of life from their parents kept relatively free of promiscuous behavior while those not so fortified did not.

What is the best way to teach sex to children?

The best way is the natural way, answering their questions as they come up. All little children are curious about body differences between boys and girls, where babies come from, and what part each parent plays in bringing about birth. As you gratify this curiosity, speaking simply and directly and using the correct names, you let them feel that all this is wholesome and natural. Sex takes its proper, not exaggerated place, in their thoughts. All the time, your own pleasant and happy marriage is the living proof to them that love and life are good and will be for them, too.

Time is of the essence in giving sex instruction to children and so is the attitude of the parents. If you grasp the opportunity to answer a child's questions in these early years while he is still in a state of innocence on the whole subject, you gain a double advantage. First you build up a body of basic information. And second you instill in the child's mind the feeling that sex is normal and natural and in no wise anything to be ashamed of. Many parents recognize the good common sense of this point of view and do determine to present the facts in just this frank and wholesome way. However, in the midst of the discussion their inherited sense of shame and fear of sex brings a flush to their faces that impresses the child more than their words. Here we have the crux of the problem of giving sex instruction. We must release our own inhibitions before we can hope to present sex in the wholesome and beautiful way it should be presented to children.

It will help to clear our minds and emotions if we take our stand on the basic proposition that sex with love is one of the highest and noblest experiences of Mankind. It is only sex outside of love that is ugly and debasing. If we thoroughly understand and accept this point of view in our own minds, we will be able to rise above the restraint and evasions that were practiced on us by our parents and set up a valid emotional pattern for our own children.

But when we come to recognize our duty in this matter, we don't necessarily rush to perform it. We keep poised and relaxed. We don't give our instruction as if it were a planned school lesson. We take our cue always from the child's questions and concerns. It is important to know what information the child is seeking. Therefore, before we talk to children about sex we must learn to listen to them. This will encourage them to speak out what is on their minds and then we can help them at the point where they need help, all the time pitching our answers to the age and understanding of the child.

Of course, you will always tell your children the clear and simple truth. Otherwise, how can they trust you? But the facts, barely presented, are not enough. It's your attitude that counts. It is your attitude which your children will absorb and act upon. Make sure always that that attitude reflects appreciation of the wonder and beauty of love and the creation of life.

As has so often been stated in this book, what you are speaks louder than what you say. If you two show that you enjoy your gender, your boys will be glad to be male and your girls to be female. They will want to be as good representatives of their sex as their parents are. The manly boy and the feminine girl are usually most attractive to the opposite gender and make a success of their boy-girl relationships.

❊ ❊ ❊

"But how did the seed get into Mommy's belly?"

Most parents handle sex instruction reasonably well until they run into this question of the father's part in procreation. Then the old sensitiveness about sex brings a blush to their faces; all their previous endeavors to keep sex free of shame and blame may now go for naught.

You'll have to face this question someday and you may as well be ready for it. It won't be difficult if you have been frank and truthful in answering *earlier and simpler questions.* Then you can, in simple and unaffected language, and yet with earnestness and warmth, explain that the father starts the baby growing inside the mother by joining his body to hers. The man and woman have come together because of their love feelings for one another. This beautiful experience is called sexual intercourse. Be careful to let it go at that. Beware of saying too much. In fact a sure and perfect rule is—just answer the child's question, no more, no less—but answer it with scrupulous truth and that touch of idealism which represents your own fine attitude toward sex.

As your child grows older you can amplify your explanation. You can say that the man and woman come together because of their love feelings. And that in order that they might express these love feelings, God gave man and woman physically different structures. They joined their bodies together to express more completely the union of their hearts and minds.

The one great error is for a parent to evade this question or to refuse to answer it. This is the poorest possible strategy. It cuts your child off from your guidance and sends him out to seek information where he can, usually from ignorant or unsavory sources whose information may be false and whose speech may be nasty. And don't avoid the issue by talking about "the birds, the bees and the flowers." Whom are you fooling? The child recognizes that you *are* evading the question and is thus as bad off as if you had refused to answer, because he feels you are hiding something naughty, something taboo, something of which he is already vaguely and instinctively aware but not sure of.

Many parents have needless fears regarding sex which they unfortunately project onto their children. Because of these fears, even the very young child's curiosity about his opposite gender playmate's differences of body structure may be considered an evil thing which must be quickly stopped.

But curiosity is the very wellspring of a child's learning. A child's curiosity about body differences should be allowed full scope. In a way it might even be welcomed, because it gives the parent opportunity to clarify and explain. When curiosity is thus wholesomely gratified, it is less likely to grow into unwholesome and nervous preoccupation.

Masturbation is another thing about which the previous generation had unwarranted fears which it transmitted to its children. The amount of harm that was done to children by scare stories regarding masturbation cannot be measured. Many psychologists say that much of our present day neurotic behavior in the field of sex, and particularly our inadequacies, may be due to fright and guilt feelings over masturbation in childhood.

It is now generally accepted that masturbation is a normal
hase of sex maturing. All children masturbate and have in every
eneration. Unhappy children masturbate to excess. In a whole-
ome home environment where there are no superstitions and
aboos on this subject, children do not masturbate to excess and
radually outgrow the habit. Your children will overcome their
ad habits and fears in the field of sex as you encourage them to
stablish happy and natural relations with their age mates of
pposite gender.

The naked children of the less civilized races have no sexual
nhibitions. True, their more primitive beliefs may foster tribal
aboos and rituals. But in the natural life, all living things, from
egetable to Man, follow God's law and Nature's command to
rocreate—"to go forth and multiply" as God told Noah in the
ible story. This magnificent command is carried in the racial
nemory of all. That is why your child in his innocence knows-
rithout-knowing much about sex. It is the parents' sacred duty
o gradually enlighten this innocence so that the child acquires
rith beauty and without hurt the pure, useful and essential
nowledge which transforms original innocence into wise and
ractical understanding and action.

Learning to like and to get along with opposite gender is one
f the most important of the developmental tasks of youth. Those
rho achieve this have the prospect of happiness in the most
nportant phase of their future existence. You will help them
chieve this happiness if you give them the right knowledge.

Summary and Suggestion

Don't let your children lose the chance to love truly and
fully because of a low concept of sex. Rather accept readily
and without reservations your duty progressively to supply
them with the necessary knowledge and to set before them
an inspiring example of married love.

Sex instruction, a task which many parents dread and for which they feel unqualified, is really easy if only you will rise above your inherited inhibitions and be at ease in your own mind when giving it. Your child is an innocent on the subject and will accept what you say without blush or sensitiveness, if only you will talk without blush or sensitiveness.

Time is of the essence in sex instruction. The more information you implant in the innocent early years, the easier it will be to give guidance and inspiration in the later, more dangerous years. From the very start, therefore, make it a point to answer all your child's questions about boy-girl difference and where do babies come from in the simplest and most unaffected manner, using the correct scientific names for all body organs or physical actions. By the time your child reaches adolescence, and is establishing his first boy-girl relationships, he will know enough to handle himself sensibly and honorably.

Try always to understand your child, to know what it is that is bothering him about sex. Listen before you talk. Answer only what is asked, simply and encouragingly, making love and sex appear beautiful and noble, as you know it to be in your own marriage.

BOOK SIX

Guidance

EVERY CHILD NEEDS TO HAVE:

*friendly help in learning how to behave
toward persons and things*

*grown ups around him who show him by
example how to get along with others*

CHAPTER I

Your Child's Good Manners
Please God and Man

FEW PARENTS realize how much a child's worldly success and spiritual health depend on plain good manners which he acquires in imitation of theirs.

There is nothing that employers will pay so much for as the ability to get along with people. Modern business is a complex of involved human relations; he who can smooth its course by his graceful manners has a most valuable talent for which the world willingly pays high.

And manners are very close to morals. In that nobly spiritual essay *The Gentleman*, Cardinal Newman defined the gentleman as "one who never inflicts pain." He it is who makes human relations sweet and pleasant; it is his ideals that hold society together. If the first commandment is "to love God—and your neighbor," good manners lead the way to fulfilling the law.

It is interesting to note in books of Quotations—jewel boxes that gather the gems of wisdom of the race—that all the wise men speak well of manners. There is no dissenting voice. If all the sages agree that good manners bring health, success, and

happiness, every good parent will want to give its benefits to his
child.

*   *   *

Charles wasn't a brain, but he got along. He had something
which opened doors for him that mere intelligence couldn't.
Charles had courtesy. He learned it from his parents.

Teachers, especially, liked Charles and were glad to help him
with his school problems. Alas, our poor school teachers! Well
mannered children are only too rare in their harried lives. No
wonder they were attracted to Charles and gave him their best
of thought and feeling. He earned it by his bright attention and
grateful smile.

The kids liked him, too. He was a nice guy to have around,
they said. Things went smoothly when he took charge. No one
was cranky or quarrelsome. He got things done.

In his post high school job Charles received promotions that
other seemingly more able employees didn't. His skill in human
relations was highly valued by his company. They had many
good uses for it. Eventually Charles went into business for himself and acquired a comfortable fortune. But he made more than
money. He made a host of friends and well wishers. His was
rich, full, interesting life all built on the talent for courtesy.

Would that parents realized the value of courtesy in the lives
of their children. Courtesy is not merely a social lubricant to
make human relations smooth and pleasant. Courtesy goes a
great deal deeper than that. Courtesy saves people from the
persistent and nagging doubt of their own worth. That is why
it is always so gratefully received. In a world of bruised and hurt
egos, courtesy is a very precious commodity and commands
a high price. You can almost insure your child's success in life by
teaching him a true and creative courtesy.

Everywhere there is the need for it because everybody has his
inferiority distresses. The big boss who thunders his orders to
his subordinates and the lowly scrubwoman who cleans his office
have one thing in common: they feel inadequate to the demand

hich life makes on them. Courtesy gives them comfort and in-
piration. Courtesy makes them do better. Smile at people and
peak them fair and they feel important, at ease in their egos.
o wonder that people are always ready to appreciate and re-
ard the giver of sincere courtesy.

The best way for parents to teach courtesy to their children
 to practice it themselves. The grace of speech and manner
iat father and mother employ toward each other, their phrases
f mutual consideration and regard, are quickly taken up by the
hildren. The marital good word is twice blessed; it gives cheer
 the married lovers; it inspires amity and cooperation among
ie children. With tact and skill, parents can teach their chil-
ren to carry the same spirit out into the world. A place to begin
 is school.

* * *

"Gordon High School does not teach manners. We teach alge-
ra, biology, American history, and many other subjects, but
nanners—no! That is something we expect the youngsters to
ave before they come here. We count on the parents to teach
iem manners."

If you were the parent whom the principal was thus admon-
hing, would you feel offended? Or would you think there
as some point to what he was saying and thank him for bring-
ig it to your attention?

The whole school enterprise would get a tremendous lift, and
 wouldn't cost the taxpayers a penny, if parents made it their
usiness to send their children to school mindful of their manners
nd particularly conscious of the special courtesy due to school
eachers. That might be just the thing to turn Education's pres-
nt winter of discontent into a more hopeful spring.

Morale is low in American schools, and when morale is low,
rue education is unlikely. The teachers can't really teach, and
o the pupils don't really learn.

To rescue education from this unhappy condition, many mu-
icipalities are taxing themselves to the limit to build new

schools and pay better salaries to teachers. All the money spent
however, will be of no avail unless morale is recovered. *You*
child's good manners are needed to help restore his school
morale.

A credit to any parent is the well-poised child who sits cheer
ful and smiling while the teacher questions or explains. He doe
not egotistically intrude while a classmate struggles to find ar
answer; he does not push or shove during change of rooms; he
responds quickly to any request for service or attention. He thu
upholds the honor of your house.

But there are some kids who mean nothing but misery to schoo
teachers. Their basic bad breeding is seen in their unrestraine
chatter, their sneaky aggression when the teacher's back i
turned, their noisy exits and entrances. And they will sell them
selves at any time for a laugh. A sad fact is that many of them
come from homes of wealth and education; their parents shoul
certainly have taught them better.

In most of America's schools today, classes are so over
crowded the teachers have to give a good deal of their time jus
to maintaining order. They are, in some instances, more lik
policemen than teachers. The children are really only hal
taught. This is a waste of half the taxpayers' money.

But if the kids, through parental guidance, had a proper reali
zation of the situation, they would be quiet, orderly and coopera
tive in the classroom. Then the teachers could give their whol
attention to teaching and the pupils would learn something. B
sending your children to school well-mannered, you will insur
their getting a good education. That's something worth thinkin
about.

You will also be doing something for your country. Americ
desperately needs more well trained, well educated, profession
workers to compete at an advantage with its powerful wel
disciplined foe, Russia. In hot war or cold, the country wit
the best schools will win. Parents are very important to ed
cation. They alone can lift our schools to the needed higher leve

Teachers are part-time parents, but parents are full tim

teachers. In the curriculum of the home, the most important subject is courtesy.

* * *

His favorite expression was: "People are no damn good!" And he always had plenty of examples to prove it.

His children heard him say this a thousand times. How did it affect them? In time, they, too, came to believe that "People are no damn good." And they, too, found plenty of examples to prove it.

There is a story of an ancient sage who sat at the gates of his city, welcoming the strangers who came in. One of them asked him:

"What kind of people live in your city?"

"What kind of people lived in the city from whence you came?" the sage inquired.

"Oh, they were terrible people: liars and thieves and cruel cut-throats who committed every manner of perversity."

"That's the kind of people you'll find in this city."

Then another stranger came by, and he, too, asked: "What kind of people live in your ctiy?"

To which the sage again queried: "What kind of people lived in your city?"

"Oh, they were very nice people—generous and brave and loving. They had faith in God and treated everyone fairly."

And again the sage replied: "That's the kind of people you'll meet in this city."

This parable has great significance for parents.

Your children learn human relations from you. If you take on the all too prevalent attitude of cynicism and doubt: All men are liars, everyone in public life is a crook, no businessman is honest —in short, that people are no damn good—they will assume a similar view.

What does this get them? A nervous, harried, contentious existence in which they are always on the lookout lest they be cheated, and by which they are sometimes led to be unethical themselves on the plea: "better do others before they do you."

But if you have attitudes of faith and good will toward all people, and teach your children the same, it may happily amaze you how much easier and pleasanter your life will be—and theirs!

For the great truth of human relationship is that everyone is ego-driven to respond to you as well, if not better, than you act toward him. Get there first with a good attitude and you nearly always receive a good response. Treat a person generously and note how determined he is to outdo your liberality.

But let a person see by the expression on your face, or by your words, that you doubt or fear him, and at once his whole self bristles up in anger at you, and he wants to do the worst toward you that he can.

With the years, many of us, because of a few bad experiences, have given up our faith in human nature. To justify our cynicism (of which we are ashamed) we aim to impose it on others, especially our children.

This is a sad mistake, because it puts our children at a great disadvantage in life. They can then draw no benefit from the vast reservoir of good will that actually exists in people, because they don't know how to call it forth. They are thus prevented from establishing happy human relations, socially and in business, which is the very foundation of a successful life.

So, stop saying: "People are no damn good." You are poisoning the minds of your children, giving them a sour and barren attitude. Your real duty is to teach your children to like people and to get along with them.

*   *   *

"Why did the man give you his seat, Mama?"

"Because he's a gentleman."

"What's a gentleman, Mama?"

If that were your five-year-old asking, how would you explain to him what a gentleman is? Would you describe it in a way to make the idea "gentleman" important to him? Or would you make it seem that a gentleman is just a nice man that gives his seat to a lady? You're passing up the chance to do your child a most significant service if you fail to impress him with the great value of courtesy in his life.

"If a man is a gentleman," said the discerning social critic Oscar Wilde, "he knows quite enough. If he's not a gentleman, all the education in the world won't help him." What do you think of this point of view? Would you want to apply it to the upbringing of your children?

In our society of rush and hurry and heartless competition, where nearly everyone's ego gets a continual kicking around, the courteous man or woman is especially appreciated. The gentleman gives people what they most crave, consideration. He's the one who has faith in us, who thinks we're worth his best attention. What a lift that gives our spirits! No wonder we value him highly and in return serve and honor him. In very fact, courtesy often commands both materially and spiritually what mere intelligence could never come to. How necessary is it then that we teach it to our children.

But in actions, not in words! We could lecture our children all day long about "thank you" and "please" and "I'll be glad to," but unless they see it illustrated in our own behavior, the words will make little impression.

Another great truth is that courtesy like charity begins at home. And how rewarding is the habitual use of courtesy there! The noise, the confusion, the conflict that are a blight on family life are by courtesy greatly reduced. Manners give your home distinction and charm.

Highest truth of all on this subject is that good manners are an expression of your spiritual self. Translate the Golden Rule "Do unto others as you would be done by," into terms of every day living and what does it mean? Good manners.

* * *

The parents in Happy Town, the American dream suburb with two cars in every garage and two chickens or pheasants in every pot, had their problems, too. One was that their well-bred children would every now and then behave like hoodlums.

Just before graduation, the senior class of the high school went on a drinking spree in the neighboring metropolis, which they were visiting supposedly to do some research study in the Museum of Natural History. The principal had to call off the senior prom as a punishment.

One Friday evening, the local movie house was, as usual, filled with the high-school crowd and their dates. Suddenly the whole lot of them went on a rampage of destructiveness, tearing the upholstery off the seats, smashing light bulbs in the washroom, breaking off tiles from the walls. Some threw eggs. The manager declared that in the future no adolescent would be admitted to his theater unless accompanied by an adult.

Could one of those misbehaving youngsters have been your son?

There are many Happy Towns in America, whose children have everything and still behave at times like hoodlums. Vandalism, delinquency, school rowdyism add up to America's No. 1 social problem, the rebellion of its youth.

Why should prosperity's youth be in rebellion?

Could it be that getting everything and giving nothing, they feel ashamed and embittered. Their strong energies turn to destroy society, because they are not called on to serve society.

American parents, moving into an era of the greatest material prosperity our country has ever known, are also, whether they know it or not, facing a period of the greatest spiritual distress our country has ever known. There will be, by all signs, more delinquency, more divorce, more mental illness in the coming decade than we have ever had before. Our material glory may turn to ashes for our children unless we learn to balance it with a spiritual ideal.

Therefore:

Soft pedal the prosperity in your home. Don't go in for the biggest car, the fanciest furnishings, the most in new gadgets. And above all, don't indulge your children with them. That swank roadster you're thinking of giving your son for graduation. Don't! Children who have everything become strangely fretful and irritable. There's nothing for them to look forward to. What's life without a dream?

And don't "pick up" after your children, doing for them what they can very well do for themselves. How can they escape becoming selfish if you are forever serving them? Let them rather serve you and the home in reasonable duties.

Encourage your children also to volunteer in school activities, church work, civic drives. Givers get strong. Givers are much happier in their egos than receivers.

Interest yourself in your son's school and school work. A recent research study shows that when parents demonstrate real interest in a child's studies, he does better with them. Absorbed in his school subjects, he is less likely to get into mischief, more willing to work for a career. Hobbies help, too.

Most important of all, practice a true, a spiritual, courtesy in the home. Your own fine manners are an inspiration to your children and a guide wherever they go. They are proud of their parents with high standards, and won't let you down by behaving otherwise on the outside.

In all this you help your growing child to find his best self. Those who have found themselves don't waste themselves by acting like hoodlums.

❋   ❋   ❋

"What our dinner table needs," exclaimed the father, laughing heartily, "is a conversation traffic cop. You kids have so many ideas on this subject, you need 'stop' and 'go' signals to give everyone a chance. And you're not letting your mother serve that nice hot apple pie she made for dessert."

His face glowed with paternal pride. What a fine brood of children he had, and what a happy interesting dinner hour they had all enjoyed together!

Are you, too, making the most of your parental opportunities at the family dinner table? The dinner hour is your best chance to unify your family, set its standards of culture, stimulate its intellectual interests, establish its spiritual ideals.

Mother sets the stage for the happy occasion by preparing a good meal, decorating the table, dolling up a bit herself, and seeing to it that the children are clean and fresh looking. Home is made attractive for the returning father.

Father, for his part, must arrive punctually and preside regularly at the head of the table, carving the roast, directing the conversation, and controlling, if necessary, the behavior of the children. Nothing can compensate for the father's absence from the dinner table, not even that million dollars you are making for your family's future welfare by overtime attention to your business.

Keep the lines of communication always open in a family and you will have a minimum of unsolved problems. Children are relieved when they can talk things over with their parents. A sympathetic and an understanding ear wins your child's gratitude and love. He is proud of his considerate parent and will never let him down by misbehaving in school or on the street. The dinner hour is an ideal time for frank and open family talk.

Good table talk also stimulates your child's intelligence and makes him a better student at school. To him that hath shall be given. The more ideas your child acquires at home, the more readily will he participate in class discussions in school. Such a child reads better, too, because he can quickly match words with thoughts.

Most valuable of all is the spiritual and moral tone you set for them in the expression of your own ideas and ideals. This doesn't mean that parents should sneak in a bit of doctrine at every possible opportunity. That could backfire in rebellion or hypocrisy.

Besides, you're too good natured to be preachy at the dinner table.

But in these happy dinner hours that you spend with your family, you gradually develop a set of principles and ideals that become the family's standards to serve the children through all their lives.

*   *   *

"But, Dad, I didn't finish my sentence."

How deeply did the father regret his discourtesy in getting up to leave the room before his son had completed what he was saying! Nor was this the first time he had done so. Absorbed in some personal or business problem oppressing him, he had taken for granted his parent right to give or withhold attention as he could.

How many parents, especially fathers, are guilty of this. For lack of a little courtesy to their children, they lose the harmony of the home and their children's sincere respect and devotion.

Courtesy always gives people an ego boost. That's why it is so good for your children. They feel proud to be worthy of their parents' full attention and respect, and act accordingly. If you want your children to possess self-assurance, their greatest need, you must make courtesy the general rule in all your relations with them.

When someone very important enters your home or office, you greet him by name, you smile warmly, you speak with interest and enthusiasm. That's the way you should treat your children. They are the most important people in your life. Their love, respect, and cooperation mean more to you than anything else in the world.

There's always time for courtesy. When you note the endless hours some households waste in petty wrangling, you realize how much time and energy might have been saved if everybody had been just reasonably polite to one another.

*   *   *

"Teach? Who, me? No, thanks, I'm through!"

Why was this competent teacher leaving the school system? Because the salary was too low?

No. Salaries of school teachers are going up. They are still not good enough, but they are getting better.

It's not the money alone that makes school teaching an unattractive profession; it's the bad manners of the present-day pupils.

Teachers say: "I'm exhausted just trying to keep order. I can't do much teaching. There's no satisfaction in the job spiritually or mentally."

At the end of a recent school year, the National Education Association published a sixty-page report entitled *Teacher Opinion on Pupil Behavior*. Over 4,000 classroom teachers all over the country were consulted for their views in the preparation of this report. What some of the teachers had to say about the children doesn't make pretty reading for parents: "The school kids of today are a lot of hoodlums. What they most need is discipline. Occasional whacks with a heavy ruler would help."

Parents should give this problem serious attention. Unless the teachers gladly teach, the children won't learn. Your dream of a good education for your children will come to nothing. They may get a diploma, but they won't know very much.

What can parents do to make their children behave better in school? Threaten them? Deprive them? Beat them if they misbehave, as some of the teachers suggested.

That won't do it. In fact, if you get too strict at home, you may drive your children to cut up in school as a kind of compensation. Discipline, yes, consistent and firm discipline, but not harshness. You can't beat good behavior into a spunky child. And would you want a submissive one?

You must make pleasant manners a way of life in your home, so that your children will instinctively follow them there and in school! How? By being consistently polite to your children, not in an affected, artificial way but as a natural expression of your love and regard for them. Speak low, smile, lend a listening ear.

Don't beat them down by your constant irritability, fault finding, blame. Rather build them up by your sincere appreciation and praise. Every child wants to live up to his parents' estimate of him. If you value your children highly, they won't value themselves so lowly as to behave like hoodlums in school.

Most misbehavoir is a bid for attention. Who is the child who must get himself noticed by loud talking, gum chewing, rustling papers, coming in late, mocking or defying the teacher? The child who has no confidence in his good qualities.

It is up to the parents to give their children the love, encouragement, and good cheer they need to feel valued as persons. They will then accept the school's discipline not in fear but with pride. The happy child is not a rebel. He likes to co-operate.

Summary and Suggestion

"Mind your manners," the intelligent parent says to his child. "Your manners can make or mar your fortune."

Unfortunately, not all parents have thought through the value of manners in promoting their child's happiness and success. They should know that we live in a world where manners are particularly appreciated, maybe because they are so generally lacking. Ours is a bitterly competitive society, usually with no quarter asked or given. In such a society there are many bruised egos for whom a courteous word or look, an encouraging smile, is as a balm to an aching wound. That is why manners have such a high market value. The youth who has learned the fine art of courtesy has an open sesame to business success. Especially if I thought my child lacking in the intellectual gifts that win position would I endeavor to endow him with the useful asset of courtesy, which often achieves what neither intellect nor force can hope to attain.

Courteous children could represent a parent's valuable contribution to the solution of America's educational problem, now more acute than ever. In present day overcrowded classrooms, learning is possible only if the children will be accommodating to the teacher's wishes and directions. Parents can make an invaluable contribution to

American education by sending a well-mannered child to school.

Good manners make for social success, for boy-girl success too. The well-spoken child is welcome in any home, and especially when he comes a'courting there.

Manners are close to morals. They are the essence of the Golden Rule.

———

BOOK SEVEN

Control

EVERY CHILD NEEDS TO KNOW:

that there are limits to what he is permitted to do and that his parents will hold him to these limits

that though it is all right to feel jealous or angry, he will not be allowed to hurt himself or others when he has these feelings

CHAPTER I

Discipline: How Can I
Guide My Child

IF YOU asked present-day American parents what they are most
worried about, they would no doubt answer: "The misbehavior
of our children."

It isn't only juvenile delinquency, our number one social problem which some call insoluble, that has gotten us down; it's the
behavior of our children in general—in school, at home, on the
playgrounds, in the streets.

When the Russian Sputniks sailed across the heavens and
Americans in chagrin and dismay asked: "How come they got
there ahead of us?", many declared that our schools' philosophy
of permissiveness had encouraged such lax and loose behavior
on the part of the pupils they naturally couldn't learn very much.
No wonder the Russians, with their strict school discipline over-
took us in technological knowledge.

Indeed, the National Education Association itself at recent
meetings gave serious attention to reports of teacher committees that the misbehavior of the pupils is the outstanding problem of American education, retarding all our endeavors toward

greater achievement in studies. By inference, the misbehavior of the children in school was declared to be a reflection of their bad manners and misbehavior in the home.

Many parents in irritability and anger at all this, because they are the ones that are being blamed, declare that their patience is at an end. From here on they will be more strict with their children and punish where formerly they coddled and cajoled.

It would be well that they paused before they punished.

There are reasons for children's misbehavior that have to be understood. And there are better ways than punishment for producing good behavior.

A child isn't born an angel, though in sleep he sometimes looks like one. Childhood represents the primitive period in the history of the race. A child is something of a savage: full of energy, combativeness, and selfish desires. It's natural for him to be noisy and destructive. Goodness isn't given to him at birth; it's something that he achieves and only under your wise direction.

A further fact to be kept in mind in considering the behavior, or misbehavior, of children is that ours is a society not friendly to children. For one thing, children rarely have room for the free expression of their exuberant energies. "Don't fence me in," cries the cowboy in the popular song. But we have already fenced our children in. Even in the suburbs to which many families fled to find play space for their children, the land is all built up and space for the whoop and dash of childhood games is strictly limited. Much that we call misbehavior in children is nothing but a bursting out of bounds of their cramped up energies.

In the large cities this condition is of course greatly aggravated by apartment house living. A four-room flat with paper-thin walls is certainly no place in which to raise children. Their noisy activity brings on the neighbor's wrath and if you send them out to play, what have you? Sidewalks crowded with pedestrians and streets awhirr with rushing automobiles. Next time you bawl out a child for getting out of bounds in his play, ask yourself the question: "But where could he play?"

Yes, children have strong instincts and emotions and no place to exercise them. Parents should keep that in mind as they try to curb their waywardness and raise them to be socially conforming and contributing.

But there are ways.

The two things that make children behave are our love and ✳ our good example. We may turn here or turn there and seek this or that remedy only to find that nothing else works. There is no short cut to discipline. Give love and you'll get obedience. Your child enjoys your love and will try to behave in order to continue to have it. And you can set your standards however high, as long as you yourself illustrate them without pretense or hypocrisy and make them worth-while by the reward of your love. Of course, you will also have to be patient and allow for lapses, remembering that children aren't born good but achieve goodness by our guidance and encouragement.

Why are we so helpless before our problem of juvenile delinquency? Because we haven't given American youth a square deal, and we know it. Our own guilt feelings prevent our speaking with authority to youth.

Sure, we have given them things—motor cars, fine clothing, good food, medical and dental care, and a large allowance—but have we given them our love, our patient attention, our constructive guidance? No! If we had, we could speak with authority to youth, and they would listen.

Mere strictness will never solve behavior problems of children. If we weren't so fretful and irritable over our own faults we wouldn't ask that it should. It would amaze you to find in the letters that come to my newspaper column how many parents write: "I have tried spanking him but it doesn't help." I have yet to find a parent who said it did.

Of course, you can always beat a child into temporary submission. You can out-face a child and make him cower before you. But this kind of obedience is of dubious value.

✗ A beaten down, fearsome child may grow into a weakling, a ninny or an out-and-out neurotic. Or he may nurse fierce inner feelings of hatred and rebellion against his parents that may later break forth in criminally destructive attacks on society.

This doesn't deny that children have many wayward impulses. They shout and run wild at times and may occasionally be quite destructive. You certainly have to hold them in check, letting them know that there are limits to what they can do.

✝ But the loved child is easily corrected. A mild punishment such as sending him out of the room or withholding a privilege, plus a clear explanation of what he has done wrong, is usually sufficient to bring him back to obedient behavior. He knows that you mean well by him even though you have had to correct him. Haven't you shown him that in a thousand kind and generous acts, as well as in your day by day devotion and interest? And doesn't he see in you a person who follows all the rules you have asked him to obey?

If you are sure of yourself, you need not hesitate to correct your child, to let him know what you expect of him. Give commands just once, in a quiet voice, but as though you expect them to be obeyed. You can afford to be firm, if you are also friendly.

In the Bible we learn that both the prophet Eli and the prophet Samuel had wicked sons. And so had many another patriarch. We wonder why. The Bible story is never quite clear on this subject. But one valuable truth is gleaned from these stories: Our own virtue does not guarantee the good behavior of our children. We mustn't be so lost in our own pious reflections that we cannot give our children constant loving guidance and attention. We allow them a lot of freedom, sure, and especially in adolescence when they so need to be trusted. But we always stand by ready to give help and advice if asked.

Nor do we set perfectionist standards which act as a kind of strait jacket to the young. Remember children are not born good; they become good, and only if we give them love and a worthy example.

And there's the rub! We Americans are not the best ones for

setting an example of obedience. There is a tradition of lawlessness among our people harking back to pioneer days, when our country was settled by men and women who fled to this country in rebellion against the arbitrary rule of church and state in the old country. We never quite got that out of our system. Many who don't exactly break the laws, don't seem to mind bending them, that is to buying influence, "fixing" traffic tickets, "doctoring up" expense accounts, using tricky advertising or deceptive selling techniques. You can't talk morality out of one side of your mouth and gloat over "pulling a fast one" out of the other. The conscience isn't deceived. And our children aren't deceived either.

Besides morality, it takes tact and good common sense to teach children discipline. You don't say "no" all the time; and you don't say "yes" all the time either. You learn to compromise. You correct as much as you can. You never let it become a question of your will or your child's will. Break a child's will and you ruin his self-confidence, his best weapon for making his way in the world. Break a child's will, and he can never love you.

So build a bridge of love and good will between you and your child after each correction. Let him know and feel that while you did not like what he did, you never ceased to like him.

And many acts bring their own punishment, like a tummy ache from eating too much candy, or the loss of a friend by being too quarrelsome. Point these out to your child. He'll learn.

Plan your child's day. Provide good toys, play space, and companions. Make allowance for noise by supplying demolition blocks and other playthings that can be set up and knocked down. Learn to let him alone to build and create according to his dreams, but always under your loving and watchful eye.

Express praise whenever you legitimately can, and avoid blame. Most children want to live up to their parents' estimate of them. Never make him feel small by shaming him because then he can't behave big.

And you want him to behave big, to grow out of wayward childhood into sturdy and steadfast adulthood. And that he will—if you will remember always to love him, guide him, and set him a good example.

Summary and Suggestion

The disciplining of children, which to many parents seems an impossibly difficult task, comes easy to those who can afford to be firm because they themselves are both loving and dutiful. When you have established a relationship of affection and good will with your child, when you promptly and cheerfully meet all his needs, you have given him a child's true happiness. He isn't going to throw this away lightly. He will do what you ask of him because he wants to retain this satisfying love. Discipline with love is the supreme grace of the good parent.

Fussy, critical, irritable parents, however, are in for a hard time. They do not convey the feeling of love and their child does not have the instinctive desire to obey in order to please the parent. Irritability, aptly called the vice of the virtuous, ruins many a parent's desire to discipline his children.

When children misbehave, always pause before you punish. Ask why. All misbehavior has a cause. Finding the cause and removing it is a much simpler and easier process than shouting and spanking. Don't demand obedience as something due to you, the parent, but always base your call for obedience on the general welfare of family and society

Your best bet in winning obedience is always to illustrate the behavior you ask your child to perform. The second sound practice is consistency, holding smilingly true to your standards day in and day out.

CHAPTER II

Individual Problems of
Discipline

"If you won't love me," says the misbehaving child, "I will make your life as miserable as you are making mine. But, if you will love me . . . !"

The man had married a woman "who had a child by a previous relationship." He had promised to be a good father to this child, but as the years went by and he had four other children to be father to, the foster child became unattractive to him, and in time absolutely obnoxious.

"Saul has a personality which strongly affects my activities and my interests. He is an extremely talkative child, and there is no let-up. In addition he has a loud and penetrating voice. He loves to be the center of attention. If there is a conversation between my wife and me, or any other member of the family, he has to enter into it.

"At mealtime he makes all kinds of unpleasant noises. In school he is reprimanded more than any child in his class for excessive talking, according to his own statement. If he does his homework, he insists on doing it while everyone is present, and his mother must help him with it, on the pretext that he cannot do it by himself.

"What he does actually is force his attention upon you, whether you want it or not. If I tell him to do something that he does not want to do, he will give me an argument. The net result is that when he is present, I cannot enjoy my own children, obtain the pleasure of their company, because my attention is forced on him."

How blind is the unloving heart!

All this boy's bad behavior is just a persistent bid for attention. If the father will accept his foster child as just as worthy of affection as his other children, perhaps, for a time even more so, because of the previous years of neglect, his troubles with him will certainly grow less.

How charming are the characteristics of a child when you love him! And how ugly when you don't!

A strong-willed child is instinctively hostile to a carping, critical parent and will do, and overdo, the very things the parent most dislikes. His whole ego is at stake. His pride demands that he give you blow for blow.

But if you love him, the same pride demands that he repay you in kind, giving love for love, and even more so. With his love will go his obedience, his willingness to have his faults and bad mannerisms corrected, his resolution to be as you desire him.

*   *   *

"A belt in the seat in time saves many a brat from becoming a bum."

So say the corporal punishment advocates to justify the beatings they give their children. And so say that whole school of thinkers on the subject of juvenile delinquency who demand a get-tough policy—the night stick and the jail—as the only way to conquer the present epidemic of child crime.

It's an attractive theory to many. Throughout history whenever children or youth showed a lack of respect for their elders or those in authority over them, the cry has been for discipline—

the discipline of the hand, the fist, or the rod. And, seemingly, it got results. For if you beat hard enough, didn't the child ultimately obey?

Yes, for the time being. But if we are to rely on punishment only as the deterrent to misbehavior, where, in what family or in what society, would there be enough time or energy to put down every wayward or destructive impulse that children have? Punishing would rapidly become the sole business of every parent, teacher, or child custodian.

Surely, there must be a better way to win obedience from children.

There is. That way is the training in self-discipline which enables each individual to control his own behavior, so that he not only is no burden to society but actually a contributor to its welfare.

Can children be taught self-discipline? Yes, they can. And it's easier than you think:

1. First, you must rid your mind of the corporal punishment idea. Give it up entirely. You merely stimulate the spirit of aggression in your children by being its living symbol. And your subsequent disturbed conscience nearly always drives you to go too far, as in further beatings you think to justify the first one.

2. Be a model of a decent human being yourself, kindly, industrious, courageous, one that your children can follow as their ideal. All children instinctively imitate their parents and teachers. Character, like manners, is caught not taught

3. Create a climate of love and good will in the home and the school, so that the child feels that he can trust people; that he doesn't have to fear and fight them all the time.

Everybody wants to be loved, even the most desperately misbehaving child or adult. In fact, when he is most misbehaving, that is the very time he most needs your love. Correct him, yes; but love him, too. If your love will equal his need, he'll stop misbehaving and give you the obedience you seek.

And this obedience will be real. It will come out of his own desire to please you because he enjoys your love and wants to continue to receive it. That's self-discipline, the only kind of discipline that can bring about a good family or a good society.

*   *   *

"I'll admit," the mother wrote, "that I yell at the children a lot, and so does my husband. But most of the time, they don't seem to hear unless we yell. It seems as though I am scolding or spanking most of the time."

This is a typical statement. Great numbers of parents, even the conscientious and well-meaning ones, give way to hollering and spanking when their children misbehave.

Does the misbehavior stop? For the moment, yes. But soon it starts up again, and worse than ever. Kids are tough, and under beatings get tougher. Soon they can take your worst and not mind it.

But you! You mind it. Exhausted and nervous and very likely troubled in conscience, you wish there were a better way.

There is!

The better way is to cultivate your own poise and self-confidence. When you are master of yourself, you find it easier to manage your children.

You rise above irritability. You accept the fact that noise and rough and tumble play are natural to children. Realizing this you don't let it bother you too much.

But when the children really do wrong, wantonly destroying things or abusing the little ones, you have the strength to give commands, and your kids take heed now, because they know you mean it. You're not just nagging.

Dignified, self-confident, good-humored parents don't have to holler. They get reasonable obedience—it's foolish to ask for more—on the strength of their loving but firm personalities.

The parents who yell and scream all day obviously lack self-control and other attributes of strength. Their clever kids size them up and behave accordingly. Why should the weak be obeyed?

Spanking, too, follows the law of diminishing returns. The more you spank, the more you have to spank. Soon it's an endurance test as to who can be tougher, you or your children. Kids of spunk and spirit won't give in, and kids without spunk and spirit just become more spineless. You lose in either case.

Here are some better ways:

1. Plan things to keep the children interested and busy. Provide plenty of good indoor and outdoor toys—blocks, erector sets, games of skill, bicycles, basket ball and net, skates, that give an outlet to lively energies.

2. Make room. Kids must have a place to play. You can't expect them to behave if you fence them in.

3. Encourage sociability. Companions keep the kids out of your hair and teach them the valuable lesson of "how to make friends and influence people." The "Y" and "Boy Scouts" provide organized activities and teach fine social ideals.

4. Encourage hobbies. They consume a lot of loose energy—constructively! They develop skills and talents.

5. Encourage reading and the library habit. Children who like books are never bored.

6. Finally, and most important, learn to leave them alone. When children are absorbed in their own creative tasks, with their own friends, they are too happily busy to be bothersome.

*　　*　　*

"I wish my children obeyed me as readily as yours do you. What's your secret?"

Mr. H. was too modest a man to talk about his way with children. But Mr. H. had a way that won not only their obedience but also their love and respect.

His way was no secret. You can have the same pleasant, fruitful relationship with your children, if you're willing to pay the price.

What price?

The price of dutiful parenthood.

A parent who has given his children the love and care they need, freely and unpossessively, has a clear conscience. He can speak with authority because in his soul there is no guilt. When he tells his children to do something, they know it is right and good for them to do it and so they obey. Hasn't everything this parent ever asked of them been for their or the family's welfare?

But parents who neglect their children; or who demand that they be more truthful, more courteous, more industrious than they themselves are; or who give way to harsh punishments—such parents are too troubled in conscience to issue an authoritative command.

Similarly, teachers who come to class unprepared, who "kill" the period with busy work, who continually berate and belittle, have a lot of discipline problems. The children feel no obligation to obey them as they do the devoted teachers. No one should be a teacher who doesn't really like children.

Kids have a sixth sense, the insight of innocence, that reads a grownup's mind like a book. They know who means well by them as well as who is just trying to dominate them. They recognize our self doubt by the uncertainty in our voices; they catch our ego distress whenever we give way to irritability. Why should they obey us when we don't obey ourselves?

All of us adults should understand that only as we speak with a clear conscience can we deal effectively with children. Why are we so helpless with juvenile delinquency, our Number One social problem? Because we haven't given youth a square deal—not in the home, not in the school, not in the world at large. And we know it! Our guilt paralyzes all our endeavors for the solution of this problem.

What our society most needs is the symbol of a loving but authoritative father who disciplines and guides with affectionate firmness. His children gladly obey because they know he is leading them to their kind of green pastures. Where will our society find this symbol? In the individual home, as more and more fathers, inspired by loving wives, live up to its ideal.

*   *   *

"How do you stop children from thumbsucking, bedwetting, lying, quarreling, stealing, hookey playing?" Many were the complaints of mothers about the misbehavior of their children. And though they didn't say so, the mothers wanted nice quick remedies that would surely solve the problems.

But, truth to tell, there are no nice quick remedies for the behavior problems of children. Every misbehaving child is different. And each one may have a different reason for doing what he does.

The smart parent begins by asking "Why?" Why did three-year-old Jackie try to bury his baby brother in the sand? Why does seven-year-old Sandra still wet her bed? Why does a teenager like Ted take a neighbor's automobile and go for a joy ride in it? Why does the formerly studious Joan now show no interest in studies? Why? Why?

When we know why our child misbehaves we are on the road to knowing what to do about it. Every action has a cause. Remove the cause, and you will very likely remove the bad act.

For instance, Ted may have taken the automobile to have a fling of power and pride because at school he was a failure, and at home he had received much criticism and blame for his poor school marks. But if his parents had conscientiously looked into the matter, they might have found out that Ted's trouble was due to poor reading ability. Because he had never learned to read well, Ted consistently failed in school and felt embittered and ashamed in front of his more successful school mates.

Hookey playing was inevitable and from there to gang membership and delinquency were easy steps. But if his parents had patiently and persistently sought out the cause of his school failure and done something about it—sent him to a good reading clinic for instance—the whole story might have been different.

Nearly always the why of a child's misbehavior is an unfulfilled need, usually of love, care, or attention. The loved child learns. The loved child is obedient, or at least reasonably so, for he enjoys his parents' love and wants to continue to deserve and

receive it. The loved child is also free of personality quirks fo
he has no need for substitute gratifications.

These are simple truths. Why can't parents see them?

Unfortunately parents have their own frustrations, defeats
inherited defects and complexes. And also, alas, their own dif
ficulties with each other. But if in love and devotion they would
comfort and sustain each other, they would be better able to
to unite in the sound rearing of their children.

Parental faults and weaknesses also have a why. Counselor.
must try to understand this why. Then they will be able to ad
vise and encourage the parents. They won't criticize and blame
them.

* * *

Are the British doing a better job of disciplining their childrer
than we Americans?

The British think they are. Sir Basil Henriques, Britain's fore
most expert on juvenile delinquency, declared while on a recen
visit: "Here you have the alarming spectacle of parents being
terrified of their children. Instead of using their paternal and
maternal instincts, parents rely on cheap books about psychiatry
—which they don't understand—and are afraid to repress the
child." Sir Basil deplored our failure to bring juvenile offender
to court on petty offenses, saying that this merely encouraged
them to go on to greater crimes. He called our TV "Perniciou
Poison" because of prison scenes, shootings, and stories of teen
age girls gone wrong, which our children view for endless hours
whereas in Britain the children have only one hour of special TV
programs, five to six o'clock in the evening. They are in schoo
until five and regard their studies more seriously than America'
children.

Philip Wylie, the noted American social critic and author
takes the same point of view in numerous books and articles. H
says America is a pediarchy, a land where children rule.

Some Americans retort to this by declaring that America
children have a great deal more individuality, resourcefulness

and charm than British children. They may be trying at times, but they are always likeable, lively, and interesting.

What do you think?

Would you want your children to have the proper manners, the deference for their elders, the social poise of British children? Or do you like your high-spirited, unconforming children just the way they are?

Perhaps you would want to set up a new ideal, different from both and yet including the best qualities of each pattern?

This would mean that while allowing our children a great deal of freedom of expression and a great deal of independence as to choice of leisure interests, friends, work activities we would nevertheless insist on courtesy in social relations, correct moral attitudes and behavior, and an acceptance on their part of a secondary position in the family. Some parents would find even this much control difficult, because they are uncertain of themselves and of what the best standards are. For these parents here's a hint that may help.

Base your standards of behavior not on personal vanity, your need for respect, nor even on personal convenience, your desire for peace and quiet in the home.

Rather let your ideal always be the general good, either of your family or of society as a whole. Then you can speak with authority in the assurance that your commands are for the child's welfare as well as your own.

A nice balance between the British strict and staid good manners and American unchecked freedom would create a happier, more competent child.

* * *

"The school kids of today are a lot of hoodlums. What they most need is discipline. Occasional whacks with a heavy ruler would help!"

This bitter point of view was expressed in a sixty-page report entitled "Teacher Opinion on Pupil Behavior," issued at the end of the last school year by the research division of The National

Education Association. More than 4,000 classroom teachers all over the country were consulted for their opinions in the preparation of this report.

Not all the teachers were so harsh in their judgment. Some (about one-third) thought their pupils were well behaved. But the great majority felt that behavior problems were getting steadily worse in America's schools. The pupils are impertinent and disorderly; they cheat on homework and tests; they lie and steal; some of the older ones commit serious sexual offenses. About 77% of the elementary school teachers, 63% of the junior high, and 37% of the senior high teachers were in favor of a return to corporal punishment in schools.

What are your ideas on discipline?

In the home as at school, discipline is good for children if it is definite, reasonable, and consistent. Children like discipline, even the misbehaving ones. It makes their lives orderly. Order is a comfort and a support. You know where you stand.

But discipline is never a substitute for good will and happy activity. As any school principal will tell you, those teachers who are themselves fine-mannered and who make their lessons interesting, rarely have a discipline problem. "An orderly classroom," says The Teachers' Letter, a fortnightly inspirational periodical for school teachers, "is not where there is an absence of noise, but the presence of a purpose."

The affection-ruled family, too, rarely knows discord and rebellion. Parents who have earned the love and respect of their children by their tenderness, their impartiality, their good humor, can govern with a mild, if steady hand.

When there is too much talk of discipline in a school, you can be sure that the teachers, as teachers, are mediocre. When there is too much talk of discipline in the home, you will find that the parents, as parents, are fearsome, uncertain, and inferiority distressed; themselves, very likely, the descendants of dictatorial or perfectionist parents.

The children know who loves them and respond in kind. The lesson goes well in that classroom where the teacher has won the good will of the pupils. And home, too, can be a school of fine behavior and manners with parents who understand that the loved child learns.

So, take your choice. If you want to, you can be very strict with your children and get obedience by an iron rule. Or you can be casual and good-natured about their behavior, setting an example of courtesy and co-operation and counting on their affection for you, their sound good sense, their inherent self-reliance to sustain the high standards you have set up for your household.

Child guidance as we have said is more an art than a science. The parent or teacher who has the right touch can safely choose love—not fear—as the mentor of his children's behavior.

* * *

Will the American school child be able to achieve in freedom the school discipline which in Russia is imposed by the state?

American parents should give serious thought to this question and discuss it earnestly with their children. Our very hope of survival in the War, Hot or Cold, that we are now waging with our Communist foe is at stake. Without active parent co-operation the teachers will not be able to stimulate the pupils to so dedicate themselves to their studies that we may hope to overtake the Russians in their technological lead over us.

At a recent meeting of the National Education Association, a committee of teachers declared that discipline is the Number One problem in the American classroom. Nor was this opinion lightly given. It was the product of a nationwide study. In many schools teachers complain they can't teach; that all their energies are absorbed in maintaining order. Even in so-called upper-class areas pupil misbehavior is common. No one can measure the loss to our national effort caused by this waywardness of the children.

In Russia they have no such problem. There the pupils are subject to a strict code of behavior, called "The Rules for Pupils," which the children obey because the alternative to obedience is

expulsion and the loss of all opportunity to hold any position o
honor or pay in the society. Scholastic achievement, on the othe
hand, is highly respected and rewarded. No wonder the Russia
children accomplish in ten years a breadth and depth of knowl
edge which American authorities declare to be at least equal t
what we accomplish in twelve.

Here are a few of the rules in the Russian School Code:

"It is the duty of every schoolchild: 1. To acquire knowledg
persistently in order to become an educated and cultured citize
and to be of the greatest possible service to his country.

"2. To study diligently, to be punctual in attendance and no
arrive late at classes.

"3. To obey the instructions of the school director and th
teachers without question.

"4. To sit upright during the lesson, not leaning on his elbow
and not slouching; to listen attentively to the teacher's expla
nations and the other pupils' answers, and not to talk or let hi
attention stray to other things.

"5. To take accurate notes in his assignment book of home
work scheduled for the next lesson, and to show these notes t
his parents; to do all the homework unaided."

Whether our children could function effectively under suc
a code is questionable. It is not in the Anglo-Saxon tradition.

But we had better find a good American equivalent for it.

It is not a new thing in history that a nation which discipline
its children conquered a nation which allowed its youth a wid
latitude of individual liberty. A striking example is Sparta, whos
soldiery, trained from infancy, easily defeated the more culture
but less hardy Athenians.

The Russian schoolchild is receiving a Spartan intellectua
training. The American boy and girl must go him one better, o
goodbye to our liberties.

*   *   *

"I must admit," the father told the counselor, "that my chi
dren are behaving much better now that I'm home for dinn

very day. I never believed that this could make such a differ-
nce, but it certainly does. Thanks for telling me."

This father had a flourishing retail business, which, as he said,
emanded his personal attention until closing hour, which was
ight o'clock. By the time he got home, the children had had
heir meal and were ready for bed. Frequently the exhausted
1other had tales to tell of their misbehavior during the day and
alled on the father to punish them. He hollered, he spanked.
t didn't seem to do much good. There was always more mis-
ehavior to report the next evening.

"Why don't you arrange to come home for early dinner with
our children?" he was advised. "Leave your shop to your assist-
nt for a couple of hours. Sure, you'll lose some customers; you
on't make so much money. But you'll be able to give your
oungsters the care and guidance they need."

The father thought it over. He recognized the wisdom of the
dvice and agreed to follow it.

A child's discipline is day by day. When you stand steadfastly
y, you can afford to make your discipline mild because it is con-
stent. There is no need for hysterical outbursts of blame and
arsh beatings that are so damaging to a child's personality.

Besides, a child appreciates your endeavors to train him. He
1ows you care because you take time and effort to show him
1e right and the true. Children really like discipline and are
roud of the parents who set high standards for them. Discipline
ith love is the supreme grace of a good parent.

"Train up a child in the way he should go and when he is old
e will not depart from it." This profound proverb of Solomon
intains the essence of all child development psychology. It is
rticularly significant for America's Number One social prob-
m, juvenile delinquency.

Young children will take direction, but by adolescence it is
o late. The adolescent wants to be more and more on his own.
e thinks he can manage his own life. And he can if he has had
e right upbringing. How much of the juvenile delinquency that
w hangs like a pall over our country might have been pre-

vented if parents had disciplined their children in the early years when training was more acceptable.

Yes, a child's discipline is day by day. But a parent's discipline is day by day, too. Parenthood sometimes looks like an overwhelming job. But it isn't. Give your children care and guidance day by day, always using the best knowledge at your command and you don't have to worry. They'll come out fine.

* * *

"My adolescent son and I," the troubled mother wrote, "are always arguing over things. I know that this is not good. So will you please tell me what I should do in the following matters.

"At what time should a boy of sixteen be home on week days? I say ten-thirty, but he insists that's too early. On week ends, and especially if he is going to a party, I stretch it to twelve-thirty and again he says that's too early. He doesn't want to be the first to leave.

"Should a boy that age be allowed to smoke? He has told me frankly that he does smoke on the outside, but I think he is too young to do so. What do you think?

"And what about an allowance? He never seems to have enough money. I give him a weekly allowance, but he can spend it in one night. Should I give him more?

"I don't like some of the friends he brings to the house. Should I forbid his associating with them?"

These questions are typical of what the parents of adolescents are asking. They show how unsure the parents feel in handling their maturing children.

Adolescents, too, are unsure of themselves, confused and frequently unhappy. Sometimes they put up a great show of bravado but deep down they are vastly troubled. They need a lot of love and understanding—not argument—in this period of their lives.

All adolescents want to assert their individuality. This naturally results in a certain amount of rebellion against parental authority. Parents have to expect this. Fixed rules, especially arbitrarily set by the parent, usually arouse resentment and sometimes open disobedience. Particularly galling is it to hear, "You're old enough to know better," and the next minute, "You're not old enough to do that."

But in homes where there is much emotional warmth, where parents and children have shared many happy experiences, where reasonableness has always been the rule, and self-reliance the ideal, adolescent youngsters are more poised and at peace with themselves and, therefore, more willing to talk things out with their parents.

So if you ask how much freedom for an adolescent, the answer is it depends on how you brought him up in the early years. If you have trained him in courtesy and kindness, if you have set him an example of decent social relations you can allow a lot of freedom and be fairly certain that family pride will prevent his doing anything unworthy of you. Your standards are a steadfast guide and better than all rules.

All adolescents tend to band together in groups or gangs. They take strength from numbers and follow the leader blindly, even though they may not like what he is doing. If the whole gang smokes, and it usually does, your youngster will smoke too. If the whole gang stays out late, he can't be the baby to come home early. If everybody is treating at a party, he has to spend money. But if your youngster has the right stuff in him, none of this will hurt him.

Adolescents need a lot of freedom to experiment, to test out their powers, to grow. They also need guidance. It is particularly helpful for them and you to understand that what they are experiencing is the common lot of youth throughout our society and that as others have come through to a sound maturity, so will they.

The wise parent stands back but stands by. He encourages initiative and independence, but he is always there to render advice when asked. He brings his adolescent child safely through this trying period and in return wins his abiding respect and love.

*   *   *

"What is discipline?" parents ask and they do want an answer. Teachers do, too. Parents and teachers are greatly concerned about the problem of discipline for children and find it difficult to come to conclusions in their mind on the subject because to them even the experts seem to disagree. What good is a system of discipline unless you are consistent in applying it. And how can you be consistent, if you're not sure you're right?

Some recent writers have risen in strong rebellion against the harsh discipline of a previous generation. Their eloquence has led many parents to believe that children should be allowed to grow up in a mild, permissive atmosphere with the least possible amount of correction. On the other hand there are those who are overwhelmed by the growing menace of juvenile delinquency in the United States today and feel that this great evil has come upon us because we spared the rod and spoiled the child. They want to restore the stern standards of the so-called good old days and feel that in the long run this will be best for children.

One of the soundest treatments of the subject of discipline that I have ever seen appeared in a fortnightly periodical called *The Teachers' Letter*. It begins with a summary list of questions which it then proceeds to answer. Parents and teachers would be wise to study both the questions and the answers:

"What is discipline? Is it handing out punishments? Is it using rewards? Is it being tough? Is it appealing to the child's better nature? Is it producing conformity to adult standards? Is it helping the child conform to his own standards?

"It may be any or all of these. The object of discipline is to help an individual do what is expected of him. For a child what is expected of him is determined largely by parents and teachers when he is young, by other children and adults as he grows older, and eventually, if the process is carried to its ideal end, by the individual himself in the light of his understanding of his society and the situations he faces. This is the desired end-product—self-discipline."

Even from this skeleton thesis we can see a noble concept of discipline emerging. In their early years children are guided by their parents and teachers along lines of behavior which the race has found by experience to be wise and useful. The child knows what is expected of him and he agrees to follow the set goals and limits of behavior because they seem reasonable to him. They are not subject to the whims and caprices of his adult mentors, but rather by a soundly impersonal consistency. Thus cleanliness, constructiveness, courage, can be taught and learned. When the child fails to live up to the standards that are expected of him, his parents may criticize and correct his acts, but they may not cease to show their love for him as an individual.

After a while parents and teachers relax their supervision of the child, and he draws his ideals from the group to which he belongs. Society has its standards which uphold and sustain it. The growing youth is made aware of these standards and recognizes his duty to abide by them. They are his new discipline.

All the time, however, he is developing a standard of self, a personal idealism which is his own private contract with God. "Nothing can give you peace," says Emerson, "but yourself." Nothing can give you peace but the triumph of principles. This is the self-discipline which is the end result of all his training.

In all three developmental steps the parent bears his part. In the beginning it is he who sets the basic rules for behavior and, by a benevolent consistency, causes them to become second nature. Then in adolescence, the parent by a wise self-denial withdraws his patronage of the child and encourages him to stand on his own in relationship with those of his age-group. The youth becomes strong through facing up to group standards and demands. In maturity, the individual remembers his father and his mother. Their ideals, if worthy, enkindle his ideals. And so each parent who "keeps unstained the honor of his house" is assured of immortality in the heart and mind of his descendants.

Summary and Suggestion

There are ways of outwitting disobedience and so avoiding those conflicts of will between parent and child that make for misery in the family.

1. Base all your demands for obedience on love rather than fear. In an environment of love, parent-child relationships are easy; in an environment of fear, they are strained and difficult.

2. Always set a good example. It is folly to ask a child to be better than his parents who are the model for his own behavior.

3. If you must resort to corporal punishment, do it rarely and always build a bridge afterwards of good will between you and your child. When you spank, direct your blows where they won't hurt too much and never to the face.

4. Above all things, make your discipline consistent. Don't get angry one day over something you permit on another.

5. Provide your children with interesting toys, plenty of play space, and good companions. The happily busy child is too agreeably occupied to get into trouble.

6. Encourage hobbies, reading and a great variety of outside sports.

7. Learn to leave your children alone.

Conclusion

*

What Your Child Needs

As WE began with you, so we conclude with you—as parent and mate. For what your child most needs is two parents who know how to give love to each other, to him, and to God. From that love follows the ready fulfillment of his other Mental Health needs: *acceptance, security, protection, independence, faith, guidance, control.* In that love, the parents find their own joy and security. If this book has one message to fathers and mothers aspiring to raise fine children it is this: In love all your endeavors will be easy and sure of success; without love, you'll never make it. Don't learn too late about love.

Your destiny, and that of your children, is determined by the degree that you realize that life is love. You have lived well, if you have loved well; and you have lived badly, if you have loved badly.

Some may call this a sentimental statement. Psychiatrists, however, who should know, will tell you that it is the most scientific truth. One of them, Dr. Justin L. Green, wrote recently in an article published in Newsweek: "In my twenty-five years of practice, I have yet to see a serious emotional problem in a

295

child whose parents loved each other, and whose love for the child was an outgrowth of their love."

In a world of many disturbed, unhappy, delinquent children, this is a very significant statement.

It has particular point for those parents who declare that they love their children though they do not love each other. The truth is you cannot give your children a satisfying love unless you also love each other—the more completely the better.

"And will you play the game of total love in marriage with me?" a young bride might ask her groom. "And will you help me with my ghosts, if I help you with yours?"

The "ghosts," as we noted in an earlier chapter, are the complexes, the odd qualities of mind and character all of us acquired in childhood in relation to our parents and brothers and sisters. We enter marriage, we might say, trailing clouds of glory behind us, faith, hope, and love, but we also drag along our complexes, perversities of personality and character, our doubts, our fears, our self-centeredness.

Which will win?

Love will win if we have compassion for each other's weaknesses and faith in each other's strengths. We must keep free of blame for each other's faults, knowing that this will lead only to recrimination and conflict. And we must promote each other's virtues by praise and appreciation. We draw to ourselves the good of all that we appreciate. This great spiritual truth applies with particular profit to our relationship with our marriage partner.

Indeed, there is no luxury in the world like living without blame of anyone, and certainly not of our mate. "You cannot love anyone unless you also love his faults." You love the whole person, or not at all.

And you love in fidelity, because that's the only way you can love fully. The great wonderful experience of love can be lived only with one person.

Don't be late in learning these things.

When you are most discontented with your children, is it because you are most discontented with yourself? When you catch yourself hollering at them, could you hold still for an instant and ask yourself "Now, what's wrong with me today that I act like this?"

Love, the psychologists agree, is a child's first need. Without it, he pines away and may even die. But if we are in no condition to give love, how sadly deprived will our children be! That is why it is important for parents to learn what it is that holds them back from giving love. Here is a pointed answer:

You cannot love your children unless you first love yourself. This profound concept was popularized a few years ago by Joshua Liebman in his famous book *Peace of Mind* and more recently and authoritatively by the psychoanalyst Erich Fromm. The reason is this: When you are in a state of self-doubt; when you hate yourself for your fears and weaknesses, you are too miserably depressed to have any loving thoughts left, even for your children.

But you don't have to stay in that state. God said that we can at any time start all over again. So forgive yourself and notice how much easier it is then to forgive others. And be good to yourself, allowing yourself some luxuries and privileges, so that you can more readily be good to others. particularly your children. Here are some hints that may help:

Don't punish yourself by setting up perfectionist standards. You don't have to be a perfect parent. Nobody is. But you do have to be a loving parent. Give your children a lot of tender, loving care and they'll come out all right, regardless of what system of training you use in raising them.

Have fun with your children. Love and laughter are a team. A father who spends time with his children in happy talk and play, does them more good than one who works extra hours to provide extra benefits for their future.

Beware of extreme self-sacrifice. That always does more harm than good. Your children resent being its recipient, because it makes them feel so weak to seem to need all this. Rather let them do things for you, and they'll love you more. The donor feels strong. It's good to feel strong.

Learn to let go of anxiety. There are spiritual laws that protect your children all the time. Latch on to these laws by sincere prayer, and you can give up your fretting and worrying.

When you let go of anxiety, what happens to your problem? More often than not it disappears. Sometimes, anxiety itself is the problem.

How anxiety bedevils our lives is perceived in a vague general way by most people. But its truly immense and immediate bearing on the health and happiness of the family is not sufficiently understood. Most families like most individuals can at once improve their general welfare by learning to let go of anxiety.

How?

A recent University of Wisconsin research study, much publicized, gives one of the answers. It points out that most worry is unreal because it deals with things that never happen (forty per cent), or have already happened (thirty per cent), or are so trivial that it wouldn't matter whether they happened or not (twenty-two per cent).

Only eight per cent of the things most people worry about are worth any concern. A small enough percentage, isn't it? Realizing that fact should be a help to some worriers.

But a greater help is found in the spiritual affirmation: "Let go and let God." This sentence is taken from the writings of one of the modern non-sectarian schools of religion whose phenomenal growth in recent years can only be due to the fact that they fill a great need—the need to see the psychological truth behind the religious belief. Most of us have so conventional and routine a religion, we hardly ever reach the spiritual realities. It's as though our life and our religion were two separate things. These modern apostles give new vitality to the truth that sets us free.

In their teachings, to "let go and let God" is merely to accept the fact that the universe is governed by law and that things work out if you let them. Doubt and anxiety, however, throw a monkey wrench into the delicate spiritual machinery.

Anxiety is subtly belittling to our children. It makes them feel small and unworthy. In that sense it is an egotistic gesture on our part at their expense. No wonder that children instinctively resent our anxiety over them.

So it's up to you. Your children possess a great potential of talents and abilities. They can be healthy, happy and joyous. But first they must have your faith in them. Faith begins when you let go of anxiety.

Best of all, give your children the pleasure of seeing you happy with each other. A husband who had been moodily sulking for days because his wife seemed to respond inadequately to his bids for affection, sat glumly one evening throughout the dinner hour and brusquely responded to his children's cheerful chatter. Their laughter died, and gloom settled over the whole table. Suddenly a better impulse came over him. He smiled at his wife, thanked her for the good dinner, and gave her a kiss. She responded in kind. At once the kids resumed their merry talk, gleefully gobbled up their meal, and with a romp and a cheer ran off to their own play.

Love needs a happy heart. If you want to be good to your children, be good to yourself—and to each other.

If there is one true joy in life to compensate for its endless toil and trouble, it is man-woman love in marriage. Don't miss it. Make up your mind that every day in every way you are going to make your marriage better and better. Then every day you will feel stronger, more optimistic about life in general, and better able to love your children.

Love is an energy. Filled with love's energy, you find the care and rearing of children easy. In the first place, they are dear to you as the product of your love. And secondly, they literally grow by themselves in a love-warmed home. The overflow of your mutual affections warms their hearts and yet leaves them free to develop according to the needs of their own natures.

Their personalities are not crushed by bearing the burden of your emotions.

Happy, healthy children are usually well-behaved children. In spite of all the hue and cry over the delinquency of modern youth, it still remains true that loving parents, devoted to their task, have little trouble raising moral children provided they themselves illustrate the ideals they aim to teach.

A child's happiness begins . . . how would you finish that sentence?

Would you say that a child's happiness begins in his good health, in his parents' comfortable circumstances, in his country's laws of liberty and justice? All these are good points. But they don't give the essential answer.

A child's happiness begins in the marital happiness of his parents. From this all his blessings flow. From the lack of it stem most of his problems and difficulties. And that's something to think about in a land where there is much marital unhappiness and much juvenile distress, and delinquency.

When a child has a father and a mother who are happy and satisfied in their relationship to each other, he feels a basic security. He knows that his home will not be broken up. He can play and study and grow with a free mind.

Best of all, he can be himself. His parents will not be possessive in their love for him, because they receive a very adequate emotional fulfillment from each other. They will not, as quarreling or estranged parents so often do, drive him to bitter bewilderment by competing for his favor. He will not become the plaything of one or other parent's emotions. No one who is the plaything of another's emotions can escape neurotic tendencies.

If parents realized what their quarreling does to their children they would certainly try harder to achieve a more satisfactory relationship. And they can!

What makes a good marriage? For an answer to that question, we might use the definition of love given by Havelock Ellis, the great sage on this subject: "Love is sex plus friendship."

When a married couple enjoy a satisfying sexual relationship, their love overflows to their children, enfolding them in its comforting warmth. The sexually frustrated, however, are full of nervous tensions that frequently explode into hostile acts that include the children in their fury. Basic to a good marriage is sexual fulfillment.

But marriage is more than just sex. It must include a true comradeship of ideas and ideals, the capacity to work together, to endure hardship and difficulty together, to share accomplishments with mutual appreciation of each other's contribution.

Such a good marriage does not just happen. Always it is the result of good will and sustained effort. Its achievement is possibly the truest sign of maturity in the individual that we know. No enterprise in life more fully justifies our best endeavors, for in its success is involved not only our personal destiny but the fate of all our descendants.

If in parental devotion you long to do something special for your children at whatever sacrifice to yourself, stop struggling and striving. Rather in relaxation, comfort, and faith indulge your devotion to your marriage partner, winning thereby his cooperation and support. Then find how easy it is to raise good children, and what a joy! For the great truth in child care and guidance is this: Your children's happiness begins in the happiness of your own marriage.

And this brings us to the final, the supreme truth on the subject of love. If you love God, you will find that the moral law is easy to accept for yourself. And if you accept it for yourself, gladly and gracefully, and not as something requiring desperate effort, it will be a light matter to teach it to your children. In morality, they will be strong, for they will be working with and not against the current of life.

There is a wonderful beneficence to the moral law once we understand it. It is the truth behind the world of appearances. We feel in harmony with ourselves and with all things once we accept the word of the psalmist: "Blessed is the man who walketh not in the counsels of the ungodly. But whose delight is in the law of the Lord."

And on that note we should close. Love God and each other and you'll have no trouble raising fine children who will catch the torch of life from your loving hands and pass it on to happy future generations.

Suggested Reading For Parents

NATURE IMPLANTS an instinct for the care of the child in the heart and mind of every parent. The sound parent trusts his instincts and usually finds that they do not fail him for most of the problems of child care and training.

However, in our complex and rapidly changing society, parents may be confronted with problems about which they need advice. Very often the books or pamphlets they read may do nothing more than confirm their own instincts. This is comforting and reassuring. Sometimes they provide new insight to, and practical application of, a more modern approach.

All this is very valuable, but it is not good for parents to be solely dependent on books for child care. Take the middle way; consult a sound reference work for a particular problem, but sturdily abide by your instinctive feelings for the everyday care of your child. The more you do this, the more self-confident you will feel. Self-confidence makes you a more successful parent.

Some of the best advice on the problems of children is to be found in brief booklets and folders. Many of these are published by the Government Printing Office, Washington, D.C., and by social agencies such as the National Association for Mental Health, the Child Study Association of America and the Human Relations Aids. These booklets and pamphlets have the advantage of brevity and simplicity, yet the advice they give is authoritative and can be safely followed. Many of these publications are either free, or available at slight cost.

Four particularly valuable government publications are *Infant Care*, price 15¢; *Your Child from One to Six*, 20¢; *Your Child from Six to Twelve*, 20¢; *The Adolescent in Your Family*, 25¢. For a complete list of government publications covering child care from birth to middle teens, write to Superintendent of Documents, Government Printing Office, Washington 25, D.C.

Some particularly valuable publications of the National Association for Mental Health are *Mental Health is 1, 2, 3*, price 5¢; *What Every Child Needs*, 5¢; *Eating Problems of Children*, 15¢; *Some Special Problems of Children*, 25¢; *You Don't Have to be Perfect Even If You Are a Parent*, 20¢. For a full list of Mental Health publications, write to the National Association for Mental Health, 10 Columbus Circle, New York 19, N.Y.

Some particularly valuable publications of the Child Study Association are *The Controversial Problem of Discipline*, price 30¢, *When Children Ask about Sex*, 30¢; *Facts of Life for Children*, 50¢. For a complete list of their publications, write to the Child Study Association of America, 132 E. 74th St., New York 21, N.Y.

Particularly valuable publications of Human Relations Aids are child training leaflets on *Baby Talk, Bed-Wetting, Fear, Feeding Habits, Nervous Habits, Shyness, Sleeping Habits, Stuttering, Destructiveness, Discipline, Lying and Stealing, Obedience, Preparing Your Child for School, Preparing Your Child for the Hospital, Sex*, and *Temper*. They are 5¢ each. They give precise and authoritative guidance. Also, *How to Know Your Child*, 15¢, and *Your Emotions* and *Overweight*, 15¢. For a complete list of publications, write to Human Relations Aids, 104 East 25 Street, New York, New York.

Index

*

A

Ability:
  confidence in, 216
  success, 126
Abnormality, 127, 235
Acceptance, 20, 73, 78, 95, 117
  and acquisition of conscience, 91–95
  and rejection, 73–79
  of stepchildren, 107–9
Achievement, 178
Activities, 159, 261
Adjustment, to handicap, 185–86
Admiration, 130
Adolescent in Your Family, The, 304
Adolescents, 177, 240, 242, 287–88
  disciplining, 287–88
  freedom of, 288, 289
  rebellion of, 288–89
Advice, 146
Affection, 28, 30, 55, 63, 66, 105, 110, 137
Aggression, 74, 141
Agnostics, 201
Alcoholism, 75–77 (*see also* Drinking)
Allowances, 177, 288
Allport, Floyd Henry, 61
Aloneness, 159
America, divorce and sexual preoccupation in, 243
American Sex Revolution, The, 242
Andrews, Gladys, 175
Anger, 234
Anxiety, 298, 299
Appreciation, 45, 46, 47, 49–50, 164, 165, 287, 296
  of courtesy, 259, 264
  demand for, 223–24
  law of, 46, 47, 49, 230
  of marriage partner, 236
  self, 50
Arguments, 42, 46, 179
Armour, Richard, 151
Asceticism, 231, 243
Asch, Sholem, 93
Attention, bidding for, 265, 276

B

Baker, Edwin A., 187
Basic foods, 19–20
Bedside Esquire, The, 59
Behavior, 86, 93, 94, 95, 98, 146, 300
  anti-social, 97
  bad, 90, 98 (*see also* Misbehavior)
  conscience and, 92
  example and, 271
  good, 95
  independent, 172, 173 (*see also* Independence)
  individual problems in, 275–92
  promiscuous, 229, 236, 245
  punishment and, 270, 273
  in school, 264 (*see also* Schools)
  and society, 270
  standards of, 283
  teacher personality and, 96–97
Behaviorist theory of child training, 81
Belonging, sense of, 142
Bible, 192, 201, 249, 272
Blame, avoiding, 273
Blind children, 186
Blocks, 156, 273
Boldness, 179, 181, 182, 183
Books:
  children and, 279
  suggested for parents, 303–4
Bovet, Theodore, 233
Boys, sex and, 238
Boy Scouts, 279
Britain, juvenile delinquency in, 282–83
Broken homes, 32, 39, 125
Building a Successful Marriage, 104, 135
Butterfield, Oliver McKinley, 62

C

Canadian Mental Health Association, 220
· Canadian National Institute for the Blind, 187

Career women, 52, 123
Case Against Sex Freedom, The, 242
Character, 178
Cheating, 211, 212, 213, 214–15, 216
Chesser, Eustace, 62
Chesser Report, 239, 240, 245
Children, 21, 33, 60, 67, 91, 94, 137–39
  age, sex education and, 247–48
  aggression in, 74
  alcoholism and, 75–77
  appreciation and, 49–50
  courage in, 126, 162–63
  curiosity in, 245–46, 248
  delinquent and non-delinquent, 92
  disobedient, 90
  disturbed, 97–98
  divorce and, 39, 48, 100–105, 106, 113–14
  dominated, 41, 42
  emotional needs, 20, 21, 103, 113
  emotional security and, 57, 62
  fathers and, 68, 104
  foster, 275, 276
  friendships of, 179
  furniture for, 155, 156
  handicapped, 185–93 (*see also* Handicapped children)
  independence, 171, 172
  innocence of, 249
  invalid-prone, 167
  isolates, 179
  instilling sex ideals in, 226–33, 243
  and low moral standards, 215
  moral law and, 202–3
  need for freedom to grow, 41, 110, 176, 177–78
  need for love, 25–31, 297
  need for outdoor activities, 159–60
  neurotic, 81, 126, 272
  over-privileged, 216–17
  and parental attitudes, 86
  parents and, 65–69
  patronized, 216, 217
  physical needs of, 155–61
  quiet, 219–20
  recognition of, 147

Children (*cont.*)
  rejection of, 73–79
  self-confidence in, 89, 113 (*see also* Self-confidence)
  and sense of belonging, 142
  sex questions of, 237, 245, 247–48, 250
  society and, 270–71
  success with, 66
  toys and games for, 156–60
  training of, 80–83 (*see also* Child training)
  of unfaithful parents, 53
  unwanted, 125
  wayward impulses of, 144, 272
  weak, 177
  when marriages are happy, 49
  words and, 162–67
Children's rooms, 155–56
Child Study Association of America, 304
Child training, 80–83
  appreciation for, 287
  behaviorist theory of, 81
  courtesy and good manners, 255 (*see also* Guidance; Courtesy)
  in discipline, 146
  geared to individual, 83
  for the handicapped, 185, 186
  in independence, 176–77, 179
  proper, 82–83
  in self-confidence, 163
Comic books, 183
Commands, 272
Common sense, discipline and, 273
Companionship, 273
Compensation, 121
Competition, social, 259
Complexes, 38, 62, 282
  defined, 296
  received in childhood, 38
Compliments, 148
Confidence, 216
Conscience, 28, 90, 91
  acquiring, 91–95
  defined, 92–93
  discipline and, 144

Conscience (*cont.*)
 teachers and, 96–99
 troubled, 211
Consistency, 274
Constructive toys, 156
Continence, 229
Control, 20 (*see also* Guidance; Discipline)
Controversial Problem of Discipline, The, 304
Conversation, family, 261–63
Cooperation, 62
 family, 141
 parent, 42, 129
Corporal punishment, 276–77
Counseling, 113, 117, 282
 marriage, 104–5, 130
 psychological, 120
Courage, 126, 162–63
 and independence, 176–84
 natural, 182, 183
Courtesy, 95, 97, 98, 147–54
 importance of, 254, 255
 parental, 148, 153
 psychology of, 148–49
 teaching, 255
 value of, 149, 258–59, 263
Creativity, children and, 156, 157, 158, 178
Crime, 74, 91, 97, 99, 126, 159
 adult, 214
 juvenile (*see* Juvenile delinquency)
Critical words, 164
Criticism, 150, 164–65
Curiosity, of children, 248

D

Daughters:
 of alcoholics, 76–77
 fathers and, 123
 rejected, 127, 130
 sex instruction for, 242
 when father wanted boy, 126–27
Delinquency:
 Juvenile, 74, 91, 92, 93
 potential, 97, 98–99, 126
Demands, 174, 223

Depreciation, self, 50
Depression, 129
Devotion, 65, 108
Diets, 120–21
Discourtesy, 153
Disillusionment, 61
Discipline, 143–46, 264
 and child guidance, 269–74
 concern over, 290, 291
 conscience and, 144–45
 individual problems of, 275–92
 as national problem, 285–86
 object of, 290, 291
 by punishment, 276–77
 school, 217–19
 self, 143, 150 (*see also* Self-discipline)
 tact and common sense in, 273
Disobedient child, 90
Distress, 164, 174
 emotional, 218, 219
 inferiority, 254
Disturbed child, 97–98, 117
Divorce, 35–36, 39, 48, 53, 58, 100–105
 in America, sex and, 243
 beneficial, 106, 107
 effect on later life, 127–28
 effects of, 101, 102
 emotional consequences, 113–14
 extent of, 103–4
 increase in cases, 104
 orphans of, 99, 100–105
 planning for the child, 114
Divorce settlements, 103
Domination, 41, 42, 43, 55, 141, 188–89
Doubt, 141
Drinking, 236, 260
Drug addiction, 103
Duty, 208

E

Early marriage, 229–30, 232, 239
Eating Problems of Children, 304
Education, 95, 96, 125, 255, 256, 269–70

Education (*cont.*)
  for marriage, 104
  sex (*see* Sex instruction)
Ego, 199, 208
Ego-distress, 152, 153
Egotism, 50
Elektra complex, 62
Eliot, George, 192
Ellis, Havelock, 49, 55, 226, 300
Emerson, Ralph Waldo, 176, 213, 291
Emotional distress, 218, 219
Emotional needs, 20, 21, 103
Emotional support, 130
Emotional ties, 110
Encouragement, 124, 130, 172, 271
  of handicapped children, 185–86
  to independence, 176–84 (*see also*
    Independence)
*Encyclopedia of Child Care and Guid-
    ance*, 57
Energy, 84–87, 109
Envy, 128
Esquire, 59
Ethics, 205, 213
Evasion, 248
Evil, goodness and, 144
Excessive care, 55
Expression, freedom of, 283
Extra-curricular activities, 219
Extroverts, 125

F

Face slapping, 152
Facts of Life for Children, 304
Faith, 20, 109, 197–209, 224
  action and, 209
  in children, 191, 299
  for children, 199, 201, 209–10
  health and, 207–8
  and mental attitudes, 241
  parents and, 198, 200, 201
  in people, 258
Faithfulness, 60–61, 296
Family:
  happy, 137
  alcoholism and, 76

Family (*cont.*)
  cooperation in, 62
  conversation, 261–63
  distressed, 223
  equality and individuality in, 139–
    40
  loss of, 102
  love and, 63–64
  and national strength, 243
  strengthening, 131
Family councils, 114
Family games, 148
Family life, 21
Family meals, 160
Fantasies, 118, 244
Fathers:
  children and, 68, 104, 123
  demands of job and, 67, 123
  divorced, 112–13
  instructing sons about sex, 245
  as symbols of authority, 280
Fathers-in-law, 69
Father substitutes, 111
Fault finding, 264
Faults, 44, 45, 164
Fear, 141, 149, 150, 171–72
  and natural courage, 182
  overcoming, 182 (*see also* Self-con-
    fidence)
  and self-centeredness, 206
Fighting, 179, 183
Finances, 40
Financial security, 136
Food, 25, 155, 161
Foods, basic, 19–20
Foster children, 275, 276
Foster fathers, 112, 115
Foster mothers, 115
Fresh air, 159
Friendships, 179
Fright, 179
Frigidity, 38, 39
Fromm, Erich, 297
Froude, James Anthony, 143
Frustration, 38, 46, 178, 231, 282
Furniture, children's, 155, 156

G

Games, 155, 157, 158
Gangs, 289
Gender preference, 127, 130
Generosity, 205–6
Gentleman, The, 253
Gibran, Kahlil, 191
Girls, sex and, 238
Glueck, Eleanor, 74, 92
Glueck, Sheldon, 74, 92
Golden Rule, 259, 266
Goodman, Dr. David, 84
Good manners, 253–54
Goodness, evil and, 144
Grandparents, 68, 69
Green, Dr. Justin L., 295
Group play, 159
Groups, adolescent, 289
Growth:
    unwillingness, 189
    freedom of, 41, 110, 176, 177–78
Guidance, 20, 253–66, 285
    adolescent, 289
    conversation and, 261–63
    and discipline, 269–74 (*see also*
        Discipline)
    by example, 261, 264, 271, 273, 274
    in good manners, 253–57, 258–61,
        263–66
    religious, 218
Guidance Newsletter, 151

H

Handicapped children, 185–93
    emphasizing strengths of, 187–88
    failures of, 187–88
    inspiration for, 185
    spiritual strength for, 191–92
Happiness, 66, 67, 163
    basis for, 300
    courtesy and, 148
    factors in, 135–36
    for the handicapped, 186
    moral condition and, 220
    in school, 164–65

Happiness (*cont.*)
    security and, 174
    sexual (*see* Sexual happiness)
Hardship, 110, 136
Harmony, spiritual, 210
Health, 165–66, 225
    foods and, 19–20
    promotion of, 166–67
    spiritual values and, 207–8
Henriques, Sir Basil, 282
Higher self, 92
Hobbies, 279, 292
Home life, 135–42
    and children's physical needs, 155–
        61
    and development of courtesy, 259
    negative and positive words and,
        162–67
    security in, 135–42
    spiritual ideals in, 141
    wholesomeness and, 235
Homemade toys, 156–57, 158
Homosexuality, 103
Honor, 212
Hookey playing, 281
Hostility, 125, 128, 235
Household management, 40
Housing, 92
*How to Do Nothing All by Yourself,
    Alone*, 158
"How to Know Your Child," 220
Human nature, 109
Human relations, learning, 257–58
Human Relations Aids, 304
Humiliation, 217
Humility, 74
Hunt, Leigh, 200
Husbands:
    cooperation, 42, 129
    duty to mates, 33, 34, 35, 36
    as providers, 54, 55
    sex and, 59, 60, 61
    unfaithful, 45, 52–53, 59–60
    wives and, 54–56
    and wives' faults, 45
Hypochondria, 166

Hypocrisy, 146, 198, 212, 271
Hysteria, 207

I

Ibsen, Henrik, 136, 137
Ideals, 141, 146, 212, 237
Illnesses, 76, 115, 165–66, 191
    mental, 137
    and positive health, 165
Ill temper, 150, 151, 152, 153
Immorality, 242–43
Impatience, 151
Inadequacy, 254–55
Independence, 20, 171, 283
    encouragement of, 174
    first steps toward, 176–84
    helping children attain, 179
    parental possessiveness and, 189–91
    as primary need, 180
    principles of, 178
    protection and, 171–75
Infancy, 25–27
    love and, 26–27, 29
    rejection of, 80–83
    spoiling, 27–28
Infant Care, 304
Inferiority, 179
Inferiority distresses, 254
Infidelity, 45, 52–53, 58–59, 60
    effect on mate, 45
    extent of, 53
Inhibitions, 249
Innocence, childhood, 249
Insecurity, 128
Inspiration:
    guidance and, 261
    for handicapped children, 185
Instincts, 144, 145
Interference, 179, 184
Isolates, 179
Invalidism, 165–66, 167
Inventiveness, 157
Irritability, 149–53, 274
    and discipline, 264
    in parents, 152–53
    self-confidence and, 278

Irritability (*cont.*)
    of teachers, 149, 150
    weakness and, 151
Irritability quotient, 149, 150

J

James, William, 84, 223
Jealousy, 89–90, 108
Joad, Cyril E. M., 236
Johnson, Isabel, 5, 20
Jull, Louis H., 103
Juvenile delinquency, 74, 91, 92, 103,
        137, 271
    and adult crime, 214
    in Britain, 282–83
    and fatherless homes, 114, 115
    and general behavior, 269
    love and, 93
    potential, 97, 98–99, 126
    principal reason for, 92
    rejection and, 126
    schools and, 218 (*see also* Schools)

K

Kant, Immanuel, 202
Kinsey Reports, 238, 239, 240, 243,
        245

L

Lancet, 76
Landis, Judson T., 102, 104, 135
Landis, Mary, 104, 135
Law of appreciation, 46, 47, 49, 230
Learning, 97
Legal rejection, 100–105
Libido, 230, 231
Liebman, Joshua, 297
Linzer, Edward, 5, 20
Lying, 211, 214, 281
Love, 20, 66, 69, 86, 299
    behavior and, 277–78 (*see also* Be-
        havior; Misbehavior)
    children and, 272
    child's need for, 297
    conditioning, 89, 90
    in development of conscience, 93
    and devotion, 65

Love (*cont.*)
    faithfulness in, 296
    handicapped children and, 185
    inability to, 38, 40–41
    as instrument of power, 82–89
    lack of, aggression and, 74 (*see also*
        Aggression)
    lack of faith in, 118
    in marriage, 28–29, 32–37, 63 (*see
        also* Marriage; Marriage love;
        Sexual happiness)
    obedience and, 88–90
    parents and, 28–29, 30
    and physical needs of children, 161
    security and, 135–42
    and sex, 36, 57, 61, 228, 230, 231,
        232, 246
    understanding need for, 25–31
Love-objects, 127
*Love, Skill and Mystery, a Handbook
    to Marriage*, 233
Love Without Fear, 62
Luxuries, 136

M

Macbeth, 197, 198
Mace, Dr. David R., 58
"Making of a Delinquent, The," 74, 92
Malnutrition, 123
Manners, 93, 253–54, 264–66
    courtesy and, 254, 255, 259 (*see
        also* Courtesy)
Marasmus, 26
Marriage, 32–33, 35, 36, 57–58, 301
    and adultery, 230
    early, 229–30, 232, 239
    failure in, 35–36, 38–39, 58–59
    improving, 65–66
    setting ideal of, 104
    parents and, 38–43
    second, 48
    sex and, 57, 59, 61, 62 (*see also* Sex;
        Sexual Happiness)
    and sex code, 227
    sharing in, 58
    success in, 61–62, 63–64

Marriage and Sexual Harmony, 62
Marriage counseling, 104–5, 130
Married love, 32–37, 38–40, 53, 57,
    58, 64, 68–69
Masturbation, 248, 249
Maturity:
    lack of, 127
    physical, 58
    spiritual, 42, 47, 58
Maurois, André, 58
Meals, 160, 261–62
Men:
    and marriage breakups, 61
    as providers, 54
    role of, 54, 55
Mental Health is 1, 2, 3, 304
Mental Health Way, The, 19, 224
Mental hygiene, 19, 97
Mental illness, 137
Mind Alive, 129
Miner, Julius Howard, 100
Ministers, 201
Misbehavior, 90, 95, 98, 123, 150
    as bid for attention, 265, 276
    dealing with, 281
    problem of, 269–70
    in schools, 264, 265 (*see also*
        Schools)
"Momism," 55
Money, children and, 177
Moodiness, 219, 299
Monogamy, 227
Morality, 203, 212, 273
    importance of, 203
    sexual, 226, 230
Moral law, 199, 202–3, 204, 205, 222,
    226, 301
Morals, 93, 94
Moral standards, 211–25
    happiness and, 220
    dangers in loss of, 215–16
    present-day, 214–15
    teaching of, 221–23
Moral strength, 144, 145
Mother domination, 40 (*see also* Dom-
    ination)

Mother-fixation, 110–12
Mothers, 53, 54, 55, 68
    divorced, 106–16
    energy and, 84–87
    neglectful, 123
    obedience and, 88–90 (*see also* Obedience)
    over-solicitous, 188–89
    and sex instruction for daughters, 245
Mothers-in-law, 69

N

National Association for Mental Health, 5, 12, 19, 20, 304
National Education Association, 95, 264, 269, 283–84, 285
Natural courage, 182, 183
"Needed Seven, The," 19, 20
Negative words, 162–63
Neglect, 123, 280
Nervous distress, 174
Neurotic children, 81, 126, 272
Newman, Cardinal, 253
Newsweek, 295
New York Guild for the Jewish Blind, 186, 187
Normality, 235
Nutrients, spiritual, 20
Nutrition, physical, 19–20

O

Obedience, 88–90, 144, 272, 273, 276, 277–78 (*see also* Discipline; Behavior)
Obesity, 120–21
Oedipus complex, 62
"One Thousand Juvenile Delinquents," 74
Orphans, divorce, 100–105
Over-conscientiousness, 208
Overeating, 120, 121
Overindulgence, 236, 237
Over-privileged children, 216–17
Overprotection, 55, 110, 184
    and fearsome attitudes, 178
    by mothers, 181–82

Over-solicitous mothers, 188–89
Overstreet, Bonaro, 129
Overstreet, Harry, 129
Overweight, 304

P

Parenthood, 18–19, 64, 66, 69, 127
Parents:
    aids for, 18
    background, 17–18, 21
    behavior toward children, 18
    cheating and, 213
    and children's needs, 20–21
    and children, 65–69
    and child's chances for sexual happiness, 234–35
    effect on children, 53
    energy and, 84–88
    errors of reflected in children, 244
    and handicapped child, 185
    happiness of, 135
    and independence of children, 171–72
    irritability in, 152
    juvenile delinquency and, 92
    marriage and, 38–43
    moral values and, 212
    possessiveness of, 189–91
    quarrels and, 42
    rejecting, 75, 77
    single (divorced), 106–16
    sex instruction by, 239–41
    standards of, 93, 94
    suggested reading for, 303–4
    understanding partners' faults, 44–45
    words to children, 162–67
"Parents Without Partners," 115
Pasley, Virginia, 125
Patronized children, 216, 217
Peace of Mind, 297
Perfectionism, 94, 114, 145, 150, 212, 221, 272, 297
Persistence, 144
Personal deprivation, 115
Personality distress, 103

Personal neatness, 125
Perversity, 127, 235
Petting, 241, 242
Physical maturity, 58
Physical needs, 20–21, 155–61
  nourishment, 160
  outdoor activity, 159–60
  play, 156–60
  rooms and furniture, 155–56
Play, 156–60, 219, 273
  group, 159
  lack of interest in, 219
Playgrounds, 159
Play materials, 156
Pleasure, 144, 208
Politeness, 264
Positive words, 162, 163, 165–66, 167
Possessiveness, 189–91
Potential delinquents, 97, 98–99
Poverty, 92, 115
Praise, 130, 264, 273, 296
Prayer, 114, 167
Pregnancy, unwanted, 75
Prejudices, 244
Preparing Your Child for School, 304
Preparing Your Child for the Hospital, 304
Pretense, 271
Pride, 163
Principles, 145, 199, 213
Promiscuity, 127, 128, 229–30, 236, 245
Promises, 119
Prophet, The, 191
Prosperity, 216–17, 260–61
Protection, 20, 171, 172, 173
Protectiveness, 55
Psychological counseling, 120
Public schools, 219 (*see also* Schools)
Punishment, 89, 174, 270, 273, 276–77, 297
  excessive, 272, 276, 278, 279
  self, 297

Q

Quarreling, 281, 300
Quarrels, 101, 104, 136

R

Rank, Otto, 189
Reader's Digest, 98, 238
Reading:
  children and, 279
  for parents, suggested, 303–4
Reading ability, 281
Rebellion, 74, 260
  adolescent, 288–89
  expressed in delinquency (*see* Juvenile delinquency)
  tradition of, 273
Reconciliation, 100
Recreation (*see also* Play)
  group, 159
  lack of, 92
  school and civic, 261
Rejection, 73–79, 89, 99
  cases, 117–31
  caused by alcoholism, 75–77
  crime and, 74
  defined, 74
  and development of conscience, 93
  and future parenthood, 129
  gender, 126–27
  infant, 80–83
  legal, 100–105 (*see also* Divorce)
  reasons for, 74–76
  results of, 77–78
  self, 84–87
Religion, 200–201, 202, 203, 231
  extremes in, 219
  and marital success, 239
  sex and, 231–32, 238
Religious belief, 125
Religious instruction, 199, 204, 240
Remarriage, 107–9
Repression, 182, 231, 243
Reprimands, 107
Resignation, 185
Responsibility, 144
Robertson, Dr. G. Gladstone, 76
Romantic fantasies, 118
Rooms, children's, 155–56
Roosevelt, Theodore, 67, 146
Rowdyism, 260

Russia:
  morality in, 243
  school code of, 285–86
  school discipline of, 269

S

Schools, 95, 97–99, 125, 163
  discipline in, 217–19, 269–70 (*see also* Discipline)
  lack of interest in, 219
  manners and, 255–56
  parents' interest in, 261
  public, 219
  sex instruction in, 238
  teachers (*see* Teachers)
School failures, 97, 98, 187, 188, 281
Scolding, 278
Second marriages, 48
Security, 128
  courtesy and, 147–54
  defined, 142
  discipline and, 143–46
  financial, 136
  happiness, 174
  and independence, 171, 172
  and love, 135–42 (*see also* Love)
Self-appreciation, 50
Self-assurance, importance of, 263
Self-centeredness, 206
Self-confidence, 89, 113, 163, 171, 224
  building, 182
  growth of, 180–81
Self-discipline, 143, 150
  sexual, 239
  teaching, 277–78
Self-indulgence, 144, 208
Self-pity, 163, 187
Self-rejection, 84–87
Self-reliance, 140
Self-righteousness, 209
Self-understanding, 153
Senate Report on Juvenile Delinquency, 62
Senate Subcommittee to Investigate Juvenile Delinquency, 91, 92
Separateness, 125

Separation, 53, 136
Sex, 36, 57, 59, 60
  alcoholism and, 76
  children's questions on, 237, 245, 247–48, 250
  and early marriage, 229–30, 232, 239
  effect of wrong attitudes, 235
  experimentation, 235
  function of, 57
  ignorance of, 62
  and love, 36, 57, 61, 228, 230, 231, 238, 246 (*see also* Love)
  outside of marriage, 229, 230, 232
  preference for one, 127
  pre-marital, 238, 239
  rejection and, 74–75
  and religion, 231–32, 238
  sublimation and, 239
  and unmarrieds, 229
  wife and, 59, 61
Sex code, 226–27, 230, 231
Sex ideals, 226–33, 243
Sex instruction, 234–50
  accomplishing, 245–46
  from companions, 245
  for daughters, 241–42, 244
  evading questions in, 248
  and national strength, 243
  and parental attitude, 246–48
  by parents, 239–41
  in schools, 238
  for sons, 242, 245
Sexual Behavior in the Human Male, 238
Sexual expression, 228
Sexual happiness, 300–301
  code for, 232
  importance of, 62, 227–28
  inertia and, 58
  law of appreciation and, 230
  re-education for, 243
  relationship to child's emotional security, 58–64
  role of sex code, 231
Sexual inadequacy, 59

Sexual infidelity, 45, 52–53, 58–59, 60
Sexual intercourse, children's questions about, 247, 248
Sex violations, 214
Shakespeare, William, 94, 197, 206
Sharing, 58, 139
Shyness, 172, 178, 179
Skin trouble, 121–22
Smith, Robert Paul, 158, 159
Smoking, 236, 288, 289
Sociability, 279
Society, children and, 270–71
Some Special Problems of Children, 304
Sons:
  importance of fathers to, 123, 125–26
  mother-fixation and, 110–12
  relationships with girls, 110, 111–12
  sex instruction for, 242
Sorokin, Dr. Pitrim A., 242, 243
Spanking, 276, 278
  possible results of, 272
  substitutes for, 279
Spenser, Edmund, 183
Spinsters, 128
Spiritual, definitions of, 197–98
Spiritual harmony, 210
Spiritual maturity, 42, 47, 208–9
Spiritual needs, 20, 199, 200, 202
Spiritual values, 198–204, 206
  faith (*see* Faith)
  health and, 207–8
  and moral law, 199, 202–3, 204, 205
  parents and, 198, 200
Spoiling, 27–28
Sports, 155, 159, 219
Standards, 93, 94, 144, 145
  behavioral, 283
  moral, 212–25 (*see also* Moral standards)
  perfectionist, 114, 145, 212, 221, 272
Stealing, 214
Stepchildren, 108–9

Stepfathers, 107–9
Strain, 150
Strecker, Dr. Edward Adam, 182, 234
Strictness, 271, 285
Students, cheating by, 214, 215–16
Sublimation, sexual, 239
Submissiveness, 74
Success:
  ability for, 126
  manners and, 253, 265, 266
Sunday School, 199, 200
Super-ego, 92
Sympathy, 125, 262
Sweden, sex problems and, 238–39

T

Table manners, 147, 152
Taboos, 244, 249
Tact, 273
Talkative child, 275
"Teacher Opinion on Pupil Behavior," 264, 283
Teachers, 95, 96–99, 256, 284
  and conscience, 96–99
  discipline and, 218
  dissatisfactions of, 263–65
  good manners and, 254
  influence of, 98
  irritability of, 149, 150
  mediocre, 284
  obedience and, 280
  personality of, and student behavior, 96–97
  positive and negative words of, 164–65
  and spiritual values, 198
Teachers' Letter, The, 284, 290
Teen-agers, problems of, 237–38
Television, 282
Temper, 150, 151, 152, 153
Ten Commandments, 226
Tennyson, Alfred, 192
Their Mothers' Sons, 182
Timidity:
  correcting, 182
  results of, 178

Toys, 156–59, 273
    excess, 156, 157
    homemade, 156–57, 158
Training, child, 80–83 (*see also* Child
    training)
21 Stayed, 125

U

Understanding, 136, 262
Unfaithfulness, 45, 52–53, 58–59, 60
Unhappiness, 135
Unwanted children, 75, 125

V

Vandalism, 260
Venereal disease, 238

W

Waite, Edward F., 101
Weak children, 177, 272
Weekly allowances, 177, 288
Weight problems, 120–21
What Every Child Needs, 5, 19, 180,
    304
When Children Ask About Sex, 304
*Where Did You Go? Out. What Did
    You Do? Nothing,* 158
"Why I am Faithful to My Wife," 59
Widows, 109, 110
Wilde, Oscar, 192, 230, 259
Wives:
    cooperation, 42, 129

Wives (*cont.*)
    deserted, 109
    duties to husbands, 34–35, 36
    husbands and, 54–56
    and husbands' faults, 44–45
    sex and, 59–61
    unhappy, 128
    widowed, 109, 110
Women, 51–56
    careers and, 52
    changes in role of, 52
    and children, 53, 55
    promiscuous, 127, 128 (*see als*
        Promiscuity)
    psychophysical unfulfillment, 51
        52
    remarried, 106–16
Words, 162–67
    critical, 164
    negative, 162–63
    positive, 162, 163, 165–66, 167
    of self-pity, 163
    teachers and, 164–65
Wordsworth, William, 67
Working mothers, 52, 123
Worrying, 298
Wylie, Philip, 282

Y

Yeats, William Butler, 94, 203
*You Don't Have to Be Perfect Even
    You Are a Parent,* 304
Youth, rebellion of, 260

THE AUTHOR AND HIS BOOK

DAVID GOODMAN, *family counselor, lecturer, and writer, was born in New York City, September 14, 1894. Son of Herman Goodman, linguist and bank foreign correspondent, and Celia Goodman, noted in her later years as a neighborhood sage and consultant in family problems, David Goodman was taken to Denver, Colo., at two because of his father's illness. Some first-hand knowledge of the emotional needs of children came to him at an early age. From seven until twelve, following his father's death, he was in a Cleveland orphanage, but in 1906 he rejoined his mother in New York, a woman who raised and educated her five children on her own efforts. He won a Pulitzer scholarship at De Witt Clinton High School in New York and entered Columbia University where he obtained his A.B. degree in 1917, and his A.M. in English the following year. In 1951 he received his Doctorate in Education from Teacher's College, of Columbia University. He taught at Rhodes School, one of New York's largest private high schools, from 1917 to 1922, when he formed his own private preparatory school, University Prep, which merged with Rhodes in 1929. After serving as principal to these combined schools for almost 25 years, Dr. Goodman gave up his position in 1955 to devote his full time to counseling, lecturing, and writing. His nationally syndicated column, "What's Best for Your Child," first appeared in the Bergen Evening Record, Bergen County, N.J., in 1952. Approximately 30 newspapers across the country now carry his thrice-weekly message on parent and child guidance. He is married to the former Malvina Peterson and they have two children, Lawrence, a lawyer recently graduated from Columbia Law School, and Eric, a Columbia University graduate now in business for himself. There are three grandchildren. Through them, he "rejoices in the opportunity for a 'second look' at child growth and development." The Goodmans make their home in Teaneck, New Jersey.*

A PARENT'S GUIDE TO THE EMOTIONAL NEEDS OF CHILDREN (*Hawthorn, 1959*) *was designed by Ernst Reichl and completely manufactured by George McKibbin & Son, Brooklyn, N.Y. The body type is Caledonia designed for the Linotype by W. A. Dwiggins, one of America's best-known typographers and designers.*

A HAWTHORN BOOK